John Rawls

An Introduction

PERCY B. LEHNING

CAMBRIDGE
UNIVERSITY PRESS

CAMBRIDGE UNIVERSITY PRESS
Cambridge, New York, Melbourne, Madrid, Cape Town, Singapore, São Paulo, Delhi

Cambridge University Press
The Edinburgh Building, Cambridge CB2 8RU, UK

Published in the United States of America by Cambridge University Press, New York

www.cambridge.org
Information on this title: www.cambridge.org/9780521727693

Originally published in Dutch as *Rawls* by Lemniscaat b.v., Rotterdam 2006,
© Percy B. Lehning 2006
First published in English by Cambridge University Press 2009 as
John Rawls: An Introduction © Percy B. Lehning 2009

English translation © Cambridge University Press 2009

Printed in the United Kingdom at the University Press, Cambridge

A catalogue record for this publication is available from the British Library

ISBN 978-0-521-89903-1 hardback
ISBN 978-0-521-72769-3 paperback

For Jack, in cherished memory

Contents

Preface

John Rawls (1921–2002) is considered one of the most influential political philosophers of the twentieth century. His main work, *A Theory of Justice*, published in 1971, is recognized as one of the all-time great works in moral and political philosophy.

Rawls formulates in new ways answers to age-old, perennial questions of political philosophy: "What is a just political order?" and "What does justice require of us?" In working out his ideas on justice, Rawls is inspired by the traditional idea of the social contract, as represented by Locke, Rousseau, and Kant. But in Rawls' theory, the social contract is not used to set up a particular form of government. Rather, the guiding idea is that the object of the social contract is the principles of justice for a society.

In formulating his ideas on justice, Rawls at the same time takes a position against rival ethical conceptions, especially against the utilitarianism that has been the predominant theory for much of modern moral philosophy, represented by a long line of writers such as David Hume and Adam Smith, Jeremy Bentham and John Stuart Mill, F. Y. Edgeworth and Henry Sidgwick.

The ways Rawls has worked out his ideas on justice have drawn widespread attention, not only from (political) philosophers, but also from philosophers of law, political scientists, economists, those in the field of public policy, and experts in jurisprudence. But not only academics have been inspired by Rawls' ideas. His ideas on "what justice requires" have influenced the theory of government and play a role in public political debates between, and within, political parties on policies to be pursued in so-called welfare states. It should be noted, however, that Rawls himself very seldom took a direct stand in debates on political topics. In addition, he was never a "party-political philosopher" and – even more important – neither is his work directly focused on daily political debates, or on the whim of political hype.

All of this brings two questions to the fore: Why is it that Rawls' work is considered to belong to the category of the all-time most important works of moral and political philosophy? And, second, how is it, and in what ways, that political movements, political parties, or for that matter "you and I" in our role as citizens, can be inspired by Rawls' ideas on justice? What can these ideas contribute today to public political debates that turn on the issue of how liberal democratic societies, that are characterized by a plurality of religious, philosophical, and moral beliefs and opinions, can be organized in such a way that they are at the same time stable and peaceful, as well as just?

This introduction to Rawls' theory of justice tries to answer these questions. In so doing it takes "the whole" of Rawls' work, which has now been published in its entirety, into account. It elaborates how Rawls' works hangs together, from his first publication in 1951 up to his very final ones, some fifty years later, and how and why it can be considered to be one consistent and coherent body of work. We will follow the developments in Rawls' theorizing on justice and will explain, if there are any, recasting and adaptations.

Let us be clear, then, about what this introduction is, and what it is not. It is not an overview of the literature on Rawls' theory. The motto of this introduction is rather "back to basics." The aim is to keep the focus on Rawls' own writings: it is his ideas, his arguments, and his texts on "justice" that take center stage. For one thing, it will help to clear up existing misunderstandings and misinterpretations of Rawls' theory, and to dismiss criticism of Rawls' failing to address problems not within his intended purview. This is not, of course, to say that Rawls' theory should be uncritically accepted. His theory is not immune to criticism, but it seeks fair criticism.

In a note on "My Teaching," Rawls once remarked: "When lecturing, say, on Locke, Rousseau, Kant, or J. S. Mill, I always tried to do two things especially. One was to pose their problems as they themselves saw them, given what their understanding of these problems was in their own time. ... The second thing I tried to do was to present each writer's thought in what I took to be its strongest form. I took to heart Mill's remark in his review of Sidgwick: 'A doctrine is not judged at all until it is judged in its best form'. I didn't say, not intentionally anyway, what I myself thought a writer should have said, but rather what the writer did say, supported by what I viewed as the most reasonable interpretation on the text. The text had to be known and respected, and its doctrine presented in its best form. Leaving aside the text seemed offensive, a kind of pretending."[1]

Following Rawls' lead on how to understand and appreciate the thought of important moral and political philosophers, we are not, in this introduction, concerned with "what I myself think Rawls should have said, but rather what Rawls did say, supported by what I view as the most reasonable interpretation of his texts." The effort in this introduction to Rawls' work is to lay bare what are the leading ideas in his theory of justice, a theory on which he had been working without interruption for over fifty years.

Rawls once thanked the author of this introduction "for correcting several of my false starts."[2] However, rather the opposite holds. Over many years, in innumerable and illuminating conversations, Rawls taught me how to improve my understanding of his theory. This introduction to his work is the fall-out thereof. It is dedicated to his memory.

List of abbreviations

The following abbreviations for Rawls' work appear throughout the text.

CP   *Collected Papers*, 1999, edited by Samuel Freeman, Cambridge, MA: Harvard University Press.

JaF   *Justice as Fairness: A Restatement*, 2001, edited by Erin Kelly, Cambridge, MA: Harvard University Press.

LHMP   *Lectures on the History of Moral Philosophy*, 2000, edited by Barbara Herman, Cambridge, MA: Harvard University Press.

LHPP   *Lectures on the History of Political Philosophy*, 2007, edited by Samuel Freeman, Cambridge, MA and London: The Belknap Press of Harvard University Press.

LoP   *The Law of Peoples*, 1999, including the paper "The Idea of Public Reason Revisited," Cambridge, MA: Harvard University Press.

PL   *Political Liberalism*, 1996, New York: Columbia University Press.

TJ   *A Theory of Justice*, 1971, Cambridge, MA: Harvard University Press.

TJR   *A Theory of Justice. Revised Edition*, 1999, Cambridge, MA: Harvard University Press.

"The Idea of Public Reason Revisited" is quoted in this introduction as published in *The Law of Peoples*, 129–180. Thus LoP: 129 refers to "The Idea of Public Reason Revisited." The article was originally published in 1997 in the *University of Chicago Law Review*, 64, 765–807. It has been included in the *Collected Papers* from 1999 (pp. 573–615), as well as in the newly expanded edition of *Political Liberalism* from 2005 (pp. 440–490).

1 | *Life and work*

John (Jack) Bordley Rawls was born on February 21, 1921 in Baltimore (Maryland, USA), as a child of a well-to-do family that had its roots in one of the southern states of the USA (North Carolina). His youth was spent in Baltimore, with the exception of the summers when the family stayed on the east coast, in a summer cottage south of Blue Hill (Maine). His father, William Lee Rawls (1883–1946), was a highly respected attorney and constitutional authority. His mother, Anna Abell Stump (1892–1954), came from an old Maryland family (a family that had its roots in Germany). She was for some time president of the Baltimore chapter of the then new "League of Women Voters."

Rawls had four brothers. Two of his younger brothers would die during his childhood, one of diphtheria (Bobby, who died at five years old in 1928), the other of pneumonia (Tommy, who died at two years old in 1929). Both died of diseases they had contracted from him. These experiences ("Why did I remain alive while my brothers died?"), as well as the undeserved, less-advantaged position of (both black and white) children of his own age that crossed his path, made a lifelong impression on Rawls. They made him realize the *arbitrariness of fortune* and the *unmerited contingencies of life*.

Rawls' radical perspective on human fate is a consequence of these experiences. According to him, the opportunities people have should be influenced as little as possible by "natural and social contingencies." His paradigm of injustice was slavery as it had existed in the southern states of the USA. Some judgments Rawls viewed as fixed points: ones we never expect to withdraw, as when Abraham Lincoln said: "If slavery is not wrong, nothing is wrong." Lincoln was, next to Immanuel Kant, a permanent source of inspiration. Rawls continued to study the works of both all his life. Abraham Lincoln especially was, for Rawls, a point of reference for what the philosopher Thomas Nagel has phrased "the engagement between the hope for achieving justice and the nearly overwhelming obstacles of the real world."

Rawls attended high school from 1935 to 1939 at the Kent School, an episcopalian private school for boys in Connecticut. After graduating in 1939, Rawls was admitted to Princeton University. He entered in September 1939 as a member of the "class of 1943." It was a moment that coincided with the German attack on Poland (September 1, 1939) that meant the beginning of the Second World War in Europe. Everyone around Rawls, including himself, was convinced that sooner or later the United States would participate in this war. Rawls started – in addition to his studies – deepening his knowledge on the history of the First World War and the general question of war and international justice.

Among his teachers at Princeton was Norman Malcolm, who had worked with, and was a friend of, Ludwig Wittgenstein (about whom Malcolm would publish his famous memoirs in 1958[1]). It was Malcolm who first raised in Rawls an interest in political philosophy. Rawls also took another course with Malcolm, during the spring term of 1942, on the (quasi-religious) topic of human evil. Rawls completed his BA in January 1943, *summa cum laude* in philosophy.

In the meantime, the United States had indeed started participating in the Second World War, following the attack on Pearl Harbor by Japan on December 7, 1941. A month after Rawls graduated, in February 1943, he entered the US Army as an enlisted man. He would remain one for three years. As a private of F Company of the 128th Infantry Regiment of the 32nd Division (the "Red Arrow Division"), he was sent to the Pacific theater for two years, where he served in New Guinea, taking part in the fighting in the Philippines (the 36-day Battle of Leyte and the 120-day Battle of Luzon, where he was grazed in the head by a sniper's bullet); he was still in the Pacific when American planes dropped the atomic bombs on Hiroshima and Nagasaki; and he was finally, from September 1945 onward for four months, part of the American forces occupying Japan.

During the war, many of Rawls' friends in his regiment, seventeen students of his Princeton "class of 1943," twenty-three of the year below, as well as classmates from Kent School, were killed. These events also profoundly influenced Rawls' thinking, once again with regard to "the arbitrariness of fortune," and also with regard to the *ius in bello*, the principles governing the conduct of democratic peoples at war, which establish certain lines that must not be crossed, thus formulating the moral limits of the means to be used during a war.

Fifty years after the fire-bombing of Japanese cities which began in the spring of 1945 (on Tokyo, for example), and the atomic bombing of

Hiroshima on (August 6), and shortly afterwards Nagasaki (August 9), Rawls wrote an article on these events. He could find no justification for these acts and considered them to be "very grave wrongs."[2] One of the arguments for dropping the atomic bombs was the claim that it would shorten the war. President Harry Truman thought it would, and would thereby save the lives of American soldiers. Japanese lives, military and civilian, presumably counted for less, Rawls notes. However, all the arguments given fail to justify violations of the principles of the conduct of a just war. Even if war is a kind of hell, and death a common occurrence, that ought not to mean that all of the moral and political distinctions on which just and decent civilized societies always depend should cease to hold (LoP: 100, 103). At the same time, Rawls had always been conscious of the fact that these very grave wrongs influenced his own fortune. He knew that if the atomic bombs had not been dropped, he and his fellow soldiers would certainly have had to fight a conventional campaign in Japan. These "very grave wrongs," then, contributed to the fact that he himself was "fortunate" and benefited from an *unmerited contingency*. He survived the war.[3]

Rawls left the army in January 1946 and began his graduate study in philosophy at Princeton University (on the GI Bill).[4] His intention was to write a dissertation on moral and political philosophy. This had not been his original plan. During his BA, Rawls had become interested in the religious question of why evil exists. His undergraduate honor thesis submitted to the Department of Philosophy at Princeton had as its subject "the origin of evil" ("A Brief Inquiry into the Meaning of Sin and Faith: An Interpretation Based on the Concept of Community," December, 1942). His intention had been to attend the School of Divinity and to become a minister. The war had made him change his mind. His personal war experiences in the Pacific, seeing with his own eyes the devastated city of Hiroshima after the Japanese surrender (his troop train went through the remains of Hiroshima), and, especially, hearing about the Holocaust, all brought Rawls to reconsider his religious beliefs as an orthodox episcopalian Christian. "How could I pray and ask God to help me, or my family, or my country, or any other cherished thing I cared about, when God would not save millions of Jews from Hitler? When Lincoln interprets the Civil War as God's punishment for the sin of slavery, deserved equally by North and South, God is seen as acting justly. But the Holocaust can't be interpreted in that way, and all attempts to do so that I have read of are hideous and evil. To interpret history as expressing God's will, God's will must accord with the most basic ideas of justice as we know them. For what else can the most basic justice be?" By June 1945, they led Rawls to abandon many of the main doctrines of Christianity, and eventually "to reject the idea of the supremacy of the divine will as also hideous and evil."[5]

Near the end of the war, then, Rawls had given up his plans to enter the episcopalian ministry. The cruelties and destruction of war, which he himself had also experienced, brought him to reflect once again on the question of evil, now framed as the question whether human beings have a moral nature able to be moved by justice, or whether that nature is so self-centered, amoral, and corrupt that justice lies outside the reach of human possibilities.

This negative perspective on humankind, that in fact is the basis of the Christian orthodox doctrine of original sin, would be rejected by Rawls for the whole his life. Negating this perspective on human nature, and banishing the dangers of resignation and cynicism, would be the driving force behind Rawls' philosophical reflection and work for more than fifty years. Rawls steadfastly remained of the opinion that a just society that guarantees liberty, equality, and self-respect for all its members remains within our reach. A reasonably just society, both at home and abroad, is possible.

On New Year's Eve, 1948, Rawls met in Baltimore Margaret (Mardy) Warfield Fox (born 1927). Her parents were Joseph Mickle Fox (from a distinguished old family from Philadelphia) and Ruth Louise Martin (from a respected family from Baltimore). Margaret Rawls studied art history at Pembroke College (now part of Brown University, at Providence, Rhode Island). In June 1949, two weeks after she graduated, they married in Baltimore. Four children were born to their marriage.

They spent their first summer together in Princeton, producing the index of Walter Kaufmann's *Nietzsche: Philosopher, Psychologist and Antichrist* (1950),[6] a book that was to become justifiably famous. (Rawls had always considered an index to be an important key by which a reader can "enter" a work. The index for his *A Theory of Justice* [1971], which he compiled, ran, for example, to nineteen pages; the index of his *Political Liberalism* [1993] to twenty-nine pages. But it is in their content rather than their size that they are exemplars of the role an index ought to play.)

In June 1950, at Princeton, Rawls defended his PhD thesis "A Study on the Grounds of Ethical Knowledge: Considered with Reference to Judgments on the Moral Worth of Character."[7] It focused on the issue of how in ethical questions a choice can be justified, on which procedure has to be used. Rawls formulated a method that can be called "a coherence theory of ethical justification."[8] The only way to convince someone of the correctness of a general moral principle is, according to this coherence theory, to show that one's own moral convictions in particular cases are nothing other than a specific application of that general moral principle. Rawls here laid down the foundation for what he later worked out as the ideas of "reflective equilibrium" and "considered judgments," ideas that have the capability to give someone conscious insight into their own sense of justice.

After having taught for the following two years in the Department of Philosophy at Princeton, Rawls spent the year 1952–1953 on a Fulbright Fellowship at Christ Church, Oxford. There he met with, among others, H. L. A. Hart, Isaiah Berlin, and Stuart Hampshire. That year was, from the perspective of the development of Rawls' ideas on (political) philosophy, the most important year of his life so far.

After his return to the United States he became assistant professor at Cornell University at Ithaca, where he joined his former teacher Norman Malcolm on the faculty, and where he was promoted to associate professor with tenure in 1956. Subsequently the Massachusetts Institute of Technology (MIT) in Cambridge (MA) offered him a professorship with tenure. He stayed at MIT as a professor of philosophy from 1960 to 1962. In 1962 he went to Harvard University (Cambridge, MA) to join the Philosophy Department, where he was appointed professor in philosophy, and where he would remain for the rest of his academic career.

Politically speaking, the second half of the 1960s in the United States was dominated by the Civil Rights Movement and by the Vietnam War. Rawls himself publicly took a stand with regard to the war. From the beginning he was of the opinion that the war was morally unacceptable: it was an unjust war. In the spring term of 1969 he taught a course, "Problems of War," which included, among other issues, *ius ad bellum* (i.e. under which circumstances is it justified to go to war) and *ius in bello* (i.e. how war ought to be conducted), and the related issues of the conscientious objection to serving in an unjust war, and of civil disobedience.

These latter ideas would eventually find their way into *A Theory of Justice* and his ideas on *ius ad bellum* and *ius in bello* would later be elaborated in *The Law of Peoples* (1999). Rawls' ideas on civil disobedience in particular, and the way in which he elaborated when citizens as dissenters are justified in publicly and non-violently disobeying the law, within the limits of fidelity to the law, had tremendous influence. (These ideas were first published in 1969 as "The Justification of Civil Disobedience," but had been circulating in manuscript form since September 1966.) They provided a justification for engaging in actions of dissent against the Vietnam War and for supporting the Civil Rights Movement in the United States.

The Vietnam War directly confronted university professors with another moral issue. Although there was compulsory military service for men up to the age of twenty-six, the Department of Defense had decided not to conscript students *in good standing*, the so-called "2–S" deferment. One failing grade could cause a student to be called up. Rawls considered this to be an unjust proposition: "If young men are forced to participate in the war at all, then at least the sons of the rich and the well-connected should share this fate equally with the rest. If not all fit young men are needed for the war, then the requisite number should be selected by lot."[9] It was a position defended by Rawls and seven of his colleagues from the Philosophy Department and another eight from Political Science. Proposals to get this position adopted in faculty meetings in late 1966 and early 1967 were eventually defeated. Disagreements relating to the Vietnam War continued for many years at Harvard University, and at many other places as well.

In the meantime, Rawls continued working steadily on the manuscript of *A Theory of Justice*. In August 1969, he left with the family to spend the academic year 1969–1970 at the Center for Advanced Study at Stanford University (CA), so that he could finally complete his *magnum opus*. Then, one morning in early April 1970, Rawls was called by the director of the Center, and told that a few incendiary bombs had exploded in the Center overnight. Rawls had left the latest version of his manuscript on his desk! But he was, once again, lucky: his office was spared by the fire, although the manuscript sustained severe water damage. It was dried page by page. After that Rawls went back to work, further modifying the manuscript.

When he returned to Harvard in September 1970, Rawls became chairman of the Department of Philosophy. The Vietnam War continued, and those working in the department had not only very diverse philosophical beliefs, but also diverse political opinions. The philosopher Hilary Putnam, for instance, was a member of the Maoist Progressive Labor Party, while the philosopher W. V. Quine supported the Vietnam policy of the American president, Richard Nixon. There was not a lot of time left for Rawls to finish his manuscript. When he eventually received the typeset galleys for correction from Harvard University Press, Rawls was amazed to discover its length: 587 pages, to which still had to be added the index prepared by Rawls himself. As Rawls recalled in 1991: "It's size and scope was a little mad, actually. In writing it I guessed it was about 350 pages; when it was put in galleys and the Press told me it was nearly 600 pages (587 to be exact) I was astounded."[10] Finally, at the end of 1971, *A Theory of Justice* was published, a study which had been a legendary twenty years in the making.

In later years Rawls rarely participated in public debates, and when he did so it was mainly in his role as philosopher. He had (political) opinions, but as he often said, these opinions were not arguments. He was of the opinion that in public debates philosophers are nearly always misunderstood. Although political philosophy has great influence on the lives of people, its effects are indirect and it takes years before they have become part of the moral consciousness of a society. To get acquainted with Rawls' "political" views, for instance that all citizens should have equality of access to the political process, that the (American) system of financing electoral campaigns is unacceptable, for his arguments on the issue of abortion, for these and many more one has to study the expositions given by him in his philosophical works.

One example where Rawls did participate in a public debate, be it once again in his role as philosopher, was in the context of the American debate with regard to legalized *physician-assisted suicide*. Before the Supreme Court at the end of 1997 would contemplate two cases involving state laws that banned physician-assisted suicide, a so-called friend of the court "*Brief of the Amici Curiae*" was presented to them. It was signed by Rawls and five other *amici*, the political and moral philosophers Judith Jarvis Thomson, Robert Nozick, Ronald Dworkin, Thomas Scanlon, and Thomas Nagel. It was the first time in the history of the Supreme Court that a group of philosophers, as *philosophers*, presented a brief.

To the question of whether dying patients have a right to choose death rather than continued pain and suffering, the signatories answered that they were united in their conviction that respect for the fundamental principles of liberty and justice, as well as for the American constitutional tradition, required that the answer should be that indeed such a right should be honored. Extensively the position is substantiated that: "Each individual has a right to make the 'most intimate and personal choices central to personal dignity and autonomy.' That right encompasses the right to exercise some control over the time and manner of one's death."[11]

In 1979 Rawls was promoted to the highest academic rank at Harvard, that of the James Bryant Conant University Professorship. His predecessor had been Kenneth Arrow, the Nobel Prize laureate for economics in 1972. Although he formally retired in 1991, Rawls continued teaching until 1995. In October 1995 Rawls suffered a stroke.[12] Several more would follow.

Rawls was not a person wanting to be in the limelight, or to accept public honors. There are a few exceptions, an honorary degree at Oxford University (1983), one at Princeton (1987), and one at Harvard (1997). In 1999 Rawls was a recipient of the National Humanities Medal, an honor awarded him by the president of the United States, William J. (Bill) Clinton. It was awarded to him not only for his philosophical work, which "stimulated a national revival of attention to moral philosophy," it was also an award in recognition of his profound influence as a teacher. As the laudatio mentions, Rawls "trained many members of the generation who are now the most distinguished practitioners of moral and political philosophy, and through his mentorship he has helped many women into the ranks of a male-dominated field."[13]

In November 1999, Rawls was awarded by the Royal Swedish Academy of Sciences the Rolf Schock Prize in Logic and Philosophy for *A Theory of Justice*, "which has constituted a renewal of normative ethics and political philosophy and has in an essential way contributed to the methodology for normative ethics."[14]

In 1960 the family had settled in Lexington (MA), one of the oldest townships in New England (founded in 1642), a short distance from Cambridge. For over thirty years Margaret Rawls was a town meeting member, focusing on matters of land use planning and environmental protection. Over the last few years she has spent her time on more fully pursuing her artistic career. It was in their home in Lexington that John Rawls died on November 24, 2002, at eighty-one years of age.

In 1951 Rawls published his first article, "Outline of a Decision Procedure for Ethics," which summarizes part of his dissertation.[15] Over the next twenty years he published some ten articles which can be considered as preliminary studies of the main themes eventually worked out in *A Theory of Justice*, published in 1971.

After the publication of *A Theory of Justice* it would be time to move on to a new topic, or so one would think. As Rawls himself tells us in an interview in 1991, "I had been writing it for a long time, so I would finally get it off my desk and then do something else. ... I had planned on doing some other things mainly connected with the third part of the book, which was the part I liked best, the part on moral psychology. That would not be exactly a new but a related topic. I have never gotten around to that and never will. I thought, the way things have turned out, that it would be better if I spent my time trying to state justice as fairness more convincingly and to reply to people and remove their objections. I'm not sure that's the best thing to have done, but that's what I have done. I'm a monomaniac really. I'd like to get something right. But in philosophy one can't do that, not with any confidence. Real difficulties always remain."[16]

This, then, is what Rawls did after 1971, and from this perspective one can interpret the publication of *A Theory of Justice* as the closure of a first phase in his work. The articles he published after 1971 can then be seen as an elaboration, but especially as stepping-stones for a second phase that resulted in the publication of *Political Liberalism* in 1993.

In the years after Rawls had published *A Theory of Justice*, he examined more and more the fact that a modern democratic society is characterized by a pluralism of religious, philosophical, and moral doctrines, as well as by cultural and ethnic diversity. He was of the opinion that his – in a political-theoretical sense (and thus not in a party-political meaning) – "liberal" theory of justice as he had formulated that theory in *A Theory of Justice*, did not sufficiently take this pluralism into account and had to be recast. This led to *Political Liberalism*, in which – still from a political-theoretical perspective – the issues of "justice and pluralism" are discussed. In June 1996 a paperback edition of *Political Liberalism* was published, to which Rawls had added a new Introduction. Rawls had planned after that another new paperback edition, including revisions he intended to make, but his illness prevented him from doing so. However, after his death a new paperback edition of *Political Liberalism* was published, in 2005, expanded with what Rawls himself considered to be the best statement on his ideas on "public reason and political liberalism," especially regarding the compatibility of public reason with religious views, ideas he had originally published as an article in 1997.

With *A Theory of Justice*, Rawls had formulated a theory for a modern democratic society, closed-off from the rest of the world. *Political Liberalism* did not change this perspective. Only with his monograph *The Law of Peoples*, published in 1999, did Rawls give his perspective on justice an international dimension and elaborate on what justice among peoples requires.

In his doing so, or so one can argue, a third and final phase had come to an end, the construction of Rawls' theory of justice being completed. (One should hasten to add, however, that Rawls himself would never consider any of his published texts as "final" or "completed"; they would always remain open for revision.) Although one can now discern, over time, three phases, closer examination shows that Rawls' complete work is in fact one coherent whole, with all the parts being closely related to each other. This introduction to Rawls' works will demonstrate how this is indeed the case.

Also in 1999, Rawls' *Collected Papers* were published, a volume that contains nearly all of his published articles.[17] In that same year he also published a revised edition of *A Theory of Justice*. In February and March 1975 Rawls had considerably revised the original English text of *A Theory of Justice* in preparing it for its German translation, a translation that was published later that year. The revisions – considered by Rawls to be significant improvements – have been included in all subsequent translations (at the time of writing there are some thirty), and no further revisions have been added since that time. Remarkably enough, this revised edition had not been available in English until 1999 (TJR: xvii).[18]

In this revised edition of 1999, the improvements that Rawls had originally made in 1975 have been incorporated. That we are concerned in this revised edition from 1999 with revisions that actually originate from 1975 also means that, to prevent any misunderstanding, we have changes only *within the framework* of *A Theory of Justice*. The revisions made by Rawls in 1975 have nothing to do with a recasting of the theory to be able to speak of "political liberalism," a recasting that, as we noted above, resulted in 1993 in the publication of *Political Liberalism*.

In 2000, Rawls' *Lectures on the History of Moral Philosophy* were published, lectures Rawls had been giving at Harvard over a period of some thirty years and that went through major revisions during that period. The lectures deal with questions of moral philosophy to which Kant, Hume, Leibniz, and Hegel had tried to give answers. In lecturing on these philosophers, Rawls would always try "to pose their problems as they themselves saw them, given what their understanding of these problems was in their own time."[19]

In May 2001, Rawls published *Justice as Fairness: A Restatement*. In some two hundred pages Rawls expounds in a concise manner the main features of his theory of justice. *Justice as Fairness* does not contain new developments or a recasting of his theory, but summarizes in an accessible way the final statement of his theory. In this relatively short guide through his work, Rawls once again explains which revisions to *A Theory of Justice* he considered necessary in order to be able to express in his ideas on justice the permanent pluralism of our contemporary democratic societies. At the same time it is clear that the main features of his exposition of what should be considered a just society have remained unchanged. (It should be added that *Justice as Fairness* does not contain Rawls' views on international justice. To become acquainted with those, one has to study *The Law of Peoples*.)

Rawls' *Lectures on the History of Political Philosophy* were published posthumously in 2007. These lectures derive from Rawls' written lectures and notes for a course in "Modern Political Philosophy" he taught at Harvard from the mid-1960s until his retirement in 1995. The lectures consider Hobbes, Locke, Hume, Rousseau, John Stuart Mill, and Marx (with appendixes on Henry Sidgwick and Joseph Butler). As the editor of these lectures, Samuel Freeman, notes in his "Editor's Foreword," the lectures reveal how Rawls conceived of the history of the social contract tradition, and they suggest how Rawls saw his own work in relation to that of Locke, Rousseau, and Kant, and to some degree to Hobbes as well.[20] With this publication Rawls' complete works are now publicly accessible.

Looking at this list of publications we can note that six of his books have been published in or after 1999 (and a seventh one, *Political Liberalism*, in 1993). Taking this into account, it is fair to say that debates on Rawls' theorizing on justice, triggered in 1971 by the publication of *A Theory of Justice*, should not be considered to be rounded off. Far from it.

Rawls not only formulates particular principles of justice, he also develops and works out methods for the justification of these principles. As *Political Liberalism*, the *Collected Papers*, the *Revised Edition* of *A Theory of Justice*, *The Law of Peoples*, and *Justice as Fairness: A Restatement* demonstrate, over time Rawls has not changed his principles or methods in any far-reaching way. In fact Rawls has permanently, for over fifty years, in a seemingly never-ending, continuous flow of articles and books, refined, clarified, defended against criticism, advanced and, if he considered it necessary, adapted his theory of justice.

When *A Theory of Justice* was eventually published in 1971, Rawls thought only a couple of friends would read the work and then that would be it. Things turned out otherwise, as we all now know. The ideas of Rawls have had an overwhelming influence on the development of political philosophy since 1971. It seems fair to say it gained such attention from a conjunction of circumstances, one related to the development of political philosophy as an academic discipline, the other related to political developments outside academia: the Vietnam War and the Civil Rights Movement.

In the 1950s and 1960s political philosophy was declared to be dead, or at least moribund, and it was claimed that creatively constructing a valuational frame of reference had been abandoned. The tradition seemed to have been broken. Two arguments were put forward that tried to substantiate this claim of – in the best of cases – the decline of political philosophy. The first was that the specific interpretation that in the natural sciences is given to what should be considered "science," should also be used as the decisive criterion to judge social and political "science." Starting from the assumption of the unity of sciences, adopting the so-called "scientific method" had among other things the consequence of underlining the idea that there is an insurmountable, logical (deductive) gulf between "is" and "ought." Making the step from observable facts to norms is, in this view, in principle impossible. This process of "scientification," with its positivist universe of discourse and its positivist methodological assumptions, attracted more and more adherents. In political science, for instance, it led to the application to political inquiry of what political scientists believed to be the methods of natural science. Political philosophy, which is after all a field that by definition is concerned with normative questions, came in academic circles to be considered an "unscientific activity," and it was pushed more and more into the background. It is this development that brought some people to the conclusion that political philosophy was dead or dying. This development thus meant raising the question of what *scientific* political theory, based on "the scientific method," could and could not do with the perennial questions of political philosophy. In this respect Arnold Brecht's *Political Theory. The Foundations of Twentieth-Century Political Thought*, published in 1959, had a seminal influence, especially with its account of the "Logical Gulf between Is and Ought," of "Scientific Value Relativism," and the implications of both for what the scientific method could do with values.[21] In fact, Brecht for one lamented the so-called crisis in political philosophy which was a result of these developments.

There is a second development (albeit closely connected with the first) that contributed to the debate on the life chances of political philosophy. It was the development of analytical philosophy with a linguistic dimension. Here the dilemma of political philosophy is articulated in terms of the positivist theory of linguistic meaning. The whole tradition of political philosophy rests, or so it is argued, on the mistaken belief that values could be objectively determined and rationally defended. T. D. Weldon, for instance, argued in *The Vocabulary of Politics* (1953) that such judgments, unlike empirical judgment, may have an emotional meaning but lacked cognitive status and so were matters of preference, ideology, or decision rather than matters for rational discussion.[22] Value judgments fall outside the scope of scientific knowledge. There is a clear distinction between philosophical, that is to say conceptual, analysis and empirical research. Philosophy is an activity in which the interest in research lies in conceptual analysis, not in substantial analysis. Talk on ethical judgments is replaced by talk on meta-ethical issues (largely inspired by the ordinary language philosophy coming from Oxford). Here also the tradition of political philosophy is considered an activity that has come to an end: the most rigorous and sophisticated developments in Anglo-Saxon philosophy have shown, or so it is claimed, that there can be no (political) philosophy that generates "true" knowledge.

Now the claim that political philosophy was moribund or had even deceased was of course a huge exaggeration, "a parochial comedy played out in the 1950s in Britain and America," as De Crespigny and Minogue have argued.[23] And John Plamenatz wrote in his "The Use of Political Theory" (1960): "Even in Oxford, which more perhaps than any other place in the English-speaking world is the home of political philosophy, it is often said that the subject is dead or sadly diminished in importance. I happen to have a professional interest in assuming that it is still alive."[24]

Besides, we should take note of the fact that in the middle of the twentieth century important work was published by political philosophers. One has only to think of Hannah Arendt, Hanna Pitkin, Judith Shklar, Isaiah Berlin, Friedrich Hayek, Michael Oakeshott, Karl Popper, Leo Strauss, and Eric Voeglin. And as for the requirement of scientific "value-neutrality" that – as the claim went – had undermined the grounds for the existence of political philosophy, that did not remain unanswered. Strauss, for example, argued that a "scientific" approach may have brought criteria for precision, but not for relevance.[25] However, in general, interest in these philosophers remained marginal, usually confined to a small (academic) circle. It should be added that the research methods used by them were usually not very intersubjective. The method used by Strauss, for example, could best be characterized as a hermeneutic one, if indeed it is not better described as a "closed" one.

In the meantime, growing dissatisfaction with so-called "value-free" political science, and its perceived irrelevance in ignoring or not taking a stand on important political issues (e.g. the Vietnam War, the Civil Rights Movement), brought to the fore the need to deal not only with "facts," but also with normative issues.

It is in this context that "at the right moment" *A Theory of Justice* was published. While acknowledging that it is "scientifically" impossible to prove the "correctness" of a normative opinion, this theory provided the possibility of reasoning on normative issues in an intersubjective manner. Empirical evidence is replaced by an appeal to the force of conviction using reasonable argumentation. Rawls created a common disciplinary discourse, based on the methods of argumentation and reasoning, in which everybody could freely partake, where nobody is locked out. And, in part, the ability to create this common discourse could be attributed to the fact that Rawls was familiar with meta-ethical inquiries, and was trained in the tradition of the analytical philosophy he was building upon. He combined rigorous conceptual analysis with substantive, normative concepts. Concepts and premises first have to be formulated in a clear and precise way. Next, as Rawls himself states, "clearly arguments from such premises can be fully deductive, as theories in politics and economics attest. We should strive for a kind of moral geometry with all the rigor which this name connotes" (TJ: 121; TJR: 104–105).[26] But at the same time Rawls was of the opinion that the analysis of moral concepts – though helpful – does not of itself enlighten us about the substance of moral principles: "The analysis of moral concepts and the a priori [...] is too slender a basis" for developing a moral theory or working out a substantive theory of justice (TJ: 51; TJR: 44). By introducing a notion of reasoning as a justification for reaching consensus on matters of justice, Rawls demonstrated – in the face of positivism – that there could be intersubjective, thus shared, "good reasons" for ethical conclusions on substantive matters. Rawls showed that it was possible for an academic political theorist to think about the critical and prescriptive analysis of politics as a reasonable kind of academic activity and thus that academic political theory not only ought, but can, turn to issues that ordinary citizens urgently want to agree practical judgments on; it can turn to "burning" political questions such as civil rights, just war, poverty, discrimination, etc.[27] And in his so doing, one could argue that it was Rawls who resurrected the field of political philosophy.

It was one of Rawls' Harvard colleagues, the philosopher Robert Nozick (who died in January 2000), who had as early as 1974 remarked, in an impressive statement in which he shows his admiration for Rawls' work:

A Theory of Justice is a powerful, deep, subtle, wide-ranging, systematic work in political and moral philosophy which has not seen its like since the writings of John Stuart Mill, if then. It is a fountain of illuminating ideas, integrated together into a lovely whole. Political philosophers now must either work within Rawls' theory or explain why not. The considerations and distinctions we have developed are illuminated by, and help illuminate, Rawls' masterful presentation of an alternative conception. Even those who remain unconvinced after wrestling with Rawls' systemic vision will learn much from closely studying it. I do not speak only of the Millian sharpening of one's views in combating (what one takes to be) error. It is impossible to read Rawls' book without incorporating much, perhaps transmuted, into one's own deepened view. And it is impossible to finish his book without a new and inspiring vision of what a moral theory may attempt to do and unite; of how *beautiful* a whole theory can be.[28]

Nozick himself was, of course, one of those who in the end was not convinced. His study, *Anarchy, State, and Utopia*, in which an alternative conception of justice is formulated, is in fact a fundamental critique of Rawls' position, therewith proving his point that admiration does not preclude disagreement.

2 | *A just society*

The aims of Rawls

Rawls' lifelong project has been to present a theory of justice that works out a reasonable and practical political philosophical conception for a just constitutional democratic society, a conception that, at the same time, provides a reasonably systematic alternative to utilitarianism.

Rawls reminds us that the political theorist Isaiah Berlin has famously claimed that many values can be pursued, but that core values such as "liberty" and "social justice" will eventually conflict with each other because they are irreconcilable and incommensurable (PL: 303). The full range of values is too extensive to fit any social world. Our human predicament and the tragedy of liberalism with its ideas on freedom of choice is, as Berlin long maintained, that "every choice may entail an irreparable loss." Certainly, Rawls agrees, "any system of social institutions is limited in the range of values it can accommodate, so that some selection must be made from the full range of moral and political values that might be realized. This is because any system has, as it were, but a limited social space" (JaF: 36, note 26). There exists no family of workable institutions that can allow sufficient space for the full range of values. A social world, even a just liberal society, is not achievable without loss.[1]

But this acknowledgment should not lead to resignation. On the contrary, Rawls' project is one of reconciliation. It does not relieve us, at least from Rawls' position, of our responsibility to explore the possibility – in ways existing circumstances allow – of a just social world within which permissible ways of life have a fair opportunity to maintain themselves and to gain adherents over generations (PL: 198; JaF: 155). And Rawls is convinced that a just liberal society is the one that has far more space than other social worlds. It is for this reason that he explores how the basic political, social, and economic institutions of a modern constitutional democracy should be designed such that, at the same time, the basic liberties of each person, as well as the claims of democratic equality, can be honored. His first aim is then – "by generalizing and carrying to a higher order of abstraction the traditional theory of the social contract as represented by Locke, Rousseau, and Kant" – to present an answer to this question.[2]

His second aim is to work out an account of justice that represents a reasonable systematic alternative to utilitarian thought generally (the thought that finds its inspiration in Jeremy Bentham [1748–1832] and John Stuart Mill [1806–1873]), and so to all the different versions of it that have long dominated in academic circles, and particularly in the Anglo-Saxon tradition of political thought (this especially being the case at the time *A Theory of Justice* was published in 1971). With this end in mind, the kind of utilitarianism Rawls describes is the strict classical doctrine which receives, according to Rawls, its clearest and most accessible formulation in the work of Henry Sidgwick (1838–1900) (TJ: 22; TJR: xi, 20).[3]

Rawls' primary reason for wanting to find such an alternative is "the weakness, so I think, of utilitarian doctrine as a basis for the institutions of constitutional democracy. In particular, I do not believe that utilitarianism can provide a satisfactory account of the basic rights and liberties of citizens as free and equal persons, a requirement of absolutely first importance for an account of democratic institutions" (TJR: xi–xii).

In utilitarianism, the appropriate terms of social cooperation are settled by whatever in the circumstances will achieve the greatest sum of satisfaction of the rational desires of individuals. What Rawls considers to be the striking feature of this utilitarian view of justice is "that it does not matter, except indirectly, how this sum of satisfactions is distributed among individuals any more than it matters, except indirectly, how one man distributes his satisfactions over time. The correct distribution in either case is that which yields the maximum fulfillment. Society must allocate its means of satisfaction whatever these are, rights and duties, opportunities and privileges, and various forms of wealth, so as to achieve this maximum if it can" (TJ: 26; TJR: 23).

The basic shortcoming of utilitarianism – in whatever form – is that basic rights of individuals can be sacrificed for a collective societal goal such as maximizing social welfare. It allows an unacceptable trade-off among persons: utilitarianism formulates a principle which may require lesser life prospects for some, simply for the sake of a greater sum of advantages enjoyed by others. Utilitarianism does not recognize that everyone has equal moral worth (which, as we will see, for Rawls does not entail that distributive shares have to be equal), and therefore recognizes neither the way persons are equal to each other, nor the way they differ from each other. Or, as Rawls has famously summarized his objections against utilitarianism: "Utilitarianism does not take seriously the distinction between persons" (TJ: 27; TJR: 24).

For Rawls, the idea of the equal moral worth of persons is basic: it is the equality between human beings as moral persons. "Each person possesses an inviolability founded on justice that even the welfare of society as a whole cannot override. For this reason justice denies that the loss of freedom for some is made right by a greater good shared by others. It does not allow that the sacrifices imposed on a few are outweighed by the larger sum of advantages enjoyed by many. Therefore in a just society the liberties of equal citizenship are taken as settled; the rights secured by justice are not subject to political bargaining or to the calculus of social interests" (TJ: 3–4: TJR: 3–4). A conception of justice should reflect this idea by publicly expressing men's respect for one another. Or, following Kant's view and putting it another way, this is saying that the way society is ordered should manifest men's desire to treat one another not as means only but as ends in themselves (TJ: 179; TJR: 156).

The defining characteristic of "moral persons" is their having two moral powers: to be reasonable and to be rational. The reasonable is the capacity that moral persons have to understand, to apply, and to act from (and not merely in accordance with) the principles of justice that specify the fair terms of social cooperation (persons have *a sense of justice*). The rational is the capacity that moral persons have to form, to revise, and to rationally pursue a conception of one's good (expressed by a rational plan of life) (persons have a capacity for *a conception of the good*). The basis of equality is taken to be similarity in these two respects: as creatures having a conception of their good and capable of a sense of justice (TJ: 19; TJR: 17). It is these two moral powers that represent equality between human beings as moral persons: these two powers are the basis of the equal moral worth of free and equal persons (JaF: 18–19).

As a Kantian view, Rawls' conception of justice accepts this conception of the person, and consequently that free and equal moral persons have different and opposing conceptions of the good. This conception of justice is independent of and prior to the notion of goodness, in the sense that its principles limit the conceptions of the good which are admissible in a just society: they must fit within the framework of this conception of justice. "A just social system defines the scope within which individuals must develop their aims, and it provides a framework of rights and opportunities and the means of satisfaction within and by the use of which these ends may be equitably pursued" (TJ: 31; see also TJR: 28).

We mentioned that Rawls is convinced that a just liberal society is the one that has far more space than other social worlds, that it has within itself sufficient space for ways of life, for various conceptions of the good, fully worthy of the devotion of those who affirm them. But these conceptions of the good must fit within the limits drawn by the conception of right itself – by the space it allows for the pursuit of permissible ends. To summarize these ideas in Rawls' phrase: "the right draws the limit; the good shows the point" (LHMP: 231).[4] This priority of the right over the good in Rawls' conception of justice, *justice as fairness*, turns out to be a central feature of the conception.[5]

Rawls' Kantian starting point – men's desire to treat one another not as means only but as ends in themselves – determines his perspective on society.[6] It is the major institutions of society, taken together as one scheme, that define men's rights and duties and influence their life prospects; what they can expect to be and how well they can hope to do. By major institutions Rawls understands the (political) constitution and the principal economic and social institutions: *the basic structure* of society.

This basic structure of society is conceived – for the time being – as a closed system, isolated from other societies. We start with "domestic" justice: society is "a self-contained national community" and has no relations with other societies. Its members enter it only by birth and leave only by death. Other questions, such as those of local justice and of global justice (the principles applying to international law), are not at this point Rawls' concern.

Rawls' focus is almost entirely on the basic structure as the subject of social justice. For him the basic structure is the primary subject of justice because its effects on the expectations of men are pervasive and present from the beginning of life. It is within the confines of this basic structure that people work together: by doing so, by social cooperation, a better life for all is possible. Society should be seen as *a cooperative venture for mutual advantage* between reasonable and rational human beings

(TJ: 4; TJR: 4). The way this social cooperation is organized defines the appropriate distribution of the benefits and burdens of social cooperation. The crucial question of course is what the "appropriate distribution of benefits and burdens" is. The answer is given by the principles of social justice.

Before we discuss the principles of justice that define the appropriate distribution of the advantages of social cooperation, we will first elaborate what the "benefits" and "burdens" of social cooperation are. Rawls' idea is that social cooperation does not only produce a material product (income and wealth), but produces other products as well: *primary goods*. It is these primary goods that enable free and equal persons, moved by their two moral powers, to pursue their different and (perhaps opposing) conceptions of the good. Rawls provides us with the following list of these primary goods:

(a) basic liberties as given by a list, for example: freedom of thought and liberty of conscience; freedom of association; the freedom defined by the liberty and integrity of the person, as well as by the rule of law; and finally, political liberties;
(b) freedom of movement and choice of occupation against a background of diverse opportunities;
(c) the powers and prerogatives of offices and positions of authority and responsibility, particularly those in the main political and economic institutions;
(d) income and wealth;
(e) the social bases of self-respect.[7]

All of these are "social primary goods," scarce "resources." They are the various social conditions and all-purpose means (having an exchange value) that are generally necessary to enable persons to pursue or to revise their determinate conception of the good, their own plan of life. Everyone is assured an equal liberty to pursue whatever plan of life he pleases (as long as it does not violate what justice demands). Primary goods are characterized as what persons need in their status as free and equal human beings, and as normal and fully cooperating members of society, over a complete life. They enable persons to develop and fully exercise their two moral powers.[8] *A Theory of Justice* holds that for the realization of each plan of life, however it may look, the same social primary goods are necessary. (In fact over time Rawls did not change his view in this regard.) It is the basic structure of society that distributes these social primary goods. The aim of Rawls' theory of justice is to answer how this is to be done in a way that is fair, and to specify what the fair terms of social cooperation are.

This explains the important role that the constitution and the social and economic institutions play in Rawls' theory, and why he considers the basic structure to be the primary subject of the principles of social justice, of *justice as fairness* (TJ: 54; TJR: 47). The principles of justice for institutions must not be confused with the principles which apply to individuals and their actions in particular circumstances. Rawls' theory of justice formulates the principles of how institutions, that one enters by birth and exits only by death "over a complete life" so to speak, and that influence the life prospects of individuals, distribute primary goods in a fair way.

For Rawls, persons are viewed as being capable of taking responsibility for their own ends: they are themselves responsible for becoming as happy as possible with the all-purpose means they can expect to acquire, with their share of primary goods. Because they are responsible for the choices they make themselves, they can become happier by changing their preferences or tastes. But because it is practically impossible to reach agreement on a meaningful estimate of happiness when persons carry out their life-plans, the amount of primary goods a person receives is clearly not intended as a measure of the citizens' expected overall psychological well-being. In fact, *justice as fairness* rejects the idea of comparing and maximizing satisfaction in questions of justice (CP: 370; PL: 187–188). The principles of *justice as fairness* do not even mention the amount or the distribution of welfare, even less do they strive for equal welfare (or "equal well-being"); they refer only to the distribution of liberties and the other primary goods (TJ: 327; TJR: 287).

Thus, because there cannot be agreement on how to estimate happiness as defined, say, by men's success in executing their rational plans, much less on the intrinsic value of these plans, the expectations of individuals over the course of a complete life are not being objectively measured in terms of "satisfaction" when plans are executed using these goods. It is the primary goods themselves that are used as the measure for estimating expectations. In fact, Rawls defines expectations as simply an *index of primary goods*. Interpersonal comparisons for the purposes of justice are to be made in terms of the citizens' index of primary goods, and these goods are seen as answering to their needs as citizens, as opposed to their (rational) preferences and desires (as in a utilitarian view). This index provides the possibility of interpersonal comparisons in a way that seems most likely to establish a publicly recognized *objective and common measure* that reasonable persons can accept. The point is that *justice as fairness* "does not look behind the use which persons make of the rights and opportunities available to them in order to measure, much less to maximize, the satisfactions they achieve. Nor does it try to evaluate the relative merits of different conceptions of the good. ... Once the whole arrangement is set up and going no questions are asked about the totals of satisfaction or perfection" (TJ 94; TJR: 80–81).

Justice as fairness focuses instead on inequalities in the life prospects of persons so far as these are determined by three main kinds of contingencies: *natural assets* – that is, natural talents and abilities, native endowments – as these have been developed or left unrealized, their use favored or disfavored over time by *social circumstances* – that is their social class of origin – and such *chance contingencies* as accident and good fortune, or good or bad luck (health, involuntary unemployment). Each of these three contingencies strongly influences each person's possibility of realizing his conception of the good. The aim of a just social order is a system of social cooperation that takes the effects of these contingencies (the fortunate distribution of natural endowment, the contingencies of social circumstance, and chance contingencies such as accident and good fortune) into account.

Someone's fortune in the distribution of natural assets and abilities, his intelligence, strength, and the like, these internal "resources" are the outcome of the natural lottery. The distribution of native assets is neither just nor unjust: it is simply a natural given. It is arbitrary from a moral perspective and consequently native assets are not someone's (moral) desert. Rawls' strong conviction is that distributive shares that are improperly influenced by these natural contingencies, so arbitrary from a moral point of view, should not determine the expectations of life that persons have. The principles of *justice as fairness* that regulate the basic structure and specify the duties and obligations of individuals do not mention moral desert, and there is no tendency for distributive shares to correspond to it: legitimate expectations are not to be based on moral desert.

There is as well the fundamental problem that expectations and possibilities in life are strongly influenced by social contingencies, by the social position one is born into: one's place in the political, social, or economic structure of the basic institutions of society. That this is so has nothing to do with merit: it is not "just" or "unjust" that persons are born into society at some particular position. It is, according to Rawls, one of the fixed points of our moral judgments that no one deserves his initial starting place in society, any more than one deserves his place in the distribution of natural assets. It introduces a high measure of luck in the lives of people, but it is luck that is influenced by societal institutions. What is just and unjust is the way in which institutions deal with these natural and social contingencies.

We have here reached a fundamental idea of Rawls' theory of justice, if not *the* basic one. It is his "intuitive notion ... that the basic structure contains various social positions and that men born into different positions have different expectations of life determined, in part, by the political system as well as by economic and social circumstances. In this way the institutions of society favor certain starting places over others. These are especially deep inequalities. Not only are they pervasive, but they affect men's initial chances in life; *yet they cannot possibly be justified by an appeal to the notions of merit or desert.* It is these inequalities, presumably inevitable in the basic structure of any society, to which the principles of social justice must in the first instance apply. These principles, then, regulate the choice of a political constitution and the main elements of the economic and social system" (TJ: 7; TJR: 7; emphasis added).

Now it may well be the case that what is just and unjust is the way in which institutions deal with natural and social contingencies, but this does not imply that the institutions themselves are a natural fact, or "a natural given." Institutions are not unchangeable and beyond human control. To the contrary, the way the basic structure orders society is "men-made" and is changeable.

Institutions reflect and express the dominant moral attitudes in society and influence these opinions in their turn. Rawls is of the opinion that when we focus on "moral attitudes," "moral learning," "moral development," some principles (or tendencies) of moral psychology refer to an institutional setting as being just, and as being publicly known to be such (TJ: 491; TJR: 429–430). These psychological principles state that the social learning of moral attitudes works most effectively through society-wide shared institutions and practices that are widely and publicly considered to be just. The extent to which institutions or social practices are just or unjust, and the belief people have therein, strongly influence in their turn the social attitudes and the affinity, trust, and confidence that people have between each other. And these relations of affinity, of fellow feeling, are not a fixed thing. As Rawls formulates it, we "acquire attachments to persons and institutions according to how we perceive our good to be affected by them. *The basic idea is one of reciprocity, a tendency to answer in kind.* Now this tendency is a deep psychological fact. Without it our nature would be very different and fruitful social cooperation fragile if not impossible" (TJ: 494–495; TJR: 433; emphasis added). It is certainly no exaggeration to say that this "tendency to reciprocity" is the most important psychological assumption underlying Rawls' theory of justice.[9]

Now if indeed institutions influence and form moral attitudes, then for the direction of moral learning and moral development, the specific design of these institutions becomes crucial. A just basic structure affects the way in which persons who grow up in such a society acquire an understanding of and an attachment to principles of justice. Those who are raised in a particular moral conception, as expressed by institutions and social practices, become in due course a certain kind of person and themselves express this conception in their actions and in their relations with others (TJ: 461; TJR: 404; LoP: 112 note 44). And Rawls is especially concerned with a *well-ordered society*, a society that is designed in such a way that moral sentiments can develop in conformity with *justice as fairness*.

The radical character of Rawls' theory lies in the fact that it focuses on the virtues of these basic institutions. Being born as a child of slaves or as a child of slave-owners, as a child of an unskilled laborer or as a child of a member of the entrepreneurial class, in all cases the social circumstances one is born into are essentially purely arbitrary. However, the institutions that allow slavery or capitalism are men-made. The relevant question is thus not so much whether a slave-owner is acting "justly" or "unjustly" in the sense of being a "good" or "bad" human being. The issue here is rather that the institution of "slavery" is without "virtue" and is unjust.

Rawls' theory formulates an institutional project. That is why he can open *A Theory of Justice* in the following way: "Justice is the first virtue of social institutions, as truth is of systems of thought. A theory however elegant and economical must be rejected or revised if it is untrue; likewise laws and institutions no matter how efficient and well-arranged must be reformed or abolished if they are unjust. ... Being first virtues of human activities, truth and justice are uncompromising" (TJ: 3–4; TJR: 3–4).

The basic question Rawls wants us to consider is whether we are actually interested in taking undeserved inequalities into account in the institutional design of our society: those inequalities that are arbitrary from a moral point of view. The guiding idea should be that the fate of human beings should be determined by the free choices they make when questions of how they want to organize their lives arise. It is not fair that these choices are determined by arbitrary and undeserved differences in social circumstances and neither is it fair they are determined by differences in the natural assets that are given to human beings "by nature." No one deserves his greater natural capacity nor merits a more favorable starting place in society: inequalities of birth and natural endowment are undeserved. Moral entitlements cannot be based on luck in the natural lottery or on social fortune; neither of these should weight men's share in the benefits and burdens of social cooperation.

As Rawls summarizes these ideas: "Once we decide to look for a conception of justice that prevents the use of the accidents of natural endowment and the contingencies of social circumstance as counters in a quest for political and economic advantage, we are led to [the principles of *justice as fairness*]. They express the result of leaving aside those aspects of the social world that seem arbitrary from a moral point of view" (TJR: 14).[10]

What is *not* Rawls' intention, as soon as we encounter an un-favorable situation or a disadvantage, is to immediately compensate for it. We should be careful to make a distinction between "choices" and "circumstances." Rawls' radical conception of equality as expressed in *justice as fairness* formulates not what should be done about inequalities that arise from men's voluntary actions in accordance with the principle of free association. These inequalities are allowed. It formulates what should be done about the inequalities that are involuntary: disadvantages that are not based on the voluntary choices persons make. In liberal democratic theories of justice, such as Rawls', one tries to strike a balance between respect for choices and the circumstances in which these choices are made. To find such a balance is the aim of *justice as fairness*.

A theory of social justice

Rawls starts his undertaking with two questions. In which social institutions would reasonable people be willing to cooperate without denying or abandoning their personal aims? And which rules of conduct in their relations with one another would they voluntarily recognize as binding, and which would they for the most part act in accordance with, even if these rules would in part thwart them from reaching their aims? A special characteristic of Rawls' theory is that in answering these questions two things are combined. Rawls formulates specific principles of social justice. But he also formulates at the same time a specific method that shows how these principles can be convincingly justified to us, the readers of his work.

A set of principles of social justice is required to define the appropriate distribution of the benefits and burdens of social cooperation. Rawls has a broad perspective on "social justice." Many "things" are being distributed, and this is one aspect in which Rawls' ideas differ in an important way from other theories on social justice. As mentioned, Rawls is of the opinion that social cooperation not only produces a material product (income and wealth), but also basic liberties, diverse opportunities, the powers and prerogatives of offices and positions of responsibility, and the social bases of self-respect.

More than anything else, Rawls considers society as a fair system of cooperation. As mentioned, the idea is that social cooperation makes possible for all a better life than anyone would have if each were to live solely by his own efforts. Although society is *a cooperative venture for mutual advantage*, it is typically marked by a conflict as well as by an identity of interests. There is an identity of interests since it makes possible a better life for all, and there is a conflict of interests since persons are not indifferent as to how the greater benefits produced by their collaboration are to be distributed. This is so because, as Rawls notes, in order to pursue their ends, each person prefers a larger to a lesser share (TJ: 4; TJR: 4).

The question then is what a "fair" distribution of the benefits (and burdens!) produced by all in social cooperation actually is. It is the principles of social justice that answer this question. The theory of justice assumes a definite limit on the strength of social and altruistic motivation. It supposes that individuals and groups put forward competing claims, and that while they are willing to act justly, they are not prepared to abandon their own interests (TJ: 281; TJR: 248–249). The principles of justice, then, do not require that a person should abandon or diminish his striving for more, but serve to solve the conflict of interest in the distribution of the advantages. The principles of social justice are "required for choosing among the various social arrange-ments which determine this division of advantages and for underwriting an agreement on the proper distributive shares. These principles ... provide a way of assigning rights and duties in the basic institutions of society and they define the appropriate distribution of the benefits and burdens of social cooperation" (TJ: 4; TJR: 4).

It is these requirements that define the role of justice, and the back-ground conditions that give rise to these necessities are what Rawls calls *the circumstances of justice*. These can be divided into two kinds. The *objective* circumstances may be described as the normal conditions under which human cooperation is both possible and necessary. Most notably there is the condition of moderate scarcity: "Natural and other resources are not so abundant that schemes of cooperation become superfluous, nor are conditions so harsh that fruitful ventures must inevitably break down. While mutually advantageous arrangements are feasible, the benefits they yield fall short of the demands men put forward" (TJ: 127; TJR: 110). Next there are the *subjective* circum-stances, the relevant aspects of the persons working together, with their own – different – life-plans, putting forward conflicting claims on the natural and social resources available, and thus formulating conflicting claims on the division of social advantages. Thus, in brief, the circum-stances of justice obtain whenever persons put forward conflicting claims for the division of social advantages under conditions of moder-ate scarcity (TJ: 126–128; TJR: 109–111).

Now Rawls' guiding aim is to determine which set of principles of social justice free and equal persons would assent to for solving this issue of distribution. It is by a specific method of public justification – that is a justification that we, "you and I," the readers of Rawls' work, could agree to – that these principles are worked out. It is to this procedure of justification we now turn.

Justification in *A Theory of Justice*

For the justification of the principles of justice we, the readers of Rawls' work, are invited to participate in a thought-experiment for the purpose of public and self clarification (JaF: 17). Imagine, Rawls asks us, a well-defined initial situation in which certain principles would be accepted. And "the most philosophical favored interpretation of this initial choice situation for the purpose of a theory of justice" is what Rawls has defined as the *"the original position"* (TJ: 18; TJR: 16). Imagine next that by social contract in such a purely hypothetical situation, we (or rather the parties that represent us) could agree on a set of principles to reconstruct from scratch, *de novo*, our society. And also imagine that in doing so, the parties in this original position are situated behind a *"veil of ignorance."* We, "you and I," "here and now," are asked to simulate being in this original position and to play the role of someone who, in accordance with enumerated restrictions on information, has to find the principles that free and equal persons, here and now, would consider to be the fair terms of social cooperation that should regulate the basic structures of society.

The veil of ignorance prevents the parties in the original position from knowing how the various alternative principles for ordering our social order will affect their own particular case. It removes differences in bargaining advantages so that, in this and other respects, the parties are symmetrically situated, a situation that is necessary if the parties are to be seen as representatives of free and equal persons who are to reach an agreement under conditions that are fair. The original position respects the basic precepts of formal equality: those equal (similar) in all relevant aspects are to be treated equally (similarly) (JaF: 18). To model this equality in the original position, the veil of ignorance does indeed exclude a large amount of information. As Rawls stipulates:

First of all, no one knows his place in society, his class position or social status; nor does he know his fortune in the distribution of natural assets and abilities, his intelligence and strength, and the like. Nor, again, does anyone know his conception of the good, the particulars of his rational plan of life, or even the special features of his psychology such as his aversion to risk or liability to optimism or pessimism. More than this, I assume that the parties do not know the particular circumstances of their own society. That is, they do not know its economic or political situation, or the level of civilization and culture it has been able to achieve. The persons in the original position have no information as to which generation they belong. (TJ: 137; TJR: 118)

Neither do the parties have any information about "people's race and ethnic group, sex and gender" (PL: 24–25).

Now, the reasons for the veil of ignorance go beyond mere simplicity. The arbitrariness of the world we live in must be corrected for by adjusting the circumstances of the initial contractual situation. It is precisely by banning knowledge of particulars that the outcome will not be biased by those arbitrary contingencies Rawls considers to be unfair from an ethical perspective. And thus, for the outcome to be fair, the parties must be fairly situated and treated equally as moral persons and not as persons advantaged or disadvantaged by the contingencies of their social position, the distribution of their abilities, or by luck and historical accident over the course of their lives (CP: 316). By excluding knowledge, the parties are able to satisfy the requirement of unanimity for a fair outcome.

The idea of the original position is to set up a fair procedure so that any principles agreed to will be just. The aim is to use the notion of *pure procedural justice* as a basis for the theory (TJ: 136; TJR: 118). The outcome yields the appropriate principles of justice for free and equal persons because the way the original position has been modeled means that it is a case of pure procedural justice (TJ: 120; TJR: 104). This is the meaning of Rawls' famous (and famously misunderstood) statement that he wants "to define the original position so that we get the desired solution" (TJ: 141; TJR: 122).

To enable deliberation to take place, the veil of ignorance is not so thick that all knowledge is banned. Thus the parties "know the general facts about human society. They understand political affairs and the principles of economic theory; they know the basis of social organization and the laws of human psychology. Indeed, the parties are presumed to know whatever general facts affect the choice of the principles of justice. There are no limitations on general information, that is, on general laws and theories, since conceptions of justice must be adjusted to the char- acteristics of the systems of social cooperation which they are to regulate, and there is no reason to rule out these facts" (TJ: 137–138; TJR: 119). Also it is, of course, assumed that the parties in the original position have information about the general circumstances of society: they know it exists under the circumstances of justice, both objective and subjective.

A feature of Rawls' Kantian approach in *A Theory of Justice* is that it aims at the thickest possible veil of ignorance (CP: 335). Rawls gives hardly any information at all to the parties – only that information that is just enough for them to come to a reasonable and rational agreement. Thus it is guaranteed that – in Kantian terms – there will be autono- mous, and not heteronomous agreement. Or, as Rawls formulates it, "the veil of ignorance deprives the persons in the original position of the knowledge that would enable them to choose heteronomous principles" (TJ: 252; TJR: 222).

The agreement of the parties on certain definitive principles establishes a connection between these principles and the full conception of
the person represented in the original position. In this way the content of
fair terms of cooperation for persons so conceived is ascertained. To see
how the full conception of the person is represented, two different parts
of the original position must be carefully distinguished. These parts
correspond to the two powers of moral personality, or what Rawls, as
we noted earlier, has called "the capacity to be reasonable" and "the
capacity to be rational." "While the original position as a whole represents both moral powers, and therefore represents the full conception of
the person, the parties as rationally autonomous representatives of
persons in society represent only *the rational*: the parties agree to
those principles which they believe are best for those they represent as
seen from these persons' conception of the good and their capacity to
form, revise, and rationally to pursue such a conception, so far as the
parties can know these things. The *reasonable*, or persons' capacity for
a sense of justice, the capacity to honor fair terms of social cooperation,
is represented by the various restrictions to which the parties are subject
in the original position and by the conditions imposed on their agreement" (PL: 305; emphasis added).[11] And of course one of these restrictions is a limit on information by the veil of ignorance. These restrictions
prevent the choice of the principles of justice from being influenced by
personal self-interest. Once the principles of justice adopted by the
parties are affirmed and acted on by free and equal persons in society,
they act with full autonomy.

Now, even if one would be interested only in one's own capacity to
form, to revise, and to pursue a conception of the good, and not in that
of any other person, the restrictions of the veil of ignorance prevent the
ascertainment of what one's own conception of the good is. How, then,
can the parties in the original position ascertain at all the conceptions of
the good of the persons they represent? What are the grounds for
deciding which principles to select in the original position? To solve
this issue Rawls introduces the notion of "primary goods," and enu-
merates a list of items falling under this heading. It is here that the
primary goods we discussed earlier come to play their role. Primary
goods are singled out by asking which things are generally necessary as
social conditions and all-purpose means to enable persons to pursue
their determinate conception of the good and to develop and exercise
their two moral powers. The choice of principles of justice by the parties

in the original position is not determined by egoistic, idiosyncratic desires, but by the wish to acquire primary goods that are – as just mentioned – the all-purpose means for choosing and developing one's own conception of the good. And the wish that one wants to accomplish one's own plan of life does not mean that the parties in the original position are rational egoists.

Thus the original position abstracts from the contingencies – the particular features and circumstances of persons – and eliminates the bargaining advantages of tailoring principles to one's advantage, advantages that inevitably arise over time within any society as a result of cumulative social and historical tendencies (TJ: 139–140; TJR: 120–121; JaF: 16). As Rawls argues, a principle that formulates "to each according to their threat advantage" (or "to their de facto political power," or "to their wealth," or "to their native endowments") is not a conception of justice and cannot be a basis for formulating principles of justice (TJ: 134, 141; TJR: 116, 122; JaF: 16). Contingent historical advantages, accidental influences from the past, social circumstances, and native endowments should not affect an agreement on the principles that are to regulate the basic structure from the present to the future (JaF: 16, 16 note 16).

Here we come to the core of Rawls' idea of presenting a conception of justice "which generalizes and carries to a higher level of abstraction the traditional conception of the social contract" (TJ: 3; TJR: 3).[12] In his theory of justice, the original position of equality corresponds to the state of nature in the traditional theory of the social contract. The original position is, as we have seen, the appropriate initial status quo, and so the fundamental agreement reached in it by the parties as representatives is fair. Since the content of the agreement concerns the principles of justice for the basic structure, the agreement in the original position specifies the fair terms of social cooperation between persons as free and equal. This explains the propriety of the name *justice as fairness*: it conveys the idea that the principles of justice are agreed to in an initial situation that is fair (TJ: 12; TJR: 11; JaF: 16).

In *justice as fairness* as a form of contract doctrine, contingent historical advantages and accidental influences of the past, and social circumstances and native endowments, should not affect the principles of justice. This points to the major difference with the (contract) views of Robert Nozick and of James Buchanan, as well as those of David Gauthier.[13] For example, in the conception of justice developed by

Nozick in his *Anarchy, State, and Utopia* (1974), a theory is formulated which is based on historical entitlements. In Nozick's theory, persons have basic rights, liberties, and opportunities, as secured in a basic structure, that are in fact dependent on contingencies of history, social circumstances, and the native endowments that persons have. It is precisely these elements that *justice as fairness* excludes as a basis for the principles of justice (JaF: 16, 16 note 16, 53).

Taking into consideration the conditions and the restrictions on information in the original position, and with the knowledge that persons want to realize their two moral powers (to be reasonable and to be rational), the parties in the original position now can try to reach agreement on specific principles of justice.

On which principles would reasonable and rational parties in the original position then unanimously agree? Consider the point of view of anyone in the original position. "Since it is not reasonable for him to expect more than an equal share in the division of social primary goods, and since it is not rational for him to agree to less, the sensible thing is to acknowledge as the first step a principle of justice requiring an equal distribution. Indeed, this principle is so obvious given the symmetry of the parties due to the veil of ignorance that it would occur to everyone immediately" (TJR: 130).[14] Thus the parties start with a principle requiring equal distribution of *all* social primary goods: equal basic liberties for all, as well as fair equality of opportunity, and equal division of income and wealth. Everyone should have an equal share: equality is the benchmark here. But we are not done yet. Rawls asks us to consider the following. "But even holding firm to the priority of the basic liberties and fair equality of opportunity, there is no reason why this initial acknowledgment should be final. Society should take into account economic efficiency and the requirements of organization and technology. If there are inequalities in income and wealth, and differences in authority and degrees of responsibility, that work to make everyone better off in comparison with the benchmark of equality, why not permit them?" (TJR: 130–131). It would be unreasonable for the parties to stop at equal division and not to agree on *these* kinds of inequalities. Since the parties are assumed to be mutually disinterested, and not moved by envy or spite (in contrast to persons in actual societies), "the basic structure should allow these [economic and organizational] inequalities, so long as these improve everyone's situation, including that of the least advantaged, provided that these inequalities are consistent with equal liberty and fair equality of opportunity. Because the parties start from an equal division of all social primary goods, those who benefit least have, so to speak, a veto. Taking equality as the basis of comparison, those who have gained more than others are to do so on terms that are justifiable to those who have gained the least" (TJR: 131). Thus the parties arrive at Rawls' famous *difference principle* (TJ: 150–152; TJR: 130–131; CP: 55; PL: 282). The difference principle expresses the idea that, starting from equal division, the most advantaged are not to be better off at any point to the detriment of the less well off (JaF: 124).

In the original position "the parties are mutually disinterested rather than sympathetic; but lacking knowledge of their natural assets or social situation, they are forced to view their arrangements in a general way" (TJ: 187; TJR: 163). This mutual disinterestedness, subject to a veil of ignorance, leads to the two principles of justice. The first principle is concerned with the distribution of equal basic rights and liberties. The second principle has two parts: the first part of it is concerned with the conditions of fair equality of opportunity. The second part of it is the difference principle mentioned above, the principle to distribute income and wealth.

Once again it should be kept in mind that in describing this thought experiment, the original position behind the veil of ignorance, we are dealing with a purely hypothetical situation. "Justice as fairness is badly misunderstood if the deliberations of the parties, and the motives we attribute to them, are mistaken for an account of the moral psychology, either of actual persons or of citizens in a well-ordered society" (PL: 28). It is plainly not a gathering of all actual or possible people. In describing the parties Rawls is not describing persons as we find them, and the original position is "a device of representation modeling reasonable constraints that limit the reasons the parties in their deliberations may appeal to" (JaF: 86). As the representatives that are deliberating in the original position are not "real people," the description Rawls gives of these representatives is then in no way based on a theory of human nature: a theory of human nature is not part of the framework of the original position (neither an idea that man by nature is "good," nor that he is by nature "bad") (PL: 28, 28 note 30; TJ: 120; TJR: 104; CP: 320–322; JaF: 86–87).

Reflective equilibrium and *justice as fairness*

"Real people," "we," "you and I," only come to play a role in the next round of deliberation on the principles of justice. The justification of ethical theories, although addressed to others who disagree with us, only makes sense when this justification is addressed to a specific "forum," as Rawls acknowledges. A successful justification is always connected with the shared starting points of the members of that forum. Public justification is not, then, simply a valid argument from given premises. It proceeds from some consensus: from premises that all parties in disagreement, assumed to be free and equal and fully capable of reason, may reasonably be expected to share and freely endorse (JaF: 27). As Rawls formulates it: "Being designed to reconcile by reason, justification proceeds from what all parties to the discussion hold in common. Ideally, to justify a conception of justice to someone is to give him a proof of its principles from premises that we both accept, these principles having in turn consequences that match our considered judgments. Thus mere proof is not justification. A proof simply displays logical relations between propositions. But proofs become justification once the starting points are mutually recognized, or the conclusions so comprehensive and compelling as to persuade us of the soundness of the conception expressed by their premises" (TJ: 580–581; TJR: 508). Justification, then, cannot be based on a moral vacuum: a minimum of (moral) consensus has to be present. Or, as Rawls says, "It is perfectly proper, then, that the argument for the principles of justice should proceed from some consensus. This is the nature of justification" (TJ: 581; TJR: 508–509). Rawls always makes an appeal to these presupposed elements of consensus that might lie hidden under the surface of the diverging opinions that we, the readers of his work, have. Rawls is of the opinion that some considered convictions, or considered judgments, may be accepted provisionally, though with confidence, as fixed points, ones that we never expect to withdraw. For example, Rawls is confident that religious intolerance and racial discrimination are unjust. And one of the clearest examples of a judgment viewed as a fixed point by Rawls is Lincoln's statement: "If slavery is not wrong, nothing is wrong" (TJ: 19–20; TJR: 17–18, 507; PL: 8, 124; JaF: 29; LoP: 174). These convictions are, as said, provisional fixed points. We start by looking to the public culture itself as the shared fund of implicitly recognized basic ideas and principles (PL: 8). This appeal to a shared fund is evident in many places in Rawls' work, not only in *A Theory of Justice*; it is a recurring element in all his work over the years. Thus for instance in *A Theory of Justice* he notes, "one of the aims of moral philosophy is to look for possible bases of agreement where none seem to exist. It must attempt to extend the range of some existing consensus and to frame more discriminating moral conceptions for our consideration" (TJ: 582; TJR: 509).

Rawls elaborates these ideas in what he describes as *"reflective equilibrium"* and *"considered judgments."* A situation of "reflective equilibrium" is one in which the principles which would be chosen in the original position are identical with those that match our considered judgments and thus these principles describe our sense of justice. In this matching process one tries to see how a subject could fit its various convictions into one coherent scheme. By dropping and revising some, by reformulating and expanding others, one supposes that a systematic organization can be found. Thus "justification is a matter of the mutual support of many considerations, of everything fitting together into one coherent view" (TJ: 21; TJR: 19). Here we have what we earlier labeled "the coherence theory of ethical justification."

Working on this matching process from both ends, we have to discern two variants. In the first variant we look at *principles of justice* to see if they match our considered judgments on what *we* think is just or unjust. If so, this is a good reason to accept these principles. In the second variant we wonder if principles are chosen under *conditions* that, according to our considered judgments, are fair ones. If we think that the account of the initial situation is indeed fair, this is a good reason to accept those principles. The difference between the two variants is the question on which the considered judgment is focused, on the principles themselves, or on the contractual circumstances under which the principles are chosen. In both cases our considered judgments should eventually match one or the other (TJ: 20; TJR: 18).

It is this process of going back and forth, of adjusting considered judgments on the one hand, or principles or circumstances for the choice of principles on the other, that Rawls calls "reflective equilibrium." The general question with "reflective equilibrium" is whether either the principles or the description of the conditions of the initial situation sufficiently match our considered judgments to eventually reach the status of a public justification for the formulated principles of justice. If there is for instance a discrepancy between the circumstances for the choice of principles and our considered judgments, we can adjust these circumstances to make sure they do fit our considered judgments. But this process of adjustment can also go the other way round. Reflection on the principles and the plausibility of the circumstances can also lead to a revision of our considered judgments (TJ: 20; TJR: 18).

The wider the range of all possible views, with their philosophically relevant arguments with which one might plausibly confront one's existing considered judgment, the more the kind of reflective equilibrium that Rawls is concerned with in his moral philosophy would be reached. Thus the issue here is that each of us, "you and I," "here and now," are assessing the choice of the principles of justice (*justice as fairness* or any other conception of justice) in the hypothetical original position by using as a test reflective equilibrium: How well does the view as a whole articulate our more firmly considered convictions of justice? Someone has carefully considered alternative conceptions of justice, and the force of various arguments for them. Given the wide-ranging reflection and possibly many changes of view, it is this matching process for which Rawls uses the term "*wide* reflective equilibrium."[15] It is clearly impossible to examine "all possible views with their philosophically relevant arguments." The most we can do, as Rawls suggests, is "to study the conceptions of justice known to us through the tradition of moral philosophy and any further ones that occur to us, and consider these" (TJ: 49). In this case, our considered judgments may or may not undergo a radical shift.

The upshot of all this is that the subject ends up being involved in a process of self-reflection in which he continually has to ask himself what is more important: the implication of the general principles of justice that are placed before him or his own, and maybe until now un-reflected, convictions. With regard to the initial situation, we can say that the subject can opt for two directions: he can either change the description of the initial situation or he can change his, until that moment, existing convictions.

Needless to say, for Rawls himself the original position with its veil of ignorance formulates the most convincing conditions for an initial situation that will lead to a choice of principles of justice that match our considered judgments. As already noted, for Rawls the original position is "the most philosophically favored interpretation of the initial choice situation" (TJ: 18; TJR: 16).

Do the principles of *justice as fairness* as the outcome of choice in the original position indeed match our considered judgments? Each of us, "you and I," have of course to consider for ourselves whether these principles of justice, our general convictions, and particular judgments are in line and, thus, "I," or "you," or both of us, are in wide reflective equilibrium. For his part, Rawls gives the following arguments as to why there are good reasons to think this would be the case.

We have already elaborated that one of the central aims of Rawls is to develop a theory of justice that is superior to utilitarianism. He is of the opinion that an important aspect of this superiority is that the principles of *justice as fairness* is a better way to express our considered judgments. Compared to utilitarianism this is especially the case when we ask how just institutions of a society, the basic structure, should be designed.

This premise is illustrated by Rawls with what is in his theory the first principle of justice, the principle that guarantees every person equal basic rights and liberties. It is this principle that reflects, better than a utilitarian principle, our considered judgments on liberty. After all, Rawls argues, one of our most basic considered judgments is the conviction that it is unjust that some persons would be discriminated against in the distribution of basic rights. The first principle of *justice as fairness* expresses this fixed point of our moral judgments. It is an example of a conviction that we never expect to withdraw, as are the convictions mentioned above that religious intolerance and racial discrimination are unjust and also belong to the fixed points of everybody's moral convictions (TJ: 19–20; TJR: 17–18; PL: 28, 45; JaF: 29–32).

In utilitarianism, we noted that the correct distribution is that which yields the maximum fulfillment. Society must allocate its means of satisfaction whatever these are – rights and duties, opportunities and privileges, and various forms of wealth – and regardless of how this sum of satisfactions is distributed among individuals, so as to achieve this maximum fulfillment if it can. The first principle of *justice as fairness*, on the other hand, formulates a clear basis for our considered judgments that completely rejects such a utilitarian argument, and this priority of "the right over the good" is, as noted before, a central feature of the conception of *justice as fairness*. The same kind of reasoning can be adopted for the public justification of the difference principle. This principle then formulates our considered judgments, upon due reflection, about how society should treat its least advantaged members from a social and economic perspective.

In the following sections we will have a closer look at the set-up of the original position and the way in which the principles of *justice as fairness* are, according to Rawls, actually derived from it.

Justice as fairness or utilitarianism?

Let us say that the conditions for the original position are indeed described according to our considered judgments. If we want to bring the thought experiment to a successful closure, the next question we have to ask is whether the principles of justice can actually be derived by "our representatives."

The original position is set up in such a way that the deliberation of the parties, their "natural" line of reasoning, would lead to the principles of *justice as fairness*. The two principles of justice are the solution to the problem of choice presented by the original position. But Rawls' aim goes a step further: at one and the same time he wants to also show why the parties in the original position do not opt for utilitarian principles of justice, the "opponent" of *justice as fairness*. Rawls explains (in *A Theory of Justice*, and in the *Revised Edition* of it, as well as, some thirty years later, in *Justice as Fairness: A Restatement*) that in the original position the parties are presented with a list with alternative traditional conceptions of justice – a menu as it were – from which they have to make their choice. The parties must unanimously agree on one of the alternatives that are on this menu. The "leader of the debate," Rawls, has in fact given the parties a very short list. There are only two alternatives on it: the principles of *justice as fairness* taken as a unit (thus including the difference principle), and a utilitarian principle (the principle of average utility). This utilitarian principle has, as will be discussed, two variants.

With this list now in hand, the next task of the parties is to twice make a fundamental comparison. Splitting up the work of the parties into two comparisons enables us to make a distinction between the reasons that lead the parties to the selection of the principle of equal basic liberties and the reasons the parties use to make a choice for the difference principle. In the first fundamental comparison the two principles of *justice as fairness*, taken as a unit, are compared with "the principle of average utility" as the sole principle of justice (principle U1). The principle of average utility says: "the institutions of the basic structure are to be arranged so as to maximize the average welfare of the members of society." The second fundamental comparison that the parties make is one in which the principles of *justice as fairness*, again as a unit, are compared with an alternative formed by substituting for the difference principle the principle of average utility (combined with a stipulated minimum) (principle U2). In all other respects the two principles that they have to choose between are unchanged. In this second comparison, then, the principles that have priority over the difference principle have already been accepted (equal basic liberties and fair equality of opportunity) and are included in both alternatives from which the parties have to choose. In this second fundamental comparison the parties are selecting a principle for regulating economic and social inequalities: either the difference principle or the principle of average utility combined with a stipulated minimum, "the principle of restricted utility."[16]

Thus the parties now have two consecutive tasks: first compare *justice as fairness* as a unit with principle U1; second compare *justice as fairness* as a unit with principle U2 (TJR: xiv; JaF: 96). The question to be answered by the parties in each of these pairs of comparisons is which principles to select to regulate the basic structure of society. But how are they to balance, in each comparison, the two possibilities from which a choice has to be made?

Rawls would like the original position argument to be as far as possible a deductive one, and to present the reasoning of the parties in it as "a kind of moral geometry with all the rigor that the name suggests" (TJ: 121; JaF: 133; see also TJR: 105; JaF: 82). To answer the question then, of how to balance in each comparison the two possibilities from which a choice has to be made, Rawls suggests in *A Theory of Justice* that there is a relation between his theory of justice and rigorous deductive reasoning in the social sciences and in economics. As he claims: "The theory of justice is a part, perhaps the most significant part, of the theory of rational choice" (TJ: 16; TJR: 15). With this bare rationalistic starting point Rawls connects a technique that has been developed in modern decision theory with the deduction of his principles of justice. Rawls uses this technique as a procedure for justification because he notes an *analogy* between his principles of justice and the so-called maximin rule for a rational choice under uncertainty, which is used in decision theory. This rule directs our attention to the worst that can happen under any proposed course of action, and to make a decision in the light of that. The maximin rule tells us to rank alternatives by their worst possible outcomes: we should adopt that alternative where the worst possible outcome is superior to the worst possible outcomes of all the other alternatives. This explains, as Rawls summarizes, the term "maximin": *maximum minimorum* (TJ: 152–154; TJR: 133; JaF: 97).

In elaborating this analogy between his principles and the maximin rule, Rawls argues that the way the original position is described makes it possible to speak about an analogy. More specifically, it is the veil of ignorance that makes the reasoning for the principles in the original position an act that decision theorists describe as a "rational choice under uncertainty." Rawls in fact formulates this even more definitely: "The veil of ignorance leads directly to the problem of choice under [complete] uncertainty" (TJ: 172; TJR: 149).

Let us now return to the "comparative studies" that the parties have to undertake. In the first fundamental comparison the maximin rule for choice under uncertainty is introduced by Rawls as a useful heuristic device, a rule of thumb for the parties to use to organize their deliberations (JaF: 97). In this first comparison the parties have to make a choice between alternative basic structures or "situations" in which they might possibly end up when the veil of ignorance is lifted. Which "situation" would then be the worst and least acceptable? Which bad outcome is better than the worst outcomes of the other alternative "situation"? This "best" "situation" should then be chosen.

Now recall that the parties in this first comparison have "only" to identify which choice will guarantee that the worst "situation" will be the best of the two bad outcomes that are possible. But following the maximin rule does not give them a direct answer to this question. It is an "empty" rule of thumb, because the rule does not itself specify which criteria should be used to be able to speak of the "best" bad "situation," comparing it to the bad "situation" of the alternative. The parties need specific arguments to be able to rank the available alternative "situations" as better or worse in terms of their fundamental interests, the interests of persons who are free and equal.

It is for this purpose that Rawls has formulated three conditions (or three chief features of "situations") that obtain in the original position, such that it is rational to be guided by the maximin rule when agreeing to the principles of justice for the basic structure, and that enable the parties in this comparative study to make a choice between *justice as fairness* and utilitarian principles (TJ: 154; TJR: 134; JaF: 98).

These three conditions are:

(a) the parties have no reliable basis for estimating the probabilities of the possible social circumstances that affect the fundamental interests of the persons they represent (this is so since the maximin rule takes no account of probabilities);

(b) the parties are not to be much concerned for what might be gained above what can be guaranteed (for those they represent) when adopting the alternative whose worst outcome is better than the worst outcome of all other alternatives (this is so since the maximin rule directs the parties to evaluate the alternatives only by their worst possible outcomes);

(c) the worst outcomes of all the other alternatives are significantly below the "guaranteeable level" (this is so since the maximin rule directs the parties to avoid alternatives whose worst outcomes are below the guaranteeable level) (TJ: 154–156; TJR: 134–135; JaF: 98).

Let us remember Rawls' aim. His intention is to show with this first comparison that he can defeat utilitarianism with its own weapons, so to speak, by showing that the parties in their comparative study will not choose utilitarian principles (at least not principle U1), but the principles of *justice as fairness*.

In *Justice as Fairness: A Restatement* (2001) Rawls once again uses the (slightly adapted) argument from the original position in the first comparison to elaborate the reasoning of the parties in favor of *justice as fairness* over utilitarianism, or in any case over a mild variant of it. The agreement for the first part of *justice as fairness*, to secure the basic rights and liberties equally for all, is fundamental because it would give an alternative to utilitarianism and a more appropriate moral basis for a modern democratic society. As Rawls says: "Should the two principles win in the first comparison, this aim is already in good part achieved; but should they lose, all is lost" (JaF: 97). This remark shows, once again, that utilitarianism is, for Rawls, the theory to beat.

Well, the two principles of justice don't lose and in fact the agreement for the first part of *justice as fairness* is a clear-cut one. This is so because an important role in the considerations of the parties is – according to Rawls – that the principles of *justice as fairness* better express what (especially) freedom in a modern society means than a principle of utility does; the latter being a principle that may sometimes permit or require a restriction or even suppression of the rights and liberties of some for the sake of a greater aggregate of social well-being, and a principle that may even allow a situation in which slavery or serfdom exists. The principle of utility (as the sole principle of justice) to order society will be rejected. The reasoning will favor the two principles of *justice as fairness*.

Summarizing this first comparison: given the conception of the person in *justice as fairness*, it is the requirements for the exercise of the two highest-order interests of the parties, the moral power to be reasonable and the moral power to be rational, that are reflected in the precedence the parties give to the basic rights and liberties which protect and secure the scope for the exercise of these moral powers. This is non-negotiable: agreeing to the principle of average utility would jeopardize those rights and liberties without sufficient reason (TJR: 131–132, 475–476; JaF: 45, 104).

In this first fundamental comparison, then, where the two principles of *justice as fairness* taken as a unit are compared with principle U1, the principle of average utility as the sole principle of justice, the outcome of this comparison, to wit rejecting a utilitarian principle, achieves the most fundamental aim of *justice as fairness*. At the same time it should be recognized, as Rawls himself does, that this first comparison does not give much support to the difference principle (JaF: 119). Since this principle is an indivisible part of the whole unit of *justice as fairness* and is thus by definition included in one of the alternatives of the pairwise comparison, it has in this first comparison so to speak a "free ride" (JaF: 96). Parenthetically it should be added that in balancing the two alternatives against each other, the parties use a complex argument which we leave aside here (TJ & TJR: §49; PL: 292; JaF: 97–119).

The difference principle or the maximin criterion?

We now turn to the second fundamental comparison the parties have to make. In this comparison the parties are selecting a principle for regulating social and economic inequalities. Here the comparison is between *justice as fairness* and U2. Both have an identical first part: the principles of equal basic liberties and fair equality of opportunity. In the second part of principle U2, the principle of average utility combined with a suitable social minimum is substituted for the difference principle. In U2, "the basic structure is, then, to be arranged so as to maximize average utility consistent, first, with guaranteeing the equal basic liberties … and fair equality of opportunity, and second, with maintaining a suitable social minimum" (JaF: 120). What principle should we choose in this second fundamental comparison: the difference principle, or rather the principle for maximizing average utility, with a guarantee of a social minimum, "the principle of restricted utility"? In this comparison these two principles are in direct competition with each other.

From a "Rawlsian" perspective it is clear, once again, what the outcome of the comparison between the two possible situations ought to be. The participants in the thought-experiment, deliberating under the conditions of the situation described in the original position, will conclude that, as a principle for distribution, the parties will reach unanimous agreement on the difference principle. (Here again there is a complex argumentation on how the parties balance the two alternatives against each other [JaF: 119–132]).

It is Rawls himself who notes, and correctly so, that when we have a closer look at the second fundamental comparison, "it is evident that, while I view the balance of the reasons as favoring the difference principle, the outcome is certainly less clear and decisive than in the first. The argument rests importantly on the great significance of certain features of the public political culture (for example, how it encourages the political virtues of mutual trust and cooperation) and not on plain and evident considerations of greater public good" (JaF: 133).[17] That the outcome of this comparison is less decisive in favor of the one or the other principle is easy to see, even without the help of complex technical reasoning. Using the maximin rule here is much less helpful in answering the question of which basic structure will guarantee that the worst "situation" in which one can end up is the "best of the worst" possibilities. After all, in both bad "situations" a suitable social minimum is maintained.

The idea of an initial choice situation under uncertainty has not been used only by Rawls. Economists and political theorists such as J. C. Harsanyi and J. Narveson, for example, have demonstrated that one can construct an initial situation that does not preclude an outcome of a collective choice in favor of *utilitarian* principles of justice. In doing so Harsanyi, for instance, uses the expected-utility maximization principle of Bayesian theory.[18] At the same time, these theoreticians have argued, with regard to the three conditions (or features) that Rawls claims to obtain in the original position, such that it is rational to be guided by the maximin rule that enables the parties to weigh in favor of the difference principle instead of the utilitarian principle, that none of these three conditions is convincing.

Rawls is well aware of this criticism. He has responded to it in a remarkable way. Not only is he of the opinion that the maximin rule is, on second thought, not much of a help here, in fact, in formulating the second comparison, the guidelines of the maximin rule for decision under uncertainty *are not used at all* (JaF: 96). Rawls states that, in arguing for the difference principle over other distributive principles (say a restricted principle of (average) utility, thus the case at hand), "there is no appeal at all to the maximin rule for decision under uncertainty" (JaF: 43 note 3).[19] Now this statement has, in the context of Rawls' theory of justice, an extremely important implication: the difference principle is not the same as the maximin criterion! In fact they are two very distinct things. This conclusion not only seems to come as a surprise, it also seems, at first sight, to be in flat contradiction with what Rawls himself had argued in *A Theory of Justice*.

However, since the early 1980s, Rawls has repeatedly explained that we are dealing here with a mistake. The mistake is in thinking that the parties deliberating in the original position focus on making a *rational* choice to select specific principles of justice. We have to remember here that the original position, as a device of representation, as a whole, represents both moral powers, the reasonable and the rational, and therefore the full conception of the person. In *Political Liberalism* and in *Justice as Fairness: A Restatement*, Rawls stresses these points once more. He adds that he hopes that this will prevent several misinterpretations that the original position "is intended to be morally neutral, or that it models only the notion of rationality, and therefore that *justice as fairness* attempts to select principles purely on the basis of a conception of rational choice as understood in economics or decision theory. For a Kantian view, such an attempt is out of the question and is incompatible with its conception of the person" (PL: 306 note 21).[20]

But much earlier on, in fact in the text of the 1975 revised edition of *A Theory of Justice* (an edition that, as has already been pointed out, appeared in English only in 1999), Rawls makes the following comment about terminology:

Economics may wish to refer to the difference principle as the maximin criterion, but I have carefully avoided this name for several reasons. The maximin criterion is generally understood as a rule for choice under great uncertainty ... whereas the difference principle is a principle of justice. It is undesirable to use the same name for two things that are so distinct. The difference principle is a very special criterion: it applies primarily to the basic structure of society via representative individuals whose expectations are to be estimated by an index of primary goods. ... In addition, calling the difference principle the maximin criterion might wrongly suggest that the main argument for this principle from the original position derives from an assumption of very high risk aversion. There is indeed a relation between the difference principle and such an assumption, but extreme attitudes to risk are not postulated ... and in any case, there are many considerations in favor of the difference principle in which the aversion to risk plays no role at all. Thus it is best to use the term "maximin criterion" solely for the rule of choice under uncertainty. (TJR: 72–73).[21]

What is the implication of all this? Basically it is the following: there is only a resemblance between the *idea* that underlies both the difference principle for distributive justice and the *idea* of maximin: the idea that attention should be given to the best possible outcome for the lowest position (in the case of justice, to the least advantaged in society). But, as Rawls himself has also noted, "despite the formal resemblance between the difference principle as a principle of distributive justice and the maximin rule as a rule of thumb for decisions under uncertainty," the reasoning for the *choice* of the difference principle does not rely on this rule. The formal resemblance is misleading (JaF: 94–95). The distinctions between the two principles are far more important than their formal resemblance. And, as already noted above, nor does the argument for the difference principle depend on the extreme aversion to uncertainty of the parties in the original position. This widespread idea is also a mistake, and based on an inaccurate interpretation of the reasoning for the selection of the difference principle.[22]

By now the reader may wonder about the importance of the argument that the way the difference principle should be interpreted and reasoned for is *not* based on the maximin rule. What precisely does the conclusion that the difference principle is not identical with the maximin criterion entail? The short answer is: this conclusion is of great importance. The fact that it has to be acknowledged that there is a difference between the two is essential for our eventual understanding of what are the precise implications of the application of the difference principle in *justice as fairness*.

To ground this, we have to return to the second fundamental comparison the parties have to undertake in the original position. If the selection of the difference principle is not based on the maximin rule, then on what is it based? Which arguments do the parties use? First of all, they note that "the principle of restricted utility" is a maximizing aggregative principle with no inherent tendency toward either equality or reciprocity (JaF: 122). The parties in the original position choose the difference principle because, simply put, they share the core of Rawls' ideas on *justice as fairness*, and these ideas are implicit in the difference principle, applied to the basic structure, that is "that social institutions are not to take advantage of contingencies of native endowments, or of initial social positions, or of good or bad luck over the course of life, except in ways that benefit everyone, including the least favored. This represents a fair undertaking between the citizens seen as free and equal with respect to those inevitable contingencies" (JaF: 124). According to the parties in the original position it is precisely these ideas that the difference principle expresses. Applied to the basic structure, these ideas formulate that, starting from an equal division, the more advantaged are not to be better off at any point to the detriment of the less well off. It is only if the difference principle is interpreted in this way that one is able to understand the crucial role that this principle plays in accomplishing democratic equality. And it is only by interpreting it in this way that we are able to see that the difference principle gives substance to reciprocity in the cooperation between moral persons, a fundamental idea underlying *justice as fairness*. We will elaborate this extensively later on.

The principles of justice and primary goods

Our next step is to have a closer look at the principles of justice themselves, principles that the parties have chosen in the original position, principles that, taken together as a unit, express *justice as fairness*. They define the just distribution of the burdens and benefits of social cooperation and assign rights and duties throughout the whole social structure. They do this by regulating how in society, seen as a *cooperative venture for mutual advantage*, the basic structure distributes "primary goods" in a fair way.

In proceeding, it should be noted that Rawls makes a distinction between two conceptions of *justice as fairness*, a "general" one and a "special" one. The "general conception of justice" is expressed in the following way:

All social primary goods – liberty and opportunity, income and wealth, and the [social] bases of self-respect – are to be distributed equally unless an unequal distribution of any or all of these primary goods is to the advantage of the least favored. (TJ: 303)[23]

In this "general" conception, *injustice*, then, is simply those inequalities that are not to the benefit of all (TJR: 54). The "special conception of justice" contains two principles (principle 1 and principle 2) and some prioritizing rules that prescribe a lexical order of the principles, the first principle having priority over the second. The relative weight of each principle is therewith determined.[24] The statement of the principles (P) of the "special conception of justice" read as follows:

The first principle:

P1:   Each person is to have an equal right to the most extensive total system of equal basic liberties compatible with a similar system of liberty for all (*the principle of equal liberty*).[25]

The second principle (which has two separate parts):

P2:   Social and economic inequalities are to be arranged so that they are both:

P2.1:   attached to offices and positions open to all under conditions of fair equality of opportunity (*the principle of fair equality of opportunity*);

P2.2:   to the greatest benefit of the least advantaged, consistent with the just savings principle (*the difference principle*).[26]

The priority rules (L) (which give the principles of justice their lexical order):

L1:   Principle P1 is lexically prior to principle P2 (*the priority of liberty*).

L2:   Principle P2.1 is lexically prior to principle P2.2.

L3:   Principle P2.2 is lexically prior to the principle of efficiency and to that of maximizing the sum of advantages (*the priority of justice over efficiency and welfare*) (TJ: 302; TJR: 266).

    In the following we will first elaborate the distinction between "the general conception of justice" and "the special conception of justice," and the priority rules that hang together with this distinction. The "general conception of justice" imposes no restriction on what sort of inequalities are permissible; it only requires that everyone's position be improved (TJR: 55). In the "special conception of justice" it seems as if the difference principle (P2.2) only applies to social primary goods or value (income and wealth). Also, in the lexical order of the principles for the basic structure, it has a low priority. First then, why the distinction between "general conception of justice" and "special conception of justice"?

The distinction is based on the following argument: as the general level of well-being rises, and as soon as society has reached a level of wealth in which the required societal conditions are realized, and a level of fulfillment of the basic needs and basic material wants of the poorest groups in society is adequately attained, there is among the primary goods one to which dominant importance is attached – basic rights and liberties. Rawls is of the opinion that only when a certain minimal level of wealth in society has been reached, is each person able to effectively use his fundamental rights and liberties.

Under these circumstances the reasonable and rational subject will rate his fundamental rights and liberties so high that he will not be willing to exchange even the smallest amount of them for an opportunity of gaining more economic well-being. This implies a lexical ordering of rights and liberties above other primary goods. The first priority rule (L1) holds. When the required minimal societal level of wealth for this preference to hold has not (as of yet) been reached, there will always be subjects who, if offered the opportunity, would be willing to give up some of their fundamental liberties, to be compensated by resulting social and economic gains. ("We need," Rawls adds, "not suppose anything so drastic as consenting to a condition of slavery. Imagine instead that people seem willing to forego certain political rights when the economic returns are significant" [TJR: 55].[27]) The valuation by the subject of the primary good "basic liberties" would not satisfy the first priority rule. In that case the general conception of justice would hold.

Only under extenuating circumstances are exchanges between basic liberties and economic and social gains permitted (TJ: 151–152, 542; TJR: 130–132, 476; JaF: 46–47). Or, as Rawls elaborates: "It is only when social circumstances do not allow the effective establishment of these basic rights that one can concede their limitation; and even then these restrictions can be granted only to the extent that they are necessary to prepare the way for the time when they are no longer justified. The denial of the equal liberties can be defended only when it is essential to change the conditions of civilization so that in due course these liberties can be enjoyed" (TJR: 132).[28] In other words: "under favorable circumstances" the priority of liberty holds (TJ: 543).

Also, as Rawls continues arguing in the revised edition of *A Theory of Justice*: "Thus in adopting the serial order of the two principles, the parties are assuming that the conditions of their society, whatever they are, admit the effective realization of the equal liberties. Or that if they do not, circumstances are nevertheless sufficiently favorable so that the priority of the first principle points out the most urgent changes and identifies the preferred path to the social state in which all the basic liberties can be fully instituted. The complete realization of the two principles in serial order is the long-run tendency of this ordering, at least *under reasonably fortunate conditions*" (TJR: 132; emphasis added).[29]

It should be added straight away that Rawls usually leaves aside "the general conception of justice." In the 1971 edition of *A Theory of Justice* he notes: "For the most part I shall assume that *the requisite circumstances* for the serial order (lexicographical ordering) obtain" (TJ: 152; emphasis added).[30] This assumption holds for practically all his work and "only" the two principles are examined in serial order. Thus, from the beginning and throughout, the focus is on "the special conception of justice" and "the conditions under which the absolute weight of liberty with respect to social and economic advantages, as defined by the lexical order of the two principles, would be reasonable" (TJR: 55).[31] Whenever society, then, is in circumstances where the basic liberties can be effectively established, the priority of liberty means that "a lesser or an unequal liberty cannot be exchanged for an improvement in economic well-being" (TJR: 132; see also JaF: 46–47).

We must be careful not to conflate two – related, but not identical – issues that are at play here. The first is the (empirical) issue of what level of economic wealth and income is no longer a barrier to constitutional government, and thus what level is presupposed for the priority of the basic equal liberties to hold. What is this required "minimal level of development" of a country such that the basic liberties can be effectively established? The second issue is whether "reasonably fortunate conditions," "favorable circumstances," do indeed exist in a country to enable it to reach the required level of wealth and income, the required "conditions of civilization." How does a country fare with regard to its resources in order to reach that required level?

In *A Theory of Justice*, and for that matter in its revised edition, these issues, which are relevant with regard to the "special conception of justice," are hardly discussed. It is only in later years that Rawls, with regard to the first issue, refers to empirical research done by the economist and political theorist Amartya Sen, together with the development economist Jean Drèze. This research shows that the priority of the basic equal liberties does not, contrary to much opinion, presuppose a high level of economic wealth and income.[32] With regard to the second issue, Rawls, again in later years, refers to empirical research by Sen on the causes of famine: the main problem with famine is not just food crises, thus not resources, but the failure of respective governments, of the political and social structure, to institute policies to remedy the effects of a shortfall in food production (LoP: 109).[33]

Taking up again the supposition of "reasonably fortunate conditions to obtain" in the context of the "special conception of justice," and thus in asserting the priority of basic rights and liberties, Rawls now adds that this means that "we suppose historical, economic and social conditions to be such that, *provided the political will exists*, effective political institutions can be established to give adequate scope for the exercise of those freedoms." If there are barriers to constitutional government, these "spring largely from the political culture and existing effective interests, and not from, for instance, *a lack of economic means, or education, or the many skills needed to run a democratic regime*" (JaF: 47; emphasis added). This still leaves rather vague what precisely these "historical, economic and social conditions," or these "reasonably fortunate conditions" are. We do now know, however, that in the context of a conception of justice that is formulated for the basic structure of society that is conceived of as a closed system, isolated from other societies, this society does not need a high level of economic wealth and income to be a constitutional government in which the priority rules, and thus the "special conception of justice," hold. And second, we also now know that if the required minimal level of civilization is not attained, it springs largely from a missing political will, that it is "the political culture and existing effective interests, that is to blame that there is – as of yet – no constitutional government" and that it is not "a lack of economic means, or education, or the many skills needed to run a democratic regime" that are to blame. As we have said, Rawls leaves aside for the most part the "general conception of justice" and assumes that the requisite circumstances for the serial order do obtain. We will do the same in what follows.

Focusing, then, on the "special conception of justice," a characteristic feature of *justice as fairness* is – next to the first priority rule (L1) – the second priority rule (L2). This formulates that any whimsical small increase in opportunities would be preferred to any (large) increase in, for example, income. Next we have to point to the specific conditions for the application of the difference principle. This principle (P2.2) has to be consistent with the "just savings principle." Since society is a system of cooperation between generations over time, a principle for saving is required. Rawls has in mind here the issue of justice between generations, a difficult problem that "subjects any ethical theory to severe if not impossible tests" (TJ: 284; TJR: 251). Each generation must not only maintain intact those just institutions that have been established, but it must also put aside in each period of time a suitable amount of real capital accumulation for future generations (and "capital" here has a broad meaning: net investment in machinery and other means of production, but also investment in learning and education, the environment, the gains of culture). Finding a just savings principle is one aspect of this issue. But Rawls adds that he does not believe that it is possible, at present anyway, to define precise limits on what the rate of savings should be. One thing, however, is evident to him: the classical principle of utility leads, once again, in the wrong direction, this time with regard to the questions of justice between generations. Maximizing total utility may lead to an excessive rate of accumulation (at least in the near future). The problem, however, is that "the utilitarian doctrine may direct us to demand heavy sacrifices of the poorer generations for the sake of greater advantages for later ones that are far better off. But this calculus of advantages, which balances the losses of some against benefits to others, appears even less justified in the case of generations than among contemporaries. Even if we cannot define a precise just savings principle, we should be able to avoid this sort of extreme" (TJ: 287; TJR: 253).

It is in any case an issue that has to be tackled in the original position and, in so doing, it has to preserve "the present-time-of-entry" interpretation: "we" can enter the original position, as it were, at any moment. The veil of ignorance that closes off the parties from all kinds of information, also prevents the parties from knowing to which generation they belong. They have, in other words, no information on which stage of the civilization of society they will end up in. "They have no way of telling whether it is poor or relatively wealthy, largely agricultural or already industrialized, and so on. The veil of ignorance is complete in these respects" (TJR: 254). In this situation the parties have to consider how much they want to save for future generations from the perspective of the least advantaged in each generation. Since the parties in the original position do not know to which generation they belong, each generation (because all generations are virtually represented in the original position) will choose the same savings principle. The presupposition is that, based on considerations of justice inherent in the conception of moral persons, each generation is concerned for its immediate descendants, "as fathers say care for their sons" (TJ: 288).[34] The result of this care is a just savings principle. Arrived at in the original position, it can be regarded as an understanding between generations to carry their fair share of the burden of realizing and preserving a just society, not only for contemporaries, but in an historical perspective (TJ: 289; TJR: 257).

However, as Rawls has stipulated since 1978, thus a couple of years after *A Theory of Justice* was published as well as after the revisions to it were made, the idea that parties in the original position assume they "care for their descendants" has – although it is not an unreasonable stipulation – certain difficulties: this idea changes the motivational assumption that characterizes the original position (to wit, the assumption that the parties, or "generations," are mutually disinterested and thus nothing constrains them from refusing to make any savings at all), to an other-regarding motivation which provides the parties with a reason to set aside savings for future generations, and thus to get a savings principle.

To solve this problem, Rawls advanced in 1978 a different foundation for the principle of just savings, one without the need to change the motivational assumption of the parties being mutually disinterested in the original position; a different foundation that at the same time preserves the present-time-of-entry interpretation of the original position. The question of savings must be dealt with by constraints that hold between citizens as contemporaries (and thus not as one that assumes that the parties "care for their descendants"). Rawls now claims that the correct savings principle is "that which the members of any generation (and so all generations) would adopt as the one their generation is to follow and as the principle they would want preceding generations to have followed (and later generations to follow), no matter how far back (or forward) in time" (PL: 274). This savings principle "supports legitimate complaints against our predecessors and legitimate expectations about our successors" (JaF: 160).[35] But although this may give us a savings principle that is now based on the correct reasoning of the parties in the original position, it leaves open, as before, the precise limits of what the rate of savings should be.

Summarizing the priority rules so far (L1 & L2), we see that the priority of the first principle of justice and that of the first part of the second principle – the principle of fair equality of opportunity – limits the application of the difference principle *within* generations. While the difference principle holds within generations, the principle of just saving holds between generations. The just savings principle is a constraint on the difference principle *between* generations: it limits its scope (TJ: 292; TJR: 258; JaF: 159).

With the last priority rule (L3) we reach the overall aim of Rawls' approach. This rule expresses the primacy of justice as "the first virtue of social institutions." Justice is to have absolute priority above other values, over, for example, allocative efficiency and welfare. Rawls wants to set forth a theory that enables us to understand and to assess the primacy of justice, especially by working out a conception of justice that provides a reasonably systematic alternative to utilitarianism.

As always, the aim is to formulate a conception of justice that, however much it may call upon our intuitive capacities, helps to make our considered judgments of justice converge. That is one of the reasons why these priority rules are explicitly mentioned. They are to further this end by singling out certain fundamental structural features of one's moral view. Thus the objections Rawls has against utilitarianism are expressed not only in the principles of justice themselves but also in the fact that these principles have priority to the principle of efficiency and to that of maximizing the sum of advantages.

The reasoning that underlies the principles of justice and their serial order, enable us now to picture more clearly how the principles of justice and the distribution of primary goods hang together:

– The first principle of justice has priority over the second. All persons are guaranteed *equal basic liberties*. Liberties are, under all circumstances – when the special conception of justice holds – valued higher than other primary goods.

— The first part of the second principle has priority over the second part of the second principle such that the condition of *fair equality of opportunity* is guaranteed equally for everybody. This idea of fair equality of opportunity must not be confused with the familiar notion of "careers open to talents": the requirement of a formal equality of opportunity in that all have at least the same legal rights of access to all advantaged social positions. The principle is made broader by adding a further condition which requires that positions are open not only in a formal sense, but that all should have a fair chance to attain them. Those who are at the same level of talent and ability, and who have the same willingness to use them, should have the same prospects of success regardless of their initial place in the social system, and regardless of their social background. For example, with regard to education, society should establish, among other things, fair equality of opportunities for all regardless of family income.[36]

— Subject to the constraint of holding offices and positions of authority and responsibility open, the inequalities in *income and wealth* are to be arranged for the greatest benefit of the least advantaged. Given the priority of the first principle to the second principle, and given the priority of the first part of the second principle to the second part of that principle, all persons in a well-ordered society have the same equal basic liberties, and fair equality of opportunity.

The priority rules are sufficient to resolve conflicts of principles, or at least to guide the way to a correct assignment of weights. By formulating these priority rules and by "linking" the different primary goods to the distinctive principles of justice, the reasonable and rational parties are strictly keeping the primary goods apart from each other. Thus weighing one against another has become impossible or is subject to strong limitations. We find this "separation" back in the working of the three different principles (the first principle of justice and the two parts of the second principle) of the special conception of *justice as fairness*. Principle 1 regards only basic rights and liberties. Principle 2.1 and principle 2.2 refer respectively to diverse opportunities and to the distribution of income and wealth. It follows from this that different rules of distribution or of maximizing cannot come into conflict with each other. Each primary good thus finds its place in one of the principles of justice, principles that in their turn have a serial order. Two remarks should be added here.

The first is the following: we noted that the first principle of justice (concerned with basic rights and liberties) has priority over all other principles. Now it is quite imaginable that one basic liberty can come into conflict with another basic liberty. Freedom of speech, a basic liberty, can for example conflict with the basic equal liberty of conscience. In *A Theory of Justice*, the basic liberties are to be assessed as a whole, as one system. Of course, basic liberties cannot be restricted by, or be subordinated to, the other principles of justice. But because the worth of one such basic liberty normally depends upon the specification of the other liberties, certain rules of order are necessary for regulating, for example, public debate. Without the acceptance of reasonable procedures of inquiry and rules of order for debate, freedom of speech loses its value. At many points one basic liberty will have to be balanced against another one, such that the best arrangement of the several basic liberties is found. Although basic liberties cannot be *restricted*, Rawls points out that they can be *regulated* so as to give the best total system of equal liberties for the sake of liberty itself.[37]

Basic rights and liberties within the frame of the first principle of justice then have to be guaranteed, such that freedom as equal liberty is the same for all. Here the question of compensating for a lesser than equal liberty does not arise: unequal liberties cannot be compensated for. But Rawls' ideas with regard to basic liberties do not stop here. There remains another issue, that of the *worth* of liberty: the value to individuals of the rights that the first principle defines, a worth which is not the same for everyone. Some have greater authority and wealth, and therefore greater means to achieve their aims and control the public political debate or to set the agenda for political discussion. Here, both parts of the second principle of justice (fair equality of opportunity as well as the difference principle) come into play. When they do, compensating steps are taken to preserve the "fair value" of the equal political liberties for all members of society. "The lesser worth of liberty is, however, compensated for, since the capacity of the less fortunate members of society to achieve their aims would be even less were they not to accept the existing inequalities whenever the difference principle is satisfied" (TJ: 204; TJR: 179).

In this case the basic structure allows a reconciliation of liberty and equality. Thus Rawls firmly states that, taking "the two principles together, the basic structure is to be arranged to maximize the worth to the least advantaged of the complete scheme of equal liberty shared by all. This defines the end of social justice" (TJ: 205; TJR: 179). (We will return at length to the distinct relationship the difference principle has with the fair value of political liberties in the section "Fair value of political liberties and access to the political process" in Chapter 3.)

We noted above that all social primary goods have been given a place in one of the principles of justice. But, and this is our second remark, strictly speaking this is not entirely correct. There is still one primary good missing: "the social bases of self-respect." This primary good has not been included in any of the specific principles of justice. There is an important reason for not doing so. Rawls is of the opinion that only when *all* principles of justice, taken together, are satisfied, will they have the desired effects on self-respect. In fact the confident conviction of the sense of one's own value, which depends in part on the respect shown to us by others, is even considered the most important primary good, as Rawls explicitly notes in *A Theory of Justice*. It is an opinion that over the years has remained unchanged.[38]

Taking all primary goods together, Rawls has selected basic rights and liberties, diverse opportunities, prerogatives and responsibilities of offices and positions of authority and responsibility, income and wealth, and the social bases of self-respect, because the highest-order interests in developing and exercising the two moral powers of moral persons (to be rational and to be reasonable) single out *these* primary goods and specify their relative importance. These primary goods are the social background conditions and *all-purpose means* generally necessary for forming and rationally pursuing a conception of the good, for carrying out a plan of life, whatever it may be (CP: 370). But although they are the all-purpose means for pursuing any conception of the good, there cannot of course – as mentioned earlier – "be any practical agreement on how to compare happiness as defined, say, by success in carrying out plans of life, nor, even less, any practical agreement on how to evaluate the intrinsic value of these plans" (CP: 371; JaF: 60). Interpersonal comparison can only be founded on an index of primary goods: such an index specifies citizens' shares of primary goods and refers to *objective* features of citizens' social circumstances. Citizens' expectations of primary goods over a complete life are the indicator of their *life prospects*. Primary goods answer the question of what are "basic needs" for free and equal persons who have physical and psychological capacities within a certain normal range, abstracting entirely from illness and accident. If necessary, additional measures,

especially with regard to health and medical care, can be decided on and
worked out at a later stage of decision making.[39] Rawls refers to
situations in which citizens temporarily fall below the essential capacities for being normal and fully cooperating members of society. But to
cope with these kind of situations the list of primary goods as it stands
does not, according to Rawls, need to be revised and neither do other
"primary goods," if there are such, have to be added to the list.[40]

Primary goods or basic capabilities?

The notion of primary goods addresses the moral and practical problem
of how, given different and opposing conceptions of the good persons
have, a public understanding could still be possible. Such an understanding is based on the idea that a *partial* similarity of persons' conceptions of the good is sufficient for political and social justice (CP:
361).[41] The same index of primary goods is to be used to compare
everyone's social situation, so that this index defines a public basis of
interpersonal comparison for questions of social justice: focusing on
shares of primary goods gives us an objective criterion for comparison.

As noted at the end of the preceding section, Rawls is of the opinion
that additional measures, especially with regard to normal health and
medical needs, can be dealt with "later." Perhaps, as Rawls notes, "the
social resources to be devoted to the normal health and medical needs of
[temporarily not normally active and fully cooperating] citizens can be
decided at the legislative stage in the light of existing social conditions
and reasonable expectations of the frequency of illness and accident. If a
solution can be worked out for this case, then it may be possible to
extend it to the hard cases" (CP: 368).[42]

Let us not directly follow Rawls' suggestion to deal with the issue of
"normal health and medical needs" "later," but let us pick the issue
up straight away. Is Rawls right in claiming that it is not necessary
that those "normal health and medical needs" be part of the list of the
primary goods? It is this position that has been contested by Amartya
Sen. Dealing "later" with this issue is too late, according to Sen. He
is of the opinion that Rawls is pushing not only the issue of hard
cases too far ahead, in fact completely out of sight, but also the issue
of "normal health and medical needs" as well. The way this issue is
handled by Rawls shows that his conception of "primary goods" has
shortcomings.

The issue here turns on what is precisely the target of our egalitarian concern. Rawls is skeptical about the uniformity of egalitarian concerns, hence rejecting welfare-based targets. Instead Rawls' aim is assuring people greater equality in the resources needed to pursue their ends. This is the role of the primary goods, their index focusing on shares of primary goods, providing us with an objective criterion for comparison. Now for Sen as well the issue turns on what the target of our egalitarian concern should be. His position is that the target ought to be "basic capabilities." That captures our egalitarian concern, not "primary goods." Though welfare-based accounts are mistaken about what is of ultimate concern (Sen agrees with Rawls in rejecting them), Sen rejects both welfare- and resource-based accounts in favor of his target. It is an issue that Sen has been debating with Rawls for many years. Reproducing the core of that debate can help us to clarify the role primary goods play and the propriety of their use in *justice as fairness*.

Certainly, Sen argues, the focus on primary goods "has an advantage arising from the fact that a person's actual freedom to lead a life does indeed depend fairly crucially on his or her holding of primary goods, and the index of primary goods can, to that extent, be seen as an index of freedom."[43] Primary goods support freedom of choice. There is, however, as Sen notes, a problem here. The advantages that persons possess are judged by reference to the index of primary goods. This means, for example, that expensive tastes are not grounds for more income. This is justified in Rawls' view because a person has responsibility for the choice of his own ends. This leads Sen to raise the following question: "But what about the cripple with utility disadvantage. ... The Difference Principle will give him neither more nor less on grounds of his being a cripple. His utility disadvantage will be irrelevant to the Difference Principle. This may seem hard, and I think it is."[44] The point Sen wants to drive home is that differences of needs – of which "hard cases" are just extreme examples – are pervasive and deserve a more central place in theories of justice, and thus also in Rawls' theory. Sen is of the opinion that leaving these cases out may guarantee that "mistakes" will be made.

One should note here in parentheses, and once again, that Rawls justifies the omission of "normal" medical and health needs, since he wants to *postpone* the question of how to deal with them rather than *ignore* them. The problem of how to deal with health and medical needs (both the "normal cases" and the "hard cases") is put, for the time being, aside. As mentioned, Rawls assumes that "all citizens have physical and psychological capacities within a certain normal range."

The problem Sen has with Rawls' conception of primary goods turns, however, not (only) on "postponing or not postponing" the issue of health and medical needs. Sen's criticism of Rawls' approach to primary goods goes much deeper: Rawls does not cope in any effective way with the problem of the fundamental diversity of human beings. The issue is what Sen calls one of "basic capabilities."[45] The freedom to choose between alternative functioning bundles reflects a person's "advantage," his capability "to function." This interpretation of needs and interests is often implicit in the demand for equality. This is what Sen defines as "basic capability equality."[46] To argue that resources should be devoted to remove or substantially reduce the handicap of the cripple despite there being no primary good deprivation, the case must rest on the interpretation of needs in the form of basic capabilities. *That* is the solution to the lack of freedom to choose various functionings. What then, according to Sen, Rawls' theory lacks is "some notion of 'basic capabilities'; a person being able to do certain things. The ability to move about is the relevant one here, but one can consider others, e.g., the ability to meet one's nutritional requirements, the wherewithal to be clothed and sheltered, the power to participate in the social life of the community."[47] We reach here a fundamental point in Sen's criticism: "The primary goods approach seems to take little note of the diversity of human beings. ... If people were basically very similar, then an index of primary goods might be quite a good way of judging advantage. But, in fact, people seem to have very different needs varying with health, longevity, climatic conditions, location, work conditions, temperament, and even body size (affecting food and clothing requirements). So what is involved is not merely ignoring a few hard cases, but overlooking very widespread and real differences. Judging advantage purely in terms of primary goods leads to a partially blind morality."[48] The interpersonal variations, even when they are exceptional, may call for *urgent* attention, since they may relate to especially important problems, for example the freedom of disabled people to move about freely and to take part in the life of the community. There are, Sen concludes, "widespread and ubiquitous variations in our ability to convert primary goods into functionings and well-beings."[49] The notion of urgency related to this is not fully captured by Rawls' approach. Although his approach of the holdings of primary goods provides a view of freedom of choice, it pays no attention to the diversity of human beings, certainly not in terms of "hard cases," but not even in terms of "normal health and medical needs." In that sense primary goods do not reflect sufficiently each person's freedom of choice to achieve valuable functioning and well-being equally. The summing up of this criticism is that primary goods "take inadequate note of the ideas behind positive freedom."[50] Rawls has fallen into the trap of "commodity fetishism": primary goods suffer from the "fetishist" handicap by being regarded as valuable in themselves, and not for the benefits they bestow upon the person. Even though the list of primary goods is specified by Rawls in a broad and inclusive way, encompassing rights, liberties, diverse opportunities, the powers and prerogatives of offices and positions of authority and responsibility, income and wealth, and the social bases of self-respect, it is still concerned with good things rather than with what these good things *do* to human beings.[51] The problem with Rawls' conception of primary goods is, then, that they are seen "only" as *means* to ends. "Rawls takes primary goods as the embodiment of advantage rather than taking advantage to be a *relationship* between persons and goods."[52]

Although Rawls fails to focus on "basic capabilities," Sen does not entirely reject Rawls' ideas. He is of the opinion that Rawls is "on the right track," since Sen is convinced that "[t]he focus on basic capabilities can be seen as a natural extension of Rawls's concern with primary goods, shifting attention from goods to what goods do to human beings."[53] Notable here is that Sen himself points out that Rawls, in his own discussion on primary goods, has sometimes pointed to "capabilities," although Rawls – in the terminology that Sen uses – pays attention to the goods themselves, and not to what a primary good can do for someone. Thus Sen – quite rightly – points out that Rawls talks about "the social bases of self-respect," instead of talking about "self-respect." In this instance, Sen remarks, there "are … good reasons to think that Rawls himself – contrary to what his own theory formally states – is really after something like capabilities. He motivates the focus on primary goods by discussing what the primary goods enable people to do. It is only because of his assumption – often implicit – that the same mapping of primary goods to capabilities holds for all, that he can sensibly concentrate on primary goods rather than on the corresponding capabilities."[54]

This remark suggests that in Rawls' theory – practically speaking – there may be less of a difference between "primary goods" and "basic capabilities" than Sen has in the first instance suggested. In fact there are more examples to be found in *justice as fairness* where Rawls implicitly takes into account "basic capabilities." Take, for example, Rawls' exposition on the "worth" of political liberties, and that this "worth" might not be equal for each and every person. Therefore measures have to be taken so that when a person wants to make use of his political liberties, their "fair value" has to be guaranteed. One could well argue that as far as "fair value" is related to the effective functioning of citizens in democratic politics, this is in line with Sen's ideas on capabilities. Rawls is well aware that a mere legal entitlement to political liberties is not sufficient and that attention has to be shifted, precisely as Sen had argued, "from goods to what goods do to human beings."

In 1992 Sen repeated his original criticism,[55] and in his turn Rawls once more discusses this criticism in *Political Liberalism* (PL: 182–183).[56] On the whole it seems fair to say that this debate has become slightly repetitive over the years, with Rawls pursuing his defense of the (same) list of primary goods, and Sen sticking to his idea of basic capabilities. Basically, both positions remain unchanged: Rawls stresses the function that primary goods play in assuring that the different conceptions of the good people have can, in practice, be realized. However, he recognizes the importance of Sen's idea of basic capabilities, especially when looking to the distribution of citizens' effective basic freedoms. The idea of the "fair value" of the (political) liberties attests to this. But Rawls adds an important caveat: "to apply the idea of effective basic capabilities without those or similar assumptions [as made in the use of primary goods about citizens' capabilities] calls for more information than political society can conceivably acquire and sensibly apply." Instead, Rawls continues, "by embedding primary goods into the specification of the principles of justice and ordering the basic structure of society accordingly, we may come as close as we can in practice to a just distribution of Sen's effective freedoms" (LoP: 13 note 3).

There is one issue, however, where Rawls acknowledges that Sen may be right. This concerns the "more extreme cases," the hard cases. Rawls stipulates that he puts "aside the more extreme cases of persons with such grave disabilities that they never can be normal contributing members of social cooperation" (JaF: 170). If indeed the solution for the "normal" cases he proposes cannot be extended to these hard cases, the idea of primary goods for these hard cases may have to be abandoned (CP: 368–369). In this situation "a different or a more comprehensive notion than that of primary goods … will, I believe, be necessary." And it is here that "for example, Sen's notion of an index which focuses on persons' basic capabilities may prove fruitful for this problem and serve as an essential complement to the use of primary goods" (CP: 369 note 8).[57] Perhaps Sen can elaborate, or so Rawls wonders, on how to deal with more extreme cases, and then "eventually this could be included in justice as fairness when suitably extended, or else adapted to it as an essential complementary part" (JaF: 176 note 59).[58]

In this exposition of the debate on "primary goods or basic capabilities" we have, as yet, still not answered precisely how Rawls argues that, indeed, "normal medical and health needs" can be dealt with without changing the list of primary goods, and how he can show that the index of the primary goods is in fact flexible enough, contrary to what Sen seems to think, to cope with the issue of "normal medical and health needs." Rawls, as mentioned, works out his answer "later," in the context of an ideal legislative procedure. We will return to this issue when we deal with the "four-stage sequence" (of which the legislative procedure is a part). There we will elaborate Rawls' final statement on this issue as worked out by him in *Justice as Fairness: A Restatement.*[59]

Primary goods or equal opportunity of welfare?

The issue in our exposition on "primary goods or basic capabilities" turned on what precisely the ultimate target of our egalitarian concern is. Sen's answer was "basic capabilities." But there are other views on what the appropriate target is. Take the view of so-called "luck egalitarians." Just like Sen they formulate criticisms of the primary goods (and the use Rawls makes of them) because these goods are inflexible or insensitive to some kind of variability in people. But unlike Sen, who agrees with Rawls in rejecting welfare-based accounts as mistaken about what is of ultimate concern, luck egalitarians argue that this is precisely the problem with primary goods: primary goods are insensitive to variability among the preferences people have. They argue that the target that comprehensively captures our egalitarian concerns is "equal opportunity for welfare" or "equal access to advantage."[60]

"Luck egalitarianism" or "equality of fortune" is a conception which takes the fundamental injustice to be the natural inequality in the distribution of luck. The fundamental aim of equality is to compensate people for undeserved bad luck. Luck egalitarianism relies on two moral premises: that people should be compensated for undeserved misfortunes, and that the compensation should come only from that part of others' good fortune that is undeserved. It has become, since say the late 1980s, one of the dominant theoretical positions among egalitarians. Theorists who endorse it include Richard Arneson, Gerald Cohen, Ronald Dworkin, and John Roemer.[61]

Luck egalitarians want to draw a sharp distinction between events that result from chance and those that result from people's choices. Choice here is central. Differences in distributive shares should only reflect people's free choices, after everyone has been compensated for the unfavorable circumstances he starts out with. It should not be considered a sign of injustice when inequality with respect to income and leisure reflects differences in the arduousness of different people's labors, when it reflects effort made acquiring skills and training them, or when it reflects people's preferences and choices, by contrast with people's "myriad forms of lucky and unlucky circumstance."[62]

Our egalitarian concerns require, or so it is argued, that people be aided whenever their un-chosen preferences make them worse off than others in opportunity for satisfaction. And primary goods, or so it is argued by luck egalitarians, are inflexible because they force us to ignore the legitimate complaints of people who are worse off than others because some of their preferences or values, which they have through no fault of their own, or as the result of nothing that they could control, put them at a disadvantage. For example, some people may have more expensive tastes than others and so be less efficient converters of primary goods into satisfaction or welfare. Primary goods are not responsive to this central egalitarian intuition: for the same assignment of primary goods, these people will be less well off than people with more modest tastes (or values): they may be made worse off with regard to their opportunity for welfare or satisfaction through no fault of their own.

This argument can be pushed further, by saying that our capacities for choice, our occasions for choice, and the alternatives for choice we confront, are also influenced by chance circumstances (by our natural talents, our upbringing, others' talents, upbringing, and choices, our social connections, etc.), so it is hard to say when a choice is not itself the result of "brute luck." If this argument is pushed to the limit, so to speak, we get to a "hard determinism" where nothing is left undetermined by nature; thus, our choices are themselves as much a matter of our circumstances as are our starting positions in life. It says that transfers of wealth should occur from richer to poorer without regard to either chance or choice, and should be decided purely on the basis of comparative welfare or comparative advantage.

Our present concern is with a less deterministic perspective. The issue at hand here is choice of preferences, or control over preferences that are central to egalitarian concerns, and the objection to the primary goods. It is this that makes the issue one of "primary goods or equal opportunity for welfare," or "primary goods or equal access to advantage." It seems fair to say that the development of "luck egalitarianism" was originally triggered by Rawls' theory of justice, in which a distinction is made between "choice" and "circumstances." With that distinction Rawls laid the basis for an "ambition-sensitive" but "endowment-insensitive" distribution as advocated, for example, in later years by the political theorist and philosopher of law Ronald Dworkin.[63] Rawls' distinction has also become the starting point for theorizing on "choice-sensitive" egalitarianism: inequalities that are the consequence of circumstances that we cannot be held responsible for, are unjust; in contrast, inequalities that are the consequence of "circumstances" we ourselves are responsible for are just, or at least not unjust.

Even though Rawls may have triggered this debate, he himself has hardly been a direct participant in it, in contrast to his debate with Sen on that other target of egalitarian concern, basic capabilities.[64] What Rawls has done over the years is to elaborate, not change his view on, the role primary goods play in *justice as fairness*. He has not changed his view on how they are defined, or on why they generate an objective measure for interpersonal comparison, or what it means for him to say, "we are responsible for the choices we make."

Let us have a closer look at what *justice as fairness* has to say on "choice" and "responsibility," and on variations in tastes and preferences. Earlier on we saw that, according to *justice as fairness*, citizens are themselves responsible for the choices they make, and for how they can increase, for example, their happiness by changing and adapting their preferences or tastes. Now, the first issue here is that of measuring "happiness." How are we to measure one person being happier than another person? We have already noted that, as far as Rawls is concerned, it is practically impossible to reach agreement on a meaningful estimate of happiness when persons carry out their plans of life, and the amount of primary goods a person receives is clearly not intended as a measure of citizens' expected overall psychological satisfaction. The fact that "equal opportunity for welfare" (or "equal access to advantage") may allow us to make explicit the choice of preferences does not mean it is responsive to Rawls' objections to using satisfaction as a measure of well-being for the purposes of justice.

Rawls' objections to measuring satisfaction weigh against its use in equality of opportunity for welfare. To decide, for example, that expected preference satisfaction is equal, we must make at least ordinal or co-ordinal comparisons. (We need a "principle of co-ordinal utilitarianism" which starts – as utilitarianism does generally – by regarding persons in terms of their capacities for satisfaction [CP: 376, 383].) Co-ordinal utility comparisons between the levels of satisfactions, or well-being, of different persons means that we in fact can ascertain whether two persons are equally well-off, or whether one is better off than the other, but the differences between the levels of satisfaction cannot be given a numerical measure. These levels can only be ordered as greater or less (CP: 377). It would commit us to there being some social utility function that would let us compare the level of satisfaction each person enjoys. Such a utility function would commit each of us, Rawls argues, to accepting its rankings of our overall satisfaction relative to every other person. But such a function constitutes a "shared highest-order preference function" (CP: 380).[65] On the basis of such a function, it would be "rational for [persons] to adjust and revise their final ends and desires, and to modify their traits of character and to reshape their realized abilities, so as to achieve a total personal situation ranked higher in the ordering," defined by the preference function (CP: 380).

Rawls' main argument against this idea is that this "shared highest-order preference function is plainly incompatible with the conception of a well-ordered society in justice as fairness" (CP: 381). Citizens' conceptions of the good are said to be not only opposed but incommensurable. "These conceptions of the good are incommensurable because their final ends and aspirations are so diverse, their specific content so different, that no common basis for judgment can be found" (CP: 381).[66]

It is of course to solve this issue of a common basis for judgment that Rawls introduced the idea of primary goods. They provide an objective measure for interpersonal comparison. Note in parentheses that an index of primary goods does not belong to theory in the economists' sense; it is part and parcel of the conception of *justice as fairness*, a conception in which moral persons are moved by their two highest-order interests, to realize and exercise their two powers of moral personality.

In addition it should be noted, according to Rawls, that this "controversy about interpersonal comparisons tends to obscure the real question, namely, whether the total (or average) happiness is to be maximized in the first place" (TJR: 78). Let us get back then to "the real question." As Rawls says:

It may be objected that expectations should not be defined as an index of primary goods anyway but rather as the satisfactions to be expected when plans are executed using these goods. After all, it is in the fulfillment of these plans that men gain happiness, and therefore the estimate of expectations should not be founded on the available means. Justice as fairness, however, takes a different view. For it does not look behind the use which persons make of the rights and opportunities available to them in order to measure, much less to maximize, the satisfactions they achieve. Nor does it try to evaluate the relative merits of different conceptions of the good. Instead, *it is assumed that the members of society are rational persons able to adjust their conceptions of the good to their situation.* There is no necessity to compare the worth of the conceptions of different persons once it is supposed they are compatible with the principles of justice. (TJ: 94; TJR: 80–81; emphasis added)

Now this exposition of the problems of measurement and primary goods discusses variations in citizens' conceptions of the good generally. Can we say more about variations in *tastes and preferences* in particular? Of course, for Rawls the same arguments on problems measuring "equal expected preference satisfaction" hold equally for "tastes and preferences,"[67] but even before we would reach the issue of measurement and the interpersonal comparisons of tastes and preferences, and before we would wonder if the target of our egalitarian concern ought to be "equal opportunity for welfare" (or "equal access to advantage"), there is already for Rawls a much more basic argument at play. Issues of tastes and preferences are, in the context of *justice as fairness*, issues of personal responsibility.

Imagine, as Rawls asks us to do, two persons, one of them having expensive tastes: he is distraught without expensive wines and exotic dishes (CP: 369). Imagine also that both persons have an equal share of the primary good "income." It is then evident they are not equally "satisfied." But we also know that (level of) satisfaction is not what *justice as fairness* takes into account. Using "satisfaction" does not generate a workable and objective criterion for interpersonal comparison. To find workable criteria for interpersonal comparison, Rawls has introduced the idea of primary goods. The role of this idea of primary goods is to abstract from disagreement about the components of welfare and to give us an objective, workable, and public way of interpersonal comparison. Primary goods do not, however, as explained earlier, give us a measure of psychological well-being, or of comparing satisfaction in matters of justice. The important point to note here is that the use of (the index of) primary goods *relies on the capacity to assume responsibility for our ends.* As Rawls argues, moral persons as citizens have some part in forming and cultivating their final ends and preferences. This presupposes that persons are not to be regarded as passive carriers of desires. They can be held responsible for their preferences: these are not beyond their control as propensities or cravings which simply happen. That we can be held responsible for our preferences is implied by our capacity, part of our moral power, to form, to revise, and rationally to pursue a conception of the good (CP: 369–370; PL: 186). The upshot of this argument is that variations in preferences and tastes are our own responsibility, as is, for example, an "expensive taste" (PL: 33–34, 185). Desires and wants, however intense, are not by themselves reasons in matters of justice. And thus Rawls can say that it is also "a normal part of being human to cope with the preferences our upbringing leaves us with" (PL: 185 note 15). (The presumption here is that being brought up in a wealthy family one develops – expensive – preferences accordingly.)

Rawls is quite convinced that we can take responsibility for our own ends. The aim of *justice as fairness* is, first, avoiding arbitrary sources of inequality. *Justice as fairness* seeks to mitigate the influence of social contingencies and natural fortune on the life prospects persons have. It is not concerned with inequalities that are the consequence of choices in personal *life-style*.

Assuming, second, "that there is a distribution of natural assets, [justice as fairness is concerned that] those who are at the same level of talent and ability, and have the same willingness to use them, should have the same prospects of success regardless of their initial place in the social system. In all sectors of society there should be roughly equal prospects of culture and achievement for everyone similarly

motivated and endowed" (TJR: 63). The expectations of those with
the same abilities and aspirations should not be affected by their social
class, cultural, or ethnic background. But *justice as fairness* is not
concerned with those inequalities that are a consequence of making
a personal choice not to develop one's abilities and talents, or of
showing no willingness to do so. These choices also fall under one's
own responsibility.

Thus, summarizing, taking "responsibility for our tastes and preferences, whether or not they have arisen from our actual choices, is a
special case of that responsibility. As citizens with realized moral
powers, this is something we must learn to deal with" (PL: 185). This
leaves out of the equation only the "preferences and tastes" that are
incapacitating and render someone unable to cooperate normally in
society. But these "preferences and tastes" that are "incapacitating" are
of a medical (or psychiatric) nature.[68] And with these medical cases we
are squarely back to Rawls' debate with Sen on "normal medical and
health needs," and what justice requires for those who temporarily have
fallen below the essential capacities for being normal and fully cooperating members of society. In *justice as fairness* we need only be
assured that people can function normally for them to be held responsible for their tastes and preferences. It may lead to a debate on "primary goods or basic capabilities," but, for Rawls, certainly not to a
debate on "primary goods or equal opportunity for welfare" (or to a
debate on "primary goods or equal access to advantage").

The difference principle and reciprocity

The design of the institutions of the basic structure of a well-ordered
society is governed by the idea of creating a fair system of social
cooperation between moral persons that stimulates a positive, voluntary contribution from every member of society. It is the difference
principle that plays a key role in accomplishing this. In this and the
next section we will elaborate on its role in *justice as fairness*, before
turning to the issue of designing the institutions of a just basic structure.

Rawls stresses that the basic structure is not designed to eliminate the
element of fortune in the distribution of burdens and benefits. That
distribution is, after all, in part based on the natural lottery of natural
assets and abilities, one person having more of them, another one less.
Even if an equal distribution of native endowments could be reached,

that would be more in balance with the equal worth of free and equal persons (But how to achieve this? By adopting eugenic policies? By abolishing the institution of "the family"?), Rawls rejects those kinds of "redistribution" of natural endowments. Measures to accomplish it would infringe on the fundamental integrity of the person and conflict with the idea of the equal status of men as moral persons, their equal moral worth. Persons themselves "own" their endowments and the psychological and physical integrity of persons is guaranteed by the basic rights and liberties that fall under the first principle of justice.

Now, although no one deserves his greater natural capacity nor merits a more favorable starting place in society, this is no reason to ignore these distinctions between persons. The basic structure should be arranged in such a way "that these contingencies work for the good of the least fortunate. Thus we are led to the difference principle if we wish to set up the social system so that no one gains or loses from his arbitrary place in the distribution of natural assets or his initial place in society without giving or receiving compensating advantages in return" (TJ: 102; TJR: 87).

In the scheme of social cooperation that develops in a just basic structure, everyone has a right to his natural assets. This right is covered as mentioned by the first principle under the basic liberty protecting the integrity of the person, and also – by participating in the just scheme of social cooperation – everybody is entitled to what one can legitimately expect to acquire. All this is not affected by the working of the difference principle. It is not a principle that has as its intention to "correct" the "undeserved" inequalities of birth and natural endowment, without much ado, in the direction of equality. *Justice as fairness*, in its entirety, or the difference principle as part of it, is badly misunderstood if its aim is seen to eliminate contingencies from social life, for some contingencies are inevitable (PL: 283). Although it is true that the difference principle gives some weight to the considerations singled out by "the principle of redress," it is not the same thing. The principle of redress is, as Rawls explains, the principle that claims "that undeserved inequalities call for redress; and since inequalities of birth and natural endowment are undeserved, these inequalities are to be somehow compensated for" (TJ: 100; TJR: 86). Indeed both principles, the difference principle and the principle of redress, see inequalities that are the result of social class and of natural endowments as undeserved and both principles look for ways to "redress," one way or another, these inequalities. In fact any theory of justice has to take the claims of redress into account, including *justice as fairness*. And therefore "redress" also represents one of the elements in Rawls' conception of justice.

The principle of redress "holds that in order to treat all persons equally, to provide genuine equality of opportunity, society must give more attention to those with fewer native assets and to those born into the less favorable social positions. The idea is to redress the bias of contingencies in the direction of equality. In pursuit of this principle, greater resources might be spent on the education of the less rather than the more intelligent, at least over a certain time of life, say the earlier years of school" (TJ: 100–101; TJR: 86).

Parenthetically note here that providing "genuine equality of opportunity" and the idea of redressing "the bias of contingencies" in the direction of equality – according to Rawls the core ideas of "the principle of redress" – show a close similarity to the ideas formulated by so-called "luck egalitarian theorists." As discussed earlier, they hold that the role of a conception of justice is to formulate that, and how, the results of natural and social contingencies should be equalized, or at least neutralized.

Now, Rawls stresses, however, that the difference principle "is not of course the principle of redress" (TJ: 101; TJR: 86). The difference principle does "not require society to try to even out handicaps as if all were expected to compete on a fair basis in the same race. But the difference principle would allocate resources in education, say, so as to improve the long-term expectation of the least favored. If this end is attained by *giving more attention to the better endowed, it is permissible*; otherwise not" (TJ: 101; TJR: 86–87; emphasis added).[69]

And, as Rawls continues, "although the difference principle is not the same as the principle of redress, it does achieve some of the intent of the latter principle. It transforms the aims of the basic structure so that the total scheme of institutions no longer emphasizes social efficiency and technocratic values" (TJ: 101; TJR: 87). Here we get to the kernel of how to deal with the inequalities of natural assets in the context of *justice as fairness*: "The difference principle represents, in effect, an agreement to regard the distribution of natural talents [the differences between persons] as in some respects a common asset and to share in the greater social and economic benefits made possible by the complementarities of this distribution. Those who have been favored by nature, whoever they are, may gain from their good fortune only on terms that improve the situation of those who have lost out" (TJR: 87).[70] This is the core of the idea of reciprocity and it is the difference principle – applied to the basic structure of a well-ordered society – that expresses this (TJ: 14, 102; TJR: xv, 13, 88; JaF: 49, 76). The fair terms of social cooperation specify an idea of reciprocity. In a well-ordered society the principles of justice as fairness "with the difference principle, with its implicit reference to equal division as a benchmark, formulate an idea of reciprocity between citizens" (PL: 17).[71]

And it is here that we also get to the core of the meaning of "a well-ordered society." Whilst it may look at first sight as if the – unequal – distribution of natural talents and unequal life chances could disrupt the harmonious relations between "free and equal moral persons," it is in effect the principles of *justice as fairness*, especially the difference principle, that guarantee a "harmony of interests." The way the difference principle expresses this "harmony of interests" should be elaborated. How can the undeniable fact that there are differences between persons in their natural endowments be combined with the idea of reciprocity in social cooperation between persons that are in a moral sense equal? The answer is: by focusing on the unequal effects that are the outcome of these natural inequalities. And this is the essence of Rawls' idea of democratic equality, in which the difference principle is embedded.

The formulation of the difference principle – "social and economic inequalities are to be arranged so that they are to the greatest benefit of the least advantaged" – brings to the fore that Rawls' conception of justice, right from the start, focuses on the least advantaged members of society. But the difference principle does not prescribe that the position of the least advantaged has to be improved by (equalizing) measures that level out differences between the most and the least advantaged members of society. On the contrary, there is nothing against a situation in which some groups in society continue to have a bigger share in the amount of primary goods that are available to them. However, if that is the case, it has to be established that this inequality compensates the least advantaged for the fact that they are, relatively speaking, so sparingly treated. It is the most advantaged groups in society that have to prove that this is indeed the case. They have to show in a convincing manner that each reform of the institutions of the basic structure which would have (more) equalizing effects (for example by a change in the tax scheme) would irrevocably have as its outcome a decline in the position of the worse off. That is, it has to be shown that if the expectations of the more advantaged would be decreased, the prospects of the least advantaged would likewise fall. Actual existing differences in power, in income and wealth, can only be justified in this way. Inequalities in the basic structure are permissible only if each person benefits from them. If it can be demonstrated that this situation holds, one can speak of "compensating advantages." It is a situation in which compensation works both ways: there exists reciprocity in the distribution of the burdens and benefits of social cooperation. Differences in, for example, income compensate the more favored on the one hand for their greater efforts and sacrifices (for instance little leisure time), and compensate the less advantaged on the other hand, because they also profit from the differences in income. We assume that in this situation it has been established that the least advantaged are receiving more primary goods than would be the case in each and every other possible situation where primary goods (income, for instance) would be distributed in a more egalitarian direction. The intuitive idea of democratic equality is that the social order is not to establish and secure the more attractive prospects of those better off unless doing so is to the advantage of those less fortunate. Democratic equality, however, does not require equalizing wealth or income. On the other hand, the difference principle does formulate a limit to the inequalities that can be justified in a society: it has to be shown empirically that these inequalities contribute to improving the expectations of the least advantaged members of society. The higher expectations of those better situated are just, if and only if that is the case (TJ: 75; TJR: 65).

The dilemma on which the difference principle turns is that there are different combinations of total production and degrees of equality: there exists a trade-off between how much is produced and the way it is distributed. The starting point is that in an economy with specific possibilities of production (given its technology and the available factors of production), there are two choices: a large product that goes hand in hand with an unequal distribution, or a small(er) product with a (more) equal distribution. Under these circumstances, and assuming we can measure the extent to which particular arrangements of the basic structure determine this trade-off (for instance the way a specific tax scheme influences this), one could strive for reforms of the existing social and economic institutions such that a greater product would be available for distribution, while the unequal distribution that accompanies it is such that the position of persons in the lowest positions – compared to their actual situation – improves. From the perspective of the difference principle this kind of reform of institutions would be considered just.

Rawls' argument with regard to the difference principle is based on a simple assumption: compensating inequalities hang together with differences in productivity that are caused by the effect of differences in rewards that influence the willingness to work (the amount of time someone wants to spend on productive labor). The inequalities of rewards of dissimilar labor productivity that are the outcome of the arrangements of an ideal market are seen by Rawls – to a certain extent – as an incentive. If one would allow the more talented only a tiny advantage in income (and in other remunerations such as prestige, or responsibility at the workplace), it could be the case that these persons would not be sufficiently motivated to acquire the special skills, experience, and training, and special know-how, which tend to earn a premium (i.e. for which firms are willing to pay more to those with these characteristics because their productivity is greater). It could undermine the supply of qualified individuals, and it could also be the case that talented persons would not look for the work in which they would be most useful to society.

Wanting to reduce the existing differences in reward that are sanctioned by the market could, or so this argument goes, demonstrably lead to lower productive efforts of the most talented individuals in society. Insufficient incentives could affect the productivity of the whole economy and thus also have a negative effect on the position of those who are worse off. Rawls summarizes these ideas in the following way: "Supposedly ... the greater expectations allowed to entrepreneurs encourages them to do things which raise the prospects of laboring class. Their better prospects act as incentives so that the economic process is more efficient, innovation proceeds at a faster pace, and so on. Eventually the resulting material benefits spread throughout the system and to the least advantaged. I shall not consider how far these things are true. The point is that something of this kind must be argued if these inequalities are to be just by the difference principle" (TJ: 78).[72]

Rawls points out that institutional corrections to the distributive outcomes of market mechanisms may have as a consequence that the life prospects of each and every person decline. Such corrections would be, according to the difference principle, unjust. On the other hand, the same principle points to the importance of a redistribution policy that, as far as possible, uses the (economic) incentives of the "competitive market." In the case that inequalities in (financial) rewards do indeed have these stimulating incentive effects, one can speak in two ways of compensating inequalities. First, the less favored are compensated for the fact that they are situated in the position of the worse off. Second, the more favored are compensated for their greater productivity. Their greater expectations "presumably cover the costs of training or answer to organizational requirements, thereby contributing to the general advantage" (TJR: 136).[73] Essential to the difference principle is that it entails the idea that inequalities are justified if these inequalities play a functional role in enhancing greater life prospects for the least advantaged. This happening is the result of the way in which the complete set of legitimate expectations of individual citizens is honored by the institutions of the basic structure.

It is clear that the justice of distributive shares depends on the background institutions and on how they allocate total income, wages, and other income plus transfers. Accordingly, Rawls does not claim that all inequalities in (income) rewards that are the result of market exchanges can be defended by making an appeal to the dreaded effect of negative incentives. There is with reason strong objection to the competitive determination of total income, since it ignores the claims of need and an appropriate standard of life. Since the market is not suited to answer these claims of need, they should be met by a separate arrangement. Therefore, as we will elaborate later, the background institutions also have to entail provisions that insure against these contingencies of the market. Indeed, the difference principle presumably requires this. But once a suitable minimum is provided by transfers, it may be perfectly fair that the rest of total income be settled by the price system, assuming that it is moderately efficient and free from monopolistic restrictions, and that unreasonable externalities have been eliminated.[74]

The difference principle and "just" inequalities

The fact that there is a relation between the gross social-economic product and income distribution is an essential presumption for the application of the difference principle to the social and economic parts of the basic structure that encompasses the means of production, markets, and the division of labor. It is this relation that makes it possible to be able to speak at all of inequalities that are actually "compensating."

But when do we have a situation in which we can speak of reciprocity? When is the harmony of social interests achieved?

The presumption that social cooperation between persons, defined by the basic structure, is mutually advantageous and also that the greater expectations of the more advantaged improve the situation of the worst off, can be illustrated with the help of the so-called "*contribution curve.*" With this curve Rawls demonstrates the relation that exists between the expectations of those who are better off (measured in, for example, the primary good income) and those who are worse off (see Figure 2.1).

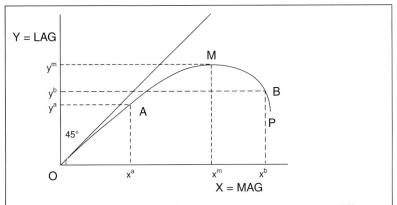

Figure 2.1 Social cooperation, the contribution curve, and the difference principle

In this figure, the distances along the two axes are measured in terms of an index of (social) primary goods. The expectations in terms of primary goods of the more advantaged group (MAG) are on the *x*-axis, and those of the less advantaged group (LAG) on the *y*-axis.

The point O, the origin, represents the point at which all (social) primary goods are distributed equally. At this point O, the total amount of primary goods to be distributed equally is, compared to all other feasible distributions, the smallest. All points on the 45° line represent equal distribution, but the further we move from this point O along the 45° line, the more there is to distribute.

A basic assumption in the following is that social cooperation between persons is productive. This assumption is expressed in the figure by the OP curve: *the contribution curve*. There are different OP curves for different schemes of cooperation. A particular contribution curve (OP) goes hand in hand with a particular scheme of social cooperation. One scheme of cooperation might be more productive than another scheme: it leads to a higher output. In that situation, the total amount of primary goods to be distributed increases. The contribution curve illustrates this relationship between total production and distribution.

The OP curve represents the contribution to the expectations of the less advantaged by the greater expectations of the more advantaged, measured in terms of an index of primary goods (measured here in a heuristic way as a person's prospect of the primary good income and wealth over a complete life). At the origin, both groups receive, as Rawls stipulates, the same remuneration. The OP curve is always below the 45° line, since the more advantaged are always better off. Thus below this 45° line we find the set of unequal distributions where the remuneration of the more advantaged group is larger than that of the less advantaged group.

In our example, the OP curve indicates the returns of the more and less advantaged, when only (schedules of) wages and salaries are changed. The curve demonstrates that the less advantaged gain (although not equally) from the greater expectations of the better off (and thus from increasing inequalities) only on the upward rising part of the contribution curve. On this segment of the curve, both the expectations of the better off, and those of the worse off, increase. Moving along the OP curve, beyond the maximum point M, on the downward sloping part of the curve inequalities are increasing even more. But although the index of the more advantaged group increases, that of the less advantaged group starts to decline.

The contribution curve provides the set of feasible distributions, but by itself does not tell us which distributions out of this set can be called "just." *Justice as fairness* provides the answer as to what choice to make from this set of feasible distributions. In *justice as fairness* it is assumed not only that social cooperation between persons is productive, but also that social cooperation as defined by the basic structure is mutually advantageous. And in *justice as fairness* the difference principle formulates how claims to goods produced in social cooperation are to be shared among those who produce them: the greater index of primary goods for one group (the more advantaged) is justified only insofar as it adds to the index of the less favored. As total production increases and both groups gain, the idea of reciprocity, which is a principle of mutual benefit, is fulfilled. These (increasing) inequalities are "permissible" inequalities.

This situation is the case along the upward rising part of the OP curve: here not only the expectations of the more advantaged group rise, but also those of the less favored group. Even higher expectations for the more advantaged raise the expectations of those in the lower position. This part of the curve is *just throughout*, but not the best just arrangement. (Thus, for instance, at point A, where there is no equal share in the output between the more advantaged group (X^a), and the less advantaged group (Y^a), this unequal division nevertheless represents not an unjust scheme: these unequal remunerations are just).

Society aims for the best just arrangement. Thus we can move further along the upward rising part of the OP curve. The best just arrangement is reached at point M, where the OP curve is at its maximum. It is here that the reciprocity implicit in the difference principle is perfectly satisfied. No changes in the expectations of those better off can improve the situation of those worse off. The best arrangement obtains. It is what Rawls calls a *perfectly just scheme*. (Thus, at point M, where there is no equal share in the output between the more advantaged group (X^m) and the less advantaged group (Y^m), this unequal division represents inequalities that are perfectly just).

Beyond the maximum point M, on the downward sloping part of the curve, the inequalities are increasing even more. Although the index of the more advantaged group increases, that of the less advantaged group starts to decline. The reciprocity implicit in the difference principle no longer obtains: the harmony of interests no longer exists. From the perspective of the difference principle this is an unjust situation. We have reached the region of unjust inequalities.

Moving along the downward sloping part of the OP curve we reach point B. This is the "Bentham point," where the sum of overall income and wealth in society ($X^b + Y^b$) is maximized. However, the difference principle is not satisfied at this point B, even though B represents a point of greater total income and wealth than M. This example is an illustration of Rawls' fundamental critique of classical utilitarianism. "A classical utilitarian ... is indifferent as to how a constant sum of benefits is distributed." Utilitarianism "allows, other things equal, larger inequalities" (TJ: 77, 78; TJR: 67).

These ideas on social cooperation, the difference principle, the contribution curve, and "just inequalities" were, more than thirty years after Rawls had formulated them for the first time, still defended by him; see TJ: 76–80, 104–105, 318–319; TJR: 65–70, 89–90, 280–281; PL: 283; JaF: 61–66; for the figure see TJ: 76; TJR: 66; JaF: 62.

From the exposition of the difference principle so far, it has become clear that Rawls is of the opinion that an unequal system of rewards, and thus an unequal distribution of, for instance, income, can be justified because the less advantaged will gain from the higher reward of the more favored. Illustrating this with the contribution curve, we can see that the less favored gain (although not equally) from the greater expectations of the better off (and thus from increasing inequalities) only on the upward rising part of the contribution curve. On this segment of the curve the expectations of both the better off and the worse off increase. Total production increases and both groups gain: there is mutual benefit as required by the idea of reciprocity and expressed in the (application of the) difference principle. These (increasing) inequalities can be justified; they are "just" or "permissible" inequalities.

This upward rising part of the curve is *just throughout*. Even higher expectations for the more advantaged would raise the expectations of those in the lowest position. It is, however, not the best just arrangement; the maximum is not yet achieved. Once that is achieved, the best arrangement obtains; it is what Rawls calls a *perfectly just scheme*. Once a society goes beyond the maximum it operates along the downward sloping part of the curve. As the more favored (still) gain, the less advantaged start to lose. These increasing inequalities are no longer positive contributions to the position of the worse off; they are unjust. On this part of the curve a harmony of interests no longer exists: the reciprocity implicit in the difference principle no longer obtains. These ideas on the contribution curve and on "just inequalities" are, more than thirty years after Rawls had formulated them for the first time, still defended by him.[75]

Given the fact that there is a relation between total production and the distribution of income, an excessive redistribution may lower the amount of income that is available for this redistribution policy. Because the productive effort someone wants to invest is limited, a tax on earned income might have the effect that persons decrease the amount of hours they are willing to spend on productive work, and consequently lower the amount they produce. Thus, attempts to achieve a just distribution can cause inefficiency. This trade-off between social justice and efficiency is traditionally the focus of the literature that is concerned with the formal analysis of the optimal tax rate.[76] This literature also has dealt extensively with the question of which optimal tax structure is required by Rawls' difference principle. The starting point here is that the shape and slope of the contribution curve is in part determined by the presumption that there is a relation between productive effort and the level of taxation. What one wants to develop is a tax scheme to raise the revenues that justice requires, that is to say a tax scheme in which the least advantaged can maximally profit from this relation. In other words, an optimum has to be found in which the minimum is to be set at that point which, taking wages into account, maximizes the expectations of the least advantaged group. The economist Kenneth Arrow, for example, has not been optimistic about finding an answer to this question: "practical implications of this research are as yet dubious, primarily because too little is known about the magnitude of the incentive effects, particularly in the upper brackets."[77]

Rawls himself implicitly seems to presuppose that the precise shape and slope of the contribution curve are known. But he pays hardly any attention to which factors, and in what way, influence its shape and slope.[78] Thus one finds next to nothing on the question of how redistribution (or taxation) policies could weaken incentives and thereby lower production. But there are several uncertainties that influence the shape and the slope of the contribution curve, uncertainties that have consequences for the application of the difference principle. In this context it has been remarked that the "shape of the contribution curve is an empirical matter, lying in the realm of positive economics. There is nothing that we can securely say about it solely on theoretical grounds."[79]

Be that as it may, and even not knowing the precise form of the contribution curve, because too little is known about the relation between (the level of) taxation of wage incomes and the magnitude of the (negative) incentive effects, illustrating the workings of the difference principle with the contribution curve makes one thing clear. As inequalities have to be compensating, the downward sloping part of the curve – the part that lies beyond the maximum – where the expectations of the more favored are (i.e. remain) increasing, while at the same time those of the less advantaged are decreasing, should be avoided. Along the downward sloping part of the curve we can no longer speak of democratic equality: this growing distance between the expectations of the most and the least advantaged is no longer compensating. It violates the principle of mutual advantage, as well as that of democratic equality. In this region of the curve there is no longer a harmony of interests, or of reciprocity. In short: these inequalities are unjust.

This analysis also illustrates, once again, that "maximin" does not represent in any way what the core idea of a "just distribution" is. The maximin criterion does not express the idea of reciprocity. It only formulates precisely what the meaning of the term "maximin" is: *maximum minimorum*, to make sure the minimum (of the least advantaged members of society, in this case) is as high as possible. As we noted, the maximin rule tells us to rank alternatives by their worst possible outcomes: we are to adopt that worst outcome which is superior to the worst outcomes of the alternatives (TJ: 152–153; TJR: 132–133). But on the question of whether there should be any restrictions on the height of the maximum (say a maximum to earned income), maximin remains silent. Any idea of "harmony of interests" plays no role when using this criterion. In contrast to the (application of the) difference principle, the maximin criterion has nothing to say about on what grounds differences between the better off and the worse off would be justified, or what the permissible range of inequalities between them is.

Designing a just basic structure: the four-stage sequence

Let us return to the parties in the original position. Although they have unanimously agreed on the principles of justice, in fact their work is not yet over. They now have the task of designing the institutional form, a basic structure, which best "fits" the principles of *justice as fairness*. With the lexical ordering of the principles in hand (given by the priority rules), they now have to make a selection from the set of possible alternative basic structures. The (hypothetical) choice of a basic structure by the parties could then proceed as follows:

— the basic structure in which the most basic rights and liberties are provided, is best;
— of each pair of possible basic structures with the same amount of basic rights and liberties, the basic structure which offers most opportunities is best;
— of each pair of basic structures with the same amount of basic rights and liberties, and the same amount of opportunities, the basic structure in which the inequalities in *income and wealth* are arranged for the greatest benefit of the least advantaged, is best.

The best alternative from the set of possible basic structures will be chosen in the original position. That is the structure that "fits" the demands of the principles of *justice as fairness*. Now, this is just shorthand for the elaboration of the work the parties are involved in, *after* their agreement in the original position on the principles of justice. Once the principles of justice are selected, however, the parties do not completely pull away the veil of ignorance, and they do not directly return to their place in society. That is much too big a step from "original position," to "a well-ordered society." Rawls in fact introduces an elaboration of the original position and imagines several intermediate stages: "the four-stage sequence" which formulates an order of agreements and enactments to design the appropriate basic structure in several steps.[80] There is a division of labor between stages, in which each stage deals with different questions of social justice. This division roughly corresponds to the two parts of the basic structure. The priority of the first principle to the second one is reflected in two of the sequences of decision making: designing a constitution takes place before the design of just laws, statutes, and policies.

In these intermediate stages, the veil of ignorance is lifted little by little. Thus Rawls guarantees that in the process of designing a basic structure for a well-ordered society, the flow of information is determined at each stage by what is required in order to apply the principles of justice intelligently to the specific question of justice at hand, while at the same time any knowledge that is likely to give rise to bias and distortion and to set men against one another is ruled out. The notion of the rational and impartial application of principles defines the kind of knowledge that is admissible (TJ: 200; TJR: 175–176). By slowly pulling away part of the veil in each stage, the knowledge and information that the parties have gradually increase. The veil has several layers, so to speak, each with its own amount of information. In the first stage, that of the original position, the parties are given only a very limited amount of information that enables them to eventually choose from the alternative conceptions of justice the principles of *justice as fairness*.

In the second and third stages, limitations on knowledge can be relaxed, since the principles of justice are already chosen. In the final, fourth stage, the veil has been completely lifted: everyone has complete access to all of the facts. No limits on knowledge remain since the full system of rules has now been adopted and applies to persons by virtue of their characteristics and circumstances. Now there is specific information about particular individuals: they do know their own social position, their place in the distribution of natural attributes, and their conception of the good.

The idea of the four-stage sequence is part of a moral theory. It is essential to keep in mind, as Rawls asks us to do, that the four-stage sequence is a device for helping us in applying the principles of justice. This scheme is part of the theory of *justice as fairness*. And once again, just as with the thought-experiment of the original position, we are dealing with a hypothetical construction. The four-stage sequence is not an account of how constitutional conventions and legislatures actually proceed, except insofar as political agents are influenced by the conception of justice in question.

The starting point is (again, or rather still) the specific conception of moral persons, the ideal of social cooperation, and the question of how the two highest-order moral interests of persons should be expressed in the constitution and legislation. The principles of justice having already been agreed on, the problem now is to formulate a scheme that will assist us in applying them. The four-stage sequence does this by setting out a series of points of view from which the different problems of justice are to be settled, problems the parties are confronted with when designing a basic structure in which the principles of justice in a political order will actually be able to work. In these stages, the parties give body to institutions such as the constitution and the major social and economic institutions, in each stage inheriting the constraints adopted in the preceding ones.

Turning now to the first stage of the "four-stage sequence," this in fact concerns the original position itself, where the principles of *justice as fairness* are chosen by the parties. In this stage a *method* is formulated about how the design of the normative rules of the game should take place, and in this same stage it is worked out what the *content* of the rules of that game are, rules that are the result of the application of that specific method: in our case the result is the principles of *justice as fairness*. In the foregoing we have already dealt extensively with this stage, albeit without calling it "the first stage" of the four-stage sequence.

What we may not have stressed enough, however, is that in this "pre-constitutional" stage, that of the original position, we have an example of *pure procedural justice*. There is no independent criterion to judge if the outcome is the right result. There is a fair or correct procedure that guarantees that the result is fair or correct whatever it happens to be (provided, of course, that the procedure has been properly followed). The background circumstances define a fair procedure. And a fair procedure passes this fairness on to the result. It is the way the original position is set up, with the veil of ignorance that guarantees this (TJ: 85–86; TJR: 74; PL: 72–73). As Rawls notes: "the aim is to characterize this situation [in the original position] so that the principles that would be chosen, whatever they turn out to be, are acceptable from a moral point of view" (TJ 120; TJR: 104). Or more specifically with regard to pure procedural justice: "The idea of the original position is to set up a fair procedure so that any principles agreed to will be just. The aim is to use the notion of pure procedural justice as a basis of theory" (TJ: 136; TJR: 118). And, to repeat, it is in order to do this that the parties are situated behind a veil of ignorance. And it is in this context that, as quoted before, Rawls can say, "We want to define the original position so that we get the desired solution" (TJ: 141; TJR: 122).

The task that lies ahead of the parties in the next stages is to set up and to impartially administer a just system of surrounding institutions such that this notion of pure procedural justice applies to distributive shares. Only against the background of a just basic structure, including a just political constitution and a just arrangement of economic and social institutions, will the requisite just procedure exist.

Now, Rawls supposes that after the parties have adopted the principles of justice in the original position, they move on to a constitutional convention; they are "delegates," so to speak, to such a convention. However, the parties don't enter the second stage, the constitutional convention, empty-handed, because they know the independent criterion with which they must judge the results of their deliberation in this constitutional convention: the two principles of justice, chosen in the original position. Thus the choice situation is no longer one of pure procedural justice, but, in this constitutional convention, it is one of *perfect procedural justice*. To explain: perfect procedural justice has two characteristics. First, there is an independent criterion for the desired outcome, a criterion defined separately from and prior to the procedure which is to be followed. In our case the independent criterion is defined by the principles of *justice as fairness*. And, second, it is possible to devise a procedure that is sure to give the desired outcome: a result that is just according to that criterion, in other words that conforms to *justice as fairness* (TJ: 85, 197–198; TJR: 74, 172; PL: 72).

It is important to remember that this stage is an extension of the hypothetical idea of the original position, and thus the work that the parties as "delegates" are undertaking in this constitutional convention is "to characterize a just constitution and not to ascertain which sort of constitution would be adopted, or acquiesced in, under more or less realistic (though simplified) assumptions about political life, much less on individualistic assumptions of the kind characteristic of economic theory" (TJ: 197 note 2; TJR: 173 note 2).[81]

The task of the parties seems relatively simple in this stage. Subject to the constraints of the principles of *justice as fairness* already chosen (the independent criterion), they are to design a system for the constitutional powers of government and the basic rights of equal citizens. It is at this stage that they weigh the justice of procedures for coping with diverse political views. The parties in this constitutional convention, of course, still have no information about particular individuals: they do not know their own social position, their place in the distribution of natural attributes, or their conception of the good. But since the appropriate conception of justice has been agreed upon, the veil of ignorance is lifted a little. In "addition to an understanding of the principles of social theory, they do now know the relevant general facts about their society, that is, its natural circumstances and resources, its level of economic advance and political culture, and so on. They are no longer limited to the information implicit in the circumstances of justice" (TJ: 197; TJR: 172–173).

This enables the parties to design a constitution that satisfies the principles of justice, more specifically one that first of all establishes a secure common status of equal citizenship and realizes political justice, and is best calculated to lead to just and effective legislation. From the perspective of the ideal of perfect procedural justice, a just constitution would be a just procedure arranged to ensure a just outcome. The task of the parties, then, is to design a political process, governed by the constitution (the procedure), that results in an outcome (the body of enacted legislation), while they have in hand the principles of justice that give them the independent criterion for both procedure and outcome (TJ: 197; TJR: 173).

First then, in pursuit of this ideal of perfect procedural justice, the "problem is to design a just procedure. To do this the liberties of equal citizenship must be incorporated into and protected by the constitution. These liberties include those of liberty of conscience and freedom of thought, liberty of the person, and equal political rights" (TJ: 197; TJR: 173). The political system, which Rawls assumes to be some form of constitutional democracy (the assumption he makes throughout all his work, over all the years), would not be a just procedure if it did not embody these liberties.

Straight away, however, the parties discover that, although their aim is to find among just constitutions (those satisfying the principle of equal liberty) the one most likely to lead to just and effective legislation in view of the general facts of society (the veil being partly lifted), it turns out that there is no feasible political process which guarantees that laws enacted in accordance with it will be just (TJ: 353; TJR: 311). Any feasible political procedure may yield an unjust outcome. And thus the parties in the constitutional convention discover that their work in designing institutions is not as easy as it might have looked at first

sight. Although there is an independent criterion for the desired outcome, and although the constitution is regarded as just, the basic rights
being incorporated in it, the procedure turns out to be imperfect
because, as Rawls points out, there is in fact "no scheme of procedural
political rules which guarantees that unjust legislation will not be
enacted" (TJ: 198; TJR: 173). In the case of a constitutional regime,
or indeed of any political form, the ideal of perfect procedural justice
cannot be achieved (TJ: 198, 353; TJR: 173, 311). The best attainable
scheme is one of *imperfect procedural justice*: "while there is an independent criterion for the correct outcome, there is no feasible procedure
which is sure to lead to it" (TJ: 86; TJR: 75).[82]

Nevertheless, some constitutional schemes have a greater tendency
than others to result in unjust laws. The task, then, for the parties in
designing institutions for a well-ordered society is to select from among
the procedural arrangements that are both just and feasible those which
are most likely to lead to a just and effective legal order (TJ: 198; TJR:
173). And in selecting a specific design, the parties have to keep in mind
the purpose of the institutions, of laws and social arrangements: that is,
in the well-ordered society, to coordinate and encourage as far as
possible the conduct of individuals who are guided by their rational
plans to achieve results which, although not intended or perhaps even
foreseen by them, are nevertheless the best ones from the standpoint of
the principles of justice.[83] In designing institutions, the parties have
"artificially" to identify the beliefs and interests that individuals will
have in the well-ordered society. To solve this problem requires a
knowledge of those beliefs and interests that men are liable to have in
the well-ordered society. The parties are assumed to know these things.
And as the parties as "delegates" do not have information about particular individuals, because the veil of ignorance is only partially lifted,
the idea of the original position is not affected (TJ: 198; TJR: 173–174).

Before we can move on to the next sequence, the legislative stage, we
have to backtrack. We have to take into account not only that in
political affairs perfect procedural justice cannot be achieved, but also
that the constitutional process must rely, to a large degree, on some
form of voting. Being required to support a just constitution, we must,
according to Rawls, go along with one of its essential principles, that of
majority rule. Although at the constitutional convention the parties are
committed to the principles of justice, "they must make some conces-
sion to one another to operate a constitutional regime. Even with the

best of intentions, their opinions of justice are bound to clash. In choosing a constitution, then, and in adopting some form of majority rule, the parties accept the risks of suffering the defects of one another's knowledge and sense of justice in order to gain the advantages of an effective legislative procedure. There is no other way to manage a democratic regime" (TJ: 354–355; TJR: 312). It is evident from the preceding that the procedure of majority rule, however it is defined and circumscribed, has a subordinate place as a procedural device. The justification for it rests, as Rawls points out, "squarely on the political ends that the constitution is designed to achieve, and therefore on the two principles of justice." Rawls' assumption here is "that some form of majority rule is justified as the best available way of insuring just and effective legislation. It is compatible with equal liberty ... and possesses a certain naturalness; for if minority rule is allowed, there is no obvious criterion to select which one is to decide and equality is violated. A fundamental part of the majority principle is that the procedure should satisfy the conditions of background justice. In this case these conditions are those of political liberty – freedom of speech and assembly, freedom to take part in public affairs and to influence by constitutional means the course of legislation – and the guarantee of the fair value of these freedoms. When this background is absent, the first principle of justice is not satisfied; yet even when it is present, there is no assurance that just legislation will be enacted" (TJ: 356; TJR: 313).

Designing just legislation

In discussing the issues of imperfect procedural justice, and how to nevertheless reach just legislation, the parties "as delegates to the constitutional convention" have already been looking ahead to issues to be taken up in the third stage, that of the legislature. Now, then, it is time for the parties to move on to the legislative stage. Here the justice of laws, statutes, and policies are assessed from the position of a representative legislator who (still) does not know the particulars of those he represents. The veil of ignorance is (still) not completely lifted. In this sequence there is a "double" check, so to speak. Statutes must satisfy not only the principles of justice (the independent criterion), but also whatever limits are laid down in the constitution.

From what has been discussed so far, it is clear that until now we have not been dealing with the requirements of (the first and second part of) the second principle, the principle of fair equality of opportunity and the difference principle. Rawls' argument here is that the history of successful constitutions shows that principles that regulate economic and social inequalities, as well as other principles that involve distributive issues, are in general not fit to be part of constitutional preconditions (TJ: 198; TJR: 174; PL: 33–37; JaF: 48). But now, in the legislative stage, the time has come to bring the social and economic principles of justice into play, especially the difference principle. It dictates that social and economic policies be aimed at maximizing the long-term expectations of the least advantaged, under conditions of fair equality of opportunity, subject to equal liberties being maintained. Having already discovered that in the political process perfect procedural justice is an unrealizable ideal, and that the best attainable scheme is one of imperfect procedural justice, the parties, in their quest for the design of a just institutional background for a well-ordered society, now run into the problem that it is difficult to design just legislation, especially with regard to economic and social policies. Here the legislators are confronted squarely with the problem of how to find assurance that any enacted legislation will be just. The problem the parties stumble on now is, once again, not caused by them having information about particular individuals with partial and self-interested views. The issue rather is that reasonable differences of opinion can exist because in these cases "judgment frequently depends upon speculative political and economic doctrines and upon social theory generally. Often the best that we can say of a law or policy is that it is at least not clearly unjust. The application of the difference principle in a precise way normally requires more information than we can expect to have and, in any case, more than the application of the first principle. It is often perfectly plain and evident when the equal liberties are violated. These violations are not only unjust but can be clearly seen to be unjust: the injustice is manifest in the public structure of institutions. But this state of affairs is comparatively rare with social and economic policies regulated by the difference principle" (TJ: 199; TJR: 174). Whether the aims of the second principle are realized is far more difficult to ascertain, depending on inferences and judgment in assessing complex social and economic information (JaF: 48).

As Rawls himself underlines, this is not an indication of a weakness in his theory of justice. It is what we should expect. Despite the veil of ignorance being only partly lifted, and thus restrictions on information still holding, there is no guarantee that one will reach unanimous agreement, since the tendencies of the general social facts will often be ambiguous and difficult to assess (TJ: 201, 357; TJR: 176, 314). Since legislators can come to different conclusions there is, (even) under ideal conditions, a necessity for a vote. The majority rule has to be applied. The application of this rule in the stage of legislation is meant to provide a decision when there is reasonable disagreement between impartial legislators as to the question of which statutes, which policies, will best guarantee the working of the difference principle. The source of this reasonable disagreement (what Rawls calls *the burdens of judgment*) is that the evidence – empirical and scientific – bearing on the issue of the working of the difference principle is conflicting and complex and hard to assess and evaluate. The outcome of the majority vote is decisive.

Let us recapitulate: we are dealing here with a description of an ideal procedure. The aim is as far as possible to enact laws and policies in line with the principles of justice. What we are not doing here is describing an actual parliamentary debate in which competing political parties are trying to get their own specific ideas accepted with the help of the majority rule. In the ideal (legislative) procedure "the decision reached is not a compromise, a bargain struck between opposing parties trying to advance their ends. The legislative discussion [in this ideal situation] must be conceived not as a contest between interests, but as an attempt to find the best policy as defined by the principles of justice. I suppose, then, as part of the theory of justice that an impartial legislator's only desire is to make the correct decision in this regard, given the general facts known to him. He is to vote solely according to his judgment. The outcome of the vote gives an estimate of what is most in line with the conception of justice" (TJ: 357; TJR: 314).

Now, of course, Rawls is not such a "naive idealist" that he does not recognize that this ideal picture of the political process is not how political practice works. Generally speaking, it is precisely self- and group-interested views that are decisive. It is in this context, then, that he remarks: "In practice political parties will no doubt take different stands on these kinds of issues. The aim of constitutional design is to make sure, if possible, that the self-interest of social classes does not so distort the political settlement that it is made outside the permitted limits" (TJ: 362; TJR: 318).[84]

Let us return to the legislators: they have more work to do. They also have to deal with measures that have to be taken to guarantee the fair value of the political liberties. And there is still another task. Discussing "primary goods or basic capabilities," we have seen that the issue of care for the "normal health and medical needs" of citizens would be dealt with "later on." Now is the time, in the legislative stage. Here there is deliberation on the measures to be taken. Also, questions as to how to provide for the demands of public health and safety (for instance unpolluted drinking water, a clean environment) have to be answered here.

That legislators in this ideal setting have to deal with issues of legislation and statutes with regard to "normal" medical and health care should not be understood as if they are dealing with measures to supplement the income of the least advantaged when they cannot cover the costs of the medical care they may prefer or need. On the contrary: provision for medical care, as with primary goods generally, is to meet the needs and requirements of those who are normal and fully cooperating members of society, but whose capacities have temporarily fallen below the minimum of essential capacities for being so (by illness and accident). Free and equal moral persons are entitled to these medical and health provisions and can legitimately be expected to receive them.

In this legislative stage, the veil of ignorance being lifted enough, information is now available about the prevalence of various illnesses and their severity, the frequency of accidents and their causes, and much else. This enables the legislators to make provision, focusing on the least advantaged, within the guidelines of the difference principle for covering these needs, by including in a social minimum the costs of covering these medical and health care needs (CP: 368; JaF: 173).

Recapitulating, and remembering the debate between Rawls and Sen on "primary goods or basic capabilities," we note first of all that the list of primary goods does not need to be extended with "health and medical care." Second, in *justice as fairness*, free and equal persons should be considered to be normal and fully cooperating members of society. One condition to enable them to be so is having the opportunity to receive any necessary education. It is the principle of fair equality of opportunity that guarantees this possibility to everybody. A second condition is that one needs to be in "good" health. Thus providing conditions to enable people to be so is, in that sense, on a par with providing conditions to enable them to receive any necessary education. Health care "falls under the general means necessary to underwrite [the principle of] fair equality of opportunity and our capacity to take advantage of our basic rights and liberties, and thus to be normal and fully cooperating members of society over a complete life" (JaF: 174). The ability to be "a normal and fully cooperating member of society" provides us with the appropriate criterion that enables us "to estimate the urgency of different kinds of medical care," and to specify the relative priority of claims on medical care and public health generally with respect to other social needs and requirements.[85] Finally, it is the difference principle that should guarantee a social minimum that is of a sufficient level to take care of the eventual costs of health care and medical needs. Rawls has thus formulated an answer to the issue of how to deal with "normal health and medical needs," and therewith shown, as he himself has claimed from the outset, that the list of primary goods does not need to be extended because the index of primary goods (specified in terms of the expectations of those goods) is in fact flexible enough, contrary to what Sen might think, to be able to cope in a fair way with differences between human beings, as the example of medical and health care needs attests (JaF: 173–174).

And here the legislators have fulfilled their tasks. It is time to move on to the fourth and final stage: the judicial one. Everyone has complete access to all of the facts, there are no reasons for the veil of ignorance in any form, and all restrictions are lifted. The question at this stage is in which way the principles of the basic structure have to be interpreted, and if perhaps additional measures have to be taken such that equal cases effectively get equal treatment. The rules are applied by administrators to particular cases and laws are interpreted by members of the judiciary. Also the following of the rules by citizens generally falls into this stage, as well as how citizens have to react to potential injustices (of which some examples are worked out by Rawls in *A Theory of Justice*: the case of civil disobedience and that of conscientious refusal to serve in an unjust war). This stage will not be elaborated on here. For an exposition of the specific design of the basic structure it is not directly relevant.

Let us recapitulate: the four-stage sequence, as developed by Rawls, is a part of the theory of justice, setting out a series of points of view from which the different problems of justice are to be settled, each point "inheriting" the constraints adopted at the preceding stage, to set up just background institutions.

Justice as fairness takes as basic the notion of pure procedural justice. This is reflected in the way the original position has been designed: as a case of pure procedural justice. The hope was that, next, in designing the constitution and legislation one could proceed according to perfect procedural justice. However, as the four-stage sequence demonstrated, we are eventually able to accomplish only imperfect procedural justice. Choices in the constitutional, as well as in the legislative, stage turn out to be indeterminate in the sense that several options are open: it is not always clear which of several constitutions, or economic and social arrangements, would be chosen. The more concrete social and economic policy enacted at the legislative stage becomes, the less we can speak of pure procedural justice: the outcome at the legislative stage does not literally define the right result. But as long as the legislators are conscientiously trying to follow the principles of *justice as fairness* unanimously agreed to in the original position, the decision of the majority is authoritative, though not definitive. Although with regard to social and economic policy the difference principle remains the guide, we nevertheless have to fall back on a notion of what Rawls calls *quasi-pure procedural justice*: as long as laws and policies that are chosen are ones that lie within the permitted range, they are equally just (TJ: 201, 362; TJR: 176, 318).

But, or so one may wonder, should we not interpret this indeterminacy in the theory of justice as a defect? It is not, as is stressed by Rawls. It is what we should expect: "Justice as fairness will prove a worthwhile theory if it defines the range of justice more in accordance with our considered judgments than do existing theories, and if it singles out with greater sharpness the graver wrongs a society should avoid" (TJ: 201; TJR: 176).

Political and market processes compared

Let us bring to the fore once again, but from a different angle, the issue of the impossibility of reaching the ideal of "perfect procedural justice" in the political process, and that the best attainable scheme of procedural political rules is one of imperfect procedural justice. Following Rawls, this can be done by pointing out several differences between the ideal legislative process and the ideal market process. The idealized "design" procedure – described above – is part of Rawls' theory of justice. The more definite our conception of this procedure as it might be realized under favorable conditions, the more firm the guidance that the four-stage sequence could give to our reflections: it would be an effective instrument to help us design the appropriate institutions that the application of *justice as fairness* requires.

By confronting the ideal political procedure with the ideal market process to which it stands in contrast, Rawls clarifies the issue further. Under ideal circumstances, the market process is a perfect procedure with respect to efficiency. As Rawls elaborates: "A peculiarity of the ideal market process, as distinct from the ideal political process conducted by rational and impartial legislators, is that the market achieves an efficient outcome even if everyone pursues his own advantage. Indeed, the presumption is that this is how economic agents normally behave" (TJ: 359; TJR: 316).

Thus it holds that the ideal market process will always lead to efficiency. But, as we have seen above, with a legislative procedure, even an ideal one, the same cannot be expected: not in all instances will the procedure lead to just legislation. "Thus despite certain resemblances between markets and elections, the ideal market process and the ideal legislative procedure are different in crucial respects. They are designed to achieve distinct ends, the first leading to efficiency, and the latter if possible to justice" (TJ: 360; TJR: 316). And while, as Rawls formulates it, "the ideal market is a perfect process with regard to its objective, even the ideal legislature is an imperfect procedure. There seems to be no way to characterize a feasible procedure guaranteed to lead to just legislation" (TJ: 360; TJR: 316). As Rawls elaborates further: "in a perfect market system, an economic agent, so far as he has any opinion at all, must suppose that the resulting outcome is indeed efficient. ... But the parallel recognition of the outcome of the legislative process concerning questions of justice cannot be demanded, for although, of course, actual constitutions should be designed as far as possible to make the same determinations as the ideal legislative procedure, they are bound in practice to fall short of what is just" (TJ: 360; TJR: 316–317).

There is presently no theory on just constitutions available, seen as a procedural theory that guarantees that a just outcome will always be reached, as is the case with the theory of competitive markets, seen as a procedure that always will lead to an efficient result. The fact that there exists no such theory of just constitutions would seem to imply that "the application of economic theory to the actual constitutional process has grave limitations in so far as political conduct is affected by men's sense of justice, as it must be in any viable society, and just legislation is the primary social end. ... Certainly economic theory does not fit the ideal procedure" (TJ: 360–361; TJR: 317).[86] Put another way: *there is no analogy between the market process and the political process*. It is not surprising, then, that Rawls is opposed to the application of economic theory to constitutional and legislative processes. He rejects "the economic theory of democracy" in which this analogy is taken as a starting point.

The description of the different steps in the process of designing a well-ordered society and the application of the four-stage sequence in so doing has shown us the problems the parties will encounter in designing just political background institutions. The question remains of how to guarantee the realization in the best way possible of the principles of *justice as fairness* with regard to distributive shares.

Fair background institutions and market arrangements

What would be the proper form of economic background institutions to regulate economic activity? Which economic system would be consistent with equal liberties and fair equality of opportunity, as well as with the requirements of fair distributive shares? Rawls' sketch of the ideal scheme of economic basic institutions makes considerable use of a system of markets that function in such a way that the outcome of the economic process is just as well as efficient. This is not surprising in light of the preceding section, where it was explained that the theory of a perfectly competitive market economy is a perfect procedure that will always lead to an efficient result. Rawls holds that only by using a system of markets can the issue of just distribution be handled as a case of *pure procedural justice*. The notion of pure procedural justice remains the ideal to strive for: reliance on pure procedural justice presupposes that the basic structure satisfies the two principles of justice. Recall that, in a situation of pure procedural justice, no attempt is made to define what the outcome should be. The distribution will be just (or at least not unjust) whatever it is. And a suitably regulated competitive economy with the appropriate surrounding background institutions is an ideal scheme to realize pure procedural justice. Thereby Rawls makes the choice of a market economy as the economic order within which *justice as fairness* has to be accomplished (TJ: 274, 304, 309; TJR: 242, 268, 272).

While one of the advantages of a market economy is efficiency, this cannot of course be the only reason for this choice: after all, social justice has priority over efficiency. Neither is this choice for market arrangements based on private ownership of the instruments of production and natural resources, arguments that are sometimes used as a precondition of a "free market." There is no essential tie between the use of free markets and the private ownership of the instruments of production. Although it is true that the allocation of instruments of production and products by a market presupposes a system of firms (firms as independent decision and production units), this does not necessarily mean that the means of production are mainly privately owned. In fact, Rawls notes here the consistency of market arrangements with socialist institutions: market institutions are common to both private-property and liberal-democratic socialist regimes. "Whatever the internal nature of firms, whether they are privately or state owned, or whether they are run by entrepreneurs or by managers elected by workers, they take the prices of outputs and inputs as given and draw up their plans accordingly" (TJ: 272; TJR: 241). In noting this consistency of market arrangements with socialist institutions one has, however, to distinguish between the allocative and the distributive function of prices. "Since under socialism the means of production and natural resources are publicly owned, the distributive function is greatly restricted, whereas a private-property system uses prices in varying degrees for both purposes" (TJ: 273–274; TJR: 242). In both kinds of regime, the system of markets decentralizes the exercise of economic power. Also, both private-property and (liberal-democratic) socialist systems normally allow for the free choice of occupation and of one's place of work. There is no reason at all for the forced and central direction of labor. It is only under command systems of either kind that this freedom is overtly interfered with.

And here we come to the main reason for Rawls' choice of market arrangements: he is of the opinion that a market system – contrary to a command economy – gives the individual the largest possible set of freedoms. A significant advantage of a market system is that, given the requisite background institutions, it is consistent with equal liberties and fair equality of opportunity. And this is, of course, important for the realization of that part of the principle of fair equality of opportunity that guarantees citizens a free choice of careers and occupations (TJ: 274; TJR: 242; JaF: 67, 67 note 35).

In conclusion: an (ideal) market system is consistent with the demands of the first principle of justice, as well as with the principle of fair equality of opportunity. But the choice of a market system needs a crucial addition. Certainly, this choice may be consistent with both these principles, as well as with efficiency, but market arrangements left to themselves do not guarantee just results. These arrangements require fair background institutions that continually adjust and compensate for the inevitable tendencies away from background fairness, in order to remain consistent with the demands of the difference principle (TJ: 272–275; TJR: 240–243; PL: 267).

Let us elaborate: the role of the institutions that belong to the basic structure is to secure fair background conditions against which the actions of individuals and associations – that are all part of society as a whole – take place. Thus the distribution resulting from voluntary market transactions (even if all the ideal conditions for competitive efficiency obtain) is not, in general, fair unless the antecedent distribution of income and wealth, as well as the structure of markets, is fair. The existing wealth must have been properly acquired and all must have had fair opportunities to earn income, to learn the desired skills, and so on (TJ: 359; TJR: 316; PL: 266).

In addition, unless the basic structure is appropriately regulated and adjusted, an initially just social process will eventually cease to be just, however free and fair particular transactions may look when viewed by themselves. Therefore, even if one relies on a large element of pure procedural justice in determining distributive shares, a conception of justice "must incorporate an ideal form of the basic structure in the light of which the accumulated results of on-going social processes are to be limited and adjusted" (PL: 281).[87] Specific supporting institutions are required for this. Thus the basic structure also includes those operations that continually adjust and compensate for the inevitable tendencies away from background fairness. Examples here are such operations as income and inheritance taxation designed to even out the ownership of property (PL 268; JaF: 160–161).[88]

Taking all this into account, the issue now is the choice of supporting institutions that have to be designed to guarantee background fairness over time. Giving a summary of what has to be expected from just background institutions, the short answer is, of course, that they have to effectuate the principles of *justice as fairness*. It means that: (a) the basic structure is regulated by a just constitution that secures the liberties of equal citizenship; liberty of conscience and freedom of thought are guaranteed, and the fair value of political liberty is maintained;

(b) fair (as opposed to formal) equality of opportunity is maintained; the government tries to ensure equal chances of education and culture for persons similarly endowed and motivated, as well as the free choice of occupation; and (c) the government guarantees a social minimum (TJ: 275; TJR: 243).

There is one more important assumption that Rawls adds in working out this sketch of the background institutions. From the start his assumption is that the kind of democratic regime is a *property-owning democracy*. In this regime the productive assets "land and capital are widely though not presumably equally held" (TJ: 280; TJR: 247). (The terms, as well as some features of the idea are borrowed by Rawls from the economist James Meade.[89]) It is Rawls' supposition that with this scheme of background institutions the principles of *justice as fairness* can be realized.

In giving his sketch of the surrounding suitable supporting political and legal background institutions to guarantee that, however things might turn out, the outcome of the distributive process will result in just distributive shares, Rawls uses an idea originally developed by the economist R. A. Musgrave.[90] According to Musgrave, government may be thought of as divided into three branches, an allocation, a stabilization, and a distribution branch, with each branch consisting of various agencies, or activities thereof, that are charged with preserving certain social and economic conditions (TJ: 275; TJR: 243). Rawls adds a fourth branch, the transfer branch. The aim of these four branches of government, taken together, is to establish a society that is not so divided that one fairly small sector controls the preponderance of productive resources. Its aim is to guarantee a democratic regime in which land and capital are widely, though not presumably equally, held. In short, the aim is to guarantee the regime of a "property-owning democracy."

In working out the roles of these four government branches, that of the allocation branch is, for example, to keep the market system competitive and to prevent the formation of unreasonable market power, i.e. by preventing market monopolies. The stabilization branch strives to bring about reasonably full employment in the sense that those who want work can find it and the free choice of occupation and the deployment of finance are supported by strong effective demand. The distribution branch has to preserve an approximate justice in distributive shares by means of taxation and the necessary adjustments in the rights of property. Two aspects of this branch may be distinguished, deriving from the two principles of justice. The first is related to the first principle of justice, especially to the fair value of the political liberties. We have noted that in the legislative stage appropriate measures have to be taken that will guarantee that political liberties are distributed in a fair way. It is from this perspective that the distribution branch "imposes a number of inheritance and gift taxes, and sets restrictions on the rights of bequest. The purpose of these levies and regulations is not to raise revenue (release resources to government) but gradually and continually to correct the distribution of wealth and to prevent concentrations of power detrimental to the fair value of political liberty and fair equality of opportunity. For example, the progressive principle [of taxation] might be applied at the beneficiary's end. Doing this would encourage the wide dispersal of property which is a necessary condition, it seems, if the fair value of the equal liberties is to be maintained" (TJ: 277; TJR: 245).[91]

The second part of the distribution branch is a scheme of taxation to raise the revenues that justice requires. Social resources must be released to the government so that it can provide for public goods and make the transfer payments necessary to satisfy the difference principle, as well as the principle of fair equality of opportunity in education. Rawls notes that a proportional expenditure tax may be part of the best tax scheme, so as to carry out the second principle of *justice as fairness* (TJ: 278–279; TJR: 246; JaF: 161).

Because the competitive determination of total income ignores the claims of need and an appropriate standard of life, it is in the legislative stage that the parties also take measures to ensure that those they represent are protected against these contingencies of the market, as the difference principle requires. This is the responsibility of the transfer branch. With revenues raised by the (second part of the) distribution branch, a suitable minimum for the least advantaged is guaranteed by transfers, as well as the means that are required to provide for the needs of normal medical and health care (TJ: 277; TJR: 244–245; JaF: 162).

This completes the sketch of the system of background and supporting institutions that satisfy *justice as fairness*. Rawls is convinced that the freedom of the person is best guaranteed in a market economy, if free market arrangements are reasonably competitive and open and if they are set within a framework of principles that arrange the background institutions of a constitutional democracy, institutions that regulate the overall trends of economic events and preserve the social conditions necessary for fair equality of opportunity. If a basic structure has been designed accordingly, distributive shares will be just (or at least not unjust), whatever they are. The system remains fair over time, from one generation to the next (JaF: 51). As *justice as fairness* uses the notion of pure procedural justice, the hope is to reach as far as possible a situation of pure background procedural justice. There is no criterion for a just distribution apart from the background institutions and the entitlements that arise from actually working through the procedure. We have also noted, however, the impediments that prevent this ideal from fully being reached. Quasi-pure procedural justice, especially with regard to social and economic policy, seems to be the best we can hope for.

It is time to summarize the kernel of *justice as fairness*. It is Rawls' ambition to unite in one coherent theory the values "liberty" and "equality." But his ambitions go further. The idea of "fraternity," neglected in democratic theory, also has a place in his theory. Fraternity conveys "certain attitudes of mind and forms of conduct without which we would lose sight of the values expressed by these rights. Or closely related to this, fraternity is held to represent a certain equality of social esteem manifest in various public conventions and in the absence of manners of deference and servility" (TJ: 105; TJR: 90). Fraternity implies these things, as well as a sense of civic friendship and social solidarity.

And it is the difference principle that provides an interpretation of these underlying ideas of the principle of fraternity. In expressing the idea of reciprocity, the difference principle "does seem to correspond to a natural meaning of fraternity: namely, to the idea of not wanting to have greater advantages unless this is to the benefit of others who are less well off. ... Those better circumstanced are willing to have their greater advantages only under a scheme in which this works out for the benefit of the less fortunate" (TJ: 105; TJR: 90).

Rawls' theory, then, is an effort to reconcile the, at first sight incompatible and conflicting, traditional ideas of the French Revolution, "liberty," "equality," and "fraternity" (or "reciprocity"), by bringing them together into one coherent scheme, in one institutional framework, the basic structure of a well-ordered society. These values are united in one single normative political theory which is relevant and topical for our time: in *justice as fairness*.

3 | *Pluralism and justice*

The aim of Rawls

The basic idea behind *A Theory of Justice* is that a well-ordered society, in which the principles of *justice as fairness* are the public principles of justice endorsed by all members of that society, would be a stable political and social order. In the years after the publication of *A Theory of Justice* (1971) Rawls is more and more concerned with the fact that modern democratic societies are characterized by a plurality of incompatible – yet reasonable – comprehensive religious, philosophical, and moral doctrines, and that not one of these doctrines is affirmed by all citizens generally. In addition, Rawls now also claims that *justice as fairness* itself is presented in *A Theory of Justice* as a comprehensive (philosophical) doctrine, as *"a comprehensive liberal doctrine"*; a comprehensive doctrine being a doctrine that applies to all subjects and whose virtues cover all parts of life (PL: xxxviii note 4).[1]

But if indeed we have to acknowledge this fact of reasonable pluralism, as we have, the idea of a well-ordered society based on *justice as fairness* has a strained relationship with this pluralism. If *justice as fairness* has indeed to be considered as (a part of) only one of these comprehensive doctrines, a liberal comprehensive one, the question becomes how we are to conceive of a well-ordered society in which there is uniform acceptance of *justice as fairness*. The short answer according to Rawls is: we cannot.

The given, that reasonable pluralism is a permanent and ineradicable fact of modern democratic society, has brought Rawls to the insight that the project to work out *justice as fairness* in the way it is done in *A Theory of Justice* is unrealistic. The argument in *A Theory of Justice* relies on the premise that in the well-ordered society of *justice as fairness*, citizens hold the same (liberal) comprehensive doctrine (to which the principles of *justice as fairness* belong). But, precisely because of the fact of reasonable pluralism, this comprehensive view is not held by citizens generally and hence the argument for stability fails. Consequently, in *Political Liberalism* Rawls regards the idea of a well-ordered society, as it is formulated in *A Theory of Justice*, as impossible (PL: xviii, xlii; LoP: 179). Removing this inconsistency explains the need for revision and recasting. It sets the stage for the issues Rawls discussed from the beginning of the 1980s – as the articles in his *Collected Papers* attest – and accounts for the nature and extent of the differences between *Political Liberalism* and *A Theory of Justice*.[2]

The issue is not simply how stability can be achieved under conditions of reasonable pluralism. Formulated in that way it would give an uninteresting Hobbesian answer (PL: 391 note 27).[3] The issue is rather to strive for stability "for the right reasons." The aim is "to work out a political conception of political justice for a (liberal) constitutional democratic regime that a plurality of reasonable [comprehensive] doctrines, religious and nonreligious, liberal and nonliberal, may endorse for the right reasons" (PL: xli).[4] The text of *Political Liberalism* tries to answer the question as to the most reasonable and deepest basis of social unity available to citizens of a modern democratic society (PL: 391 note 27). *Political Liberalism* considers how, despite this fact of reasonable pluralism, social unity might come about and how to further it. In doing this, *Political Liberalism* presupposes that a reasonable, comprehensive doctrine does not reject the essentials of a constitutional democratic regime (PL: xviii; LoP: 177).

Rawls clearly conceives of the primary purpose of political philosophy as practical (as opposed to epistemological or metaphysical). It should provide bases for public justification and political agreement about basic political, and social and economic institutions. This also explains why Rawls now claims that his theory is specifically a *political* theory of justice, which is not itself a comprehensive moral theory, *nor part of one*. The problem is stated as working out a *political* conception of justice for a (liberal) constitutional democratic regime that people may endorse while they, at the same time, affirm a plurality of reasonable comprehensive doctrines, be they religious or nonreligious, liberal or nonliberal. And if this is possible at all, would citizens of such a society endorse *justice as fairness* as a political conception of justice, if indeed *justice as fairness* can be shown to not be (any longer) a comprehensive doctrine? These are the central issues that Rawls is concerned with, and working out these ideas resulted in the publication in 1993 of *Political Liberalism*. We can consider this publication to be the first summing up of what in chapter 1 has been called "the second phase" in the development of Rawls' views on justice.

In *Political Liberalism*, as well as in *A Theory of Justice*, Rawls is concerned with finding a public, generally endorsed, justification of the principles of *justice as fairness*. The difference is that in *Political Liberalism* we are concerned with the insight of what this justification requires in circumstances where there is no comprehensive doctrine that is affirmed by all, or nearly all, citizens. It is removing the inconsistency that *A Theory of Justice* concerns only a well-ordered society regulated by a single conception of justice as a comprehensive view that explains the nature and extent of the differences between *Political Liberalism* and *A Theory of Justice*.

Differences there are, but at the same time it should be stressed that the shift in the direction of a political basis of Rawls' theory has left many elements unchanged. Recasting, yes, but not repudiating the core ideas of *A Theory of Justice*. The structure and content of *justice as fairness* remain, as we will see, substantially the same (PL: xviii, xviii note 4, xliii note 8). We are still concerned with an account of con- structivism – albeit now one of political, not moral, constructivism – of which the main features are still in place. Thus, for instance, the argu- ments on the role of the original position, the meaning and content of the two principles of justice that issue from this procedure of construc- tion, the arguments about what should be considered a well-ordered society, and which principles of justice should regulate the basic struc- ture of that society, the requirements for the background institutions, all these elements have remained much the same.

This also holds for the ideas Rawls formulated in the third part of *A Theory of Justice* on (three) principles or tendencies of moral psychol- ogy, on moral development and the capacity for developing a sense of justice, in short on the moral attitudes of individuals and the role institutions play in developing them. In *Political Liberalism* these same ideas still play their role.[5] And the Kantian dimension, too, is still present.[6]

Although there is a change in perspective, with *justice as fairness* being considered a (liberal) comprehensive view in *A Theory of Justice*, while being considered a political conception in *Political Liberalism*, in both instances we start with "domestic" justice: the basic structure is that of a closed society; it is self-contained and has no relations with other societies. Its members enter it only by birth and leave only by death (PL: 12; JaF: 11). Other questions, such as those of local justice and of global justice (the principles applying to international law, or the Law of Peoples as Rawls calls it), are not dealt with in *Political Liberalism*. Just as in *A Theory of Justice*, in *Political Liberalism* questions of justice among peoples are postponed until we have an account of *political* justice for a well-ordered democratic society. All of these elements, then, are still in place in the complex process of justification of *justice as fairness* as a political conception. Taking into account the – final – unified statement of his theory that Rawls himself has given in *Justice as Fairness: A Restatement*, in 2001, we can note that all of this has remained unchanged over time. What has changed is the framework in which *justice as fairness*, now seen as a political conception, belongs: a well-ordered society characterized by a plurality of reasonable comprehensive doctrines (PL: xliii note 8).

Political liberalism and citizenship

How to maintain social unity in a society characterized by ethnic and cultural pluralism and by a diversity of religious, philosophical, and moral doctrines that are there to stay? In addition, we have to take into account that each of these religious, philosophical, and moral doctrines has at least one fundamental variant, for instance secular, Christian, or Islamic. How can citizens be united in societies with these characteristics, societies that are not only not homogenous with regard to comprehensive doctrines, but are also characterized by multicultural and/or multi-ethnic heterogeneity? How is one to conceive such a society to be cohesive and stable? What would make an alignment in such a society durable over time? If citizens not only do not share one and the same comprehensive doctrine, but if there is also no (longer a) "common heritage," a shared life-style to which citizens can refer, how then can citizenship actually create a common experience, a common identity, and solidarity for the members of that society? On what should "shared citizenship identity" be based so that it surpasses comprehensive doctrines, as well as rivalling religious, secular, or ethnic identities?

The fact that we have to acknowledge that there is no religious, philosophical, or moral doctrine shared by all citizens raises a fundamental problem: there is no general, reasonable comprehensive doctrine that can play the public role of a widely accepted basis for political justice, or that can be the basis for a shared conception of citizenship.

It is this issue that brings Rawls to make a distinction between a democratic society that creates a social space where there is room for a plurality of religious, philosophical, and moral doctrines, as well as for cultural and ethnic variety, and a society were there is space for only one comprehensive doctrine. It is in this context that Rawls considers it a serious error to not distinguish between the idea of a democratic political society and the idea of community (PL: 37; JaF: 21). The reason that not making such a distinction is considered to be an error is because, as soon as political society itself, as a whole, would be considered a "community," united in affirming one and the same comprehensive doctrine, then the oppressive use of state power is necessary to maintain that political community, regardless of which comprehensive religious, philosophical, or moral doctrine is at stake. In fact, Rawls is of the opinion that this holds for any reasonable comprehensive doctrine, whether religious or nonreligious, liberal or nonliberal. There is no exception: even a society united on a reasonable form of utilitarianism, or on the reasonable comprehensive liberalisms of Kant or John Stuart Mill, would eventually require the sanctions of state power to remain so (PL: 37; JaF: 34). From this perspective, the liberalism of *justice as fairness*, as now approached in *Political Liberalism*, should not be considered a *philosophy of man*, a comprehensive doctrine, as are the liberal moral doctrines of Kant or Mill.[7]

Political Liberalism has it own subject matter: how is a just and free society possible under conditions of deep doctrinal conflict between citizens, with no prospect of resolution (PL: xxx)? This is an issue of political justice, and *justice as fairness* gives a political-theoretical answer as to how the major institutions of a modern democratic society, its basic structure, should be designed so as to guarantee social unity and political stability. *Political Liberalism* expresses a family of political values that characteristically apply to that basic structure.

In working out "political liberalism," Rawls emphasizes the distinction between personal and political opinions, between "men" and "citizens," between the non-public, private sphere and the public domain. The moral subject of "political liberalism" is the citizen: "political liberalism" formulates a liberal democratic theory of citizenship. It is based on a minimal liberal democratic criterion: in a society characterized by plurality of many sorts, citizens cannot expect all other citizens to share their ends, although they ought to be able to expect them to respect their interests. In the absence of compelling evidence to the contrary, free and equal persons are assumed to understand their own interests better than anyone else claims to do.

Rawls differs here from the opinion of communitarian thinkers such as, for example, Michael Sandel, author of *Liberalism and the Limits to Justice*.[8] Sandel is of the opinion that someone's political ideals are at the same time his personal ideals, and that the state ought to embody the good life of its citizens. Rawls' theory is the major subject of Sandel's critique. Rawls makes, and wrongly so according to Sandel, a distinction between the public domain and the non-public "private society." Rawls affirms – as a Kantian liberal – the priority of the right to the good which depends in turn, according to Sandel, on a picture of the self given prior to its ends. But Sandel considers this image of "*the unencumbered self*" flawed. Since Rawls abandons the idea that society is a political community with a substantial ideal based on a comprehensive doctrine, and thus rejects the idea that government ought to promote virtue or shape the moral character of its citizens, and impose on some the values of others, he has to embrace this idea of an *unencumbered self* and of an individualistic, atomistic conception of social and political order. Political society is itself, in Sandel's interpretation of Rawls' ideas, no good at all, but at best a means to an individual or associational good.[9]

But, or so the rebuttal of this argument goes, Sandel incorrectly supposes that a choice has to be made between a Rawlsian vision of individual rights, with individuals solely pursuing their own ends, and an Aristotelian Principle in the theory of the good. For Rawls it is the well-ordered society of *justice as fairness* that is intrinsically good (TJ: §65; TJR: §65; PL: 203 note 33, 207). It is plainly a mistake to say that *justice as fairness* is an individualistic political conception, just as it is a mistake to think that Rawls' starting point is that of an "atomistic self." And this holds for the case where *justice as fairness* is conceived to be a liberal comprehensive doctrine, as well as when it is conceived as a political conception of justice, our present concern (LoP: 166). Contrary to what Sandel suggests, Rawls does recognize the importance that the idea of "belonging" has for persons. His theory is one in which the recognition of mutual dependence leads to mutual respect, and in which there is room for empathy, care, and attention for each other, as well as a willingness to listen to the other. It is the idea of a well-ordered society, seen as "*a social union of social unions*," that expresses this.[10] It is one of the ideas that has been, over time, an enduring element in Rawls' perspective on how to conceive of a just society. It could even be argued that, from this perspective, Rawls is rather a "communitarian" thinker than a "liberal" one, if we note that he conceives of the self as essentially social instead of as atomistic.[11]

But Rawls does stress the difference between how we see ourselves as free and equal citizens in the political domain and the way we see ourselves in the non-political domain, in the private space of our personal life or in the public space of, for example, associations. In the political domain, the *politics of rights* cannot be allowed to be replaced by the *politics of the common good*.

Justification in *Political Liberalism*

The question now is what are the requirements of the public justification of the principles of justice in a situation of conflicting and even incommensurable religious, philosophical, and moral doctrines? In what sense is the method of public justification that is being used in *Political Liberalism* different from that in *A Theory of Justice*? And, next, what principles of justice are eventually justified? Do they differ from the principles of *justice as fairness* as formulated in *A Theory of Justice*? In *Political Liberalism* the arguments in answer to these questions are developed in two stages (PL: 140–141; CP: 486).

In the first stage, Rawls sets out *justice as fairness* as a *"freestanding"* view, an account of a political (but of course moral) conception of justice that applies in the first instance to the basic structure of society, and articulates – as we will elaborate – two kinds of political values, those of political justice, and those of public reason (PL: 64). Once this is done, Rawls takes up, in the second stage of the argument, the issue of *justice as fairness* and stability.

The second stage turns to the actual situation in which societies are characterized not only by different, reasonable comprehensive doctrines, but also by their plural, diverse, multicultural, and multi-ethnic variety. This stage of the exposition considers how the well-ordered democratic society of *justice as fairness* may establish and preserve social unity and stability over time, given the reasonable pluralism characteristic of it (PL: 133). Is the political conception practicable, that is, does it come under the art of the possible? Are the precepts and ideals of *justice as fairness* indeed able to generate a stability that is secured by sufficient motivation of the appropriate kind, acquired under just institutions, and in a situation in which plural societies actually exist? (CP: 486–487). A political conception can only gain public justification if all citizens can recognize and support it, regardless of which reasonable comprehensive doctrine each of them adheres to. Can it, then, gain the support of reasonable comprehensive doctrines? And, can a just regime based on *justice as fairness* gain the support of citizens with differences of culture and nationality (PL: xl; LoP: 25, 25 note 20)? It is in this context, that of social unity and stability, that Rawls introduces the idea of *overlapping consensus*. Can the political conception of justice be the central focus of an "overlapping consensus"?

Although "stability" is the focus of *Political Liberalism*, this issue can only be taken up once the principles of justice for the basic structure are at hand. First, then, we will discuss the arguments in the first stage, the "freestanding" one. It will give us, or so we hope, the principles of justice that specify the fair terms of cooperation among citizens, as well as a specification of when a society's basic institutions are just. The aim here is to give an exposition of a political conception of justice that can be presented and expounded apart from, or without reference to, any one or other comprehensive doctrine, whatever it may be: it is neither presented as, nor derived from, such a doctrine. This is the reason Rawls speaks of a "freestanding" political conception of justice. It should be possible to present this political conception of justice without saying, or knowing, or hazarding a conjecture about, what religious, philosophical, or moral comprehensive doctrine it may belong to, or would be supported by (PL: 12–13). Accepting this conception does not, then, presuppose accepting any particular comprehensive doctrine: a political conception presents itself as a reasonable conception for the basic structure standing on its own: it is "freestanding."

A political conception that can be argued for in this way gives all citizens a basis for "*public reasoning,*" a shared reason for informed and willing political agreement with regard to the design of the basic structure of society. In formulating a political conception of justice, *Political Liberalism* seeks to present and justify a moral conception of justice (because of course a political conception is a moral conception [PL: 11–12; JaF: 26]) that is compatible with a wide range of epistemological, metaphysical, and even moral views, including non-Kantian perfectionist, intuitionist, and utilitarian ones. In formulating a political conception of justice, "political liberalism" applies the principle of toleration to philosophy itself. It leaves it to citizens themselves to settle the questions of religion, philosophy, and morals in accordance with the views they freely affirm (PL: 9–10, 154).

Political Liberalism tries to discover the values that are necessary to construct this independent, "freestanding" justification of a political conception of justice in certain fundamental ideas, seen as implicit (latent) in the public political culture of a democratic society, that comprise the political institutions of a constitutional regime and the public tradition of their interpretation, as well as basic political texts (constitutions; declarations of human rights) that are common knowledge. Society's main institutions, and their accepted forms of interpretation, are seen as a fund of implicitly shared ideas and principles. Rawls is of the opinion that we, the readers of his work in contemporary democratic societies, always have an implicit idea of justice based on this shared fund. This is evident, for instance, from the way in which in daily life the meaning of the constitutionally guaranteed rights and liberties are debated. Some of the ideas have a more fundamental character than others.

As Rawls explains (once again, as in *A Theory of Justice*, but now in the context of his exposition on "political liberalism"), *justice as fairness* starts from within this specific political tradition and uses ideas that are deeply embedded in it. The most fundamental ideas in the conception of *justice as fairness* are those of society as a fair system of cooperation over time from one generation to the next, the idea of *citizens* (those engaged in cooperation) as free and equal persons, and the idea of a well-ordered society as a society effectively regulated by a political conception of justice. Rawls adds two more fundamental ideas, ideas which we have already encountered in *A Theory of Justice*, recognizing that these two ideas are not seen as familiar to the educated common sense of the democratic tradition: that of the basic structure of such a society, and that of the original position. These are introduced for the purpose of presenting *justice as fairness* in a unified and perspicuous way (PL: 14 note 16, 25–27; JaF: 24–25).

Persons have, as free and equal citizens, two moral powers: they have a capacity for a sense of justice and they have a capacity to have, to revise, and to rationally pursue a conception of the good. They are the capacities of persons to be reasonable and rational. Having, to an essential minimum degree, these two moral powers is the basis of equality among citizens as moral persons.

Indeed, we have already come across these ideas in the arguments for *justice as fairness*, as developed in *A Theory of Justice*. But now, in *Political Liberalism*, where we are developing a *political* conception of justice, the Kantian dimension of Rawls' theory, for example, has become "thinner." The Kantian conception of the person (as free and equal, reasonable and rational) is still in place, but not without adjustments. We now no longer speak of a moral person as part of a comprehensive Kantian doctrine; now the idea of the person is represented by the "free and equal citizen." It is the "political" person of a modern democratic society, with the political rights and duties of citizenship, who stands in a political relation with his fellow citizens. But of course the citizen is also a "moral actor," because the political conception of justice is also a moral conception.

This concept of the person as citizen, for Rawls, is itself not a metaphysical or a psychological concept, but both a normative and political one (JaF: 19). As mentioned, the two moral powers give the basis of equality between citizens as moral persons. Their rights are not dependent on religion, social class, ethnicity, or gender. Citizens are free, autonomous persons. They regard themselves as being entitled to make claims on their institutions to advance their conception of the good, or to revise or even change their conception of the good. Such changes do not affect their public or legal identity as free persons, their identity as a matter of basic law (JaF: 21–22).

It is now, in the context of "political liberalism," *citizens* who need – in order to be able to fully exercise their two moral powers and to pursue their "plan of life," and possibly to revise it, as free and equal persons – specific scarce resources: "primary social goods." And, as we have already seen in the analysis of *A Theory of Justice*, these primary goods are the various social conditions and all-purpose means that are generally necessary to enable citizens to adequately pursue any conception of the good, whatever it might be (provided it falls within the range permitted by the political conception of justice) (JaF: 23, 57). *Political Liberalism* takes it that, regardless of the reasonable religious, philosophical, or moral comprehensive doctrines citizens have, and regardless of their (permissible) conceptions of the good, they require for their advancement roughly the same primary goods, that is the same basic rights and liberties, diverse opportunities, powers and prerogatives of offices and positions of authority and responsibility, and the same all-purpose means as income and wealth, with all of these supported by the same social bases of self-respect (PL: 180).

The way the "freestanding" justification proceeds also contains many elements that we are already familiar with from *A Theory of Justice*. Once again the original position (now called a "mediating conception"), with its feature of the "veil of ignorance," plays a central role. It is a heuristic device of representation, or alternatively a thought-experiment, for the purpose of public- and self-clarification to help us to order in a coherent way the fundamental ideas mentioned earlier – the idea of society as a fair system of cooperation over time, from one generation to the next, the idea of *citizens* as free and equal persons, and the idea of a well-ordered society as a society effectively regulated by a political conception of justice (PL: 25–27).

The aim of this first stage, in which we are concerned with independent justification and hence "freestanding," is to establish which set of principles best "fits" the fundamental democratic ideas that are taken as a starting point. And, precisely as is done in *A Theory of Justice*, in this "freestanding" original position a set of principles is agreed for the fair distribution of primary goods. In this original position, where the parties have to reach unanimous agreement behind the veil of ignorance, it is of course assumed that the parties have information about the general circumstances of society: they know it exists under the circumstances of justice, both objective and subjective. Thus they know that these circumstances of justice obtain whenever persons put forward conflicting claims to the division of social advantages under conditions of moderate scarcity. But now, in addition, they know that the circumstances of justice also include the fact of reasonable pluralism.

Thus, the veil of ignorance does allow the knowledge that society is characterized by the fact of pluralism, that is, that a plurality of comprehensive doctrines exists in society (though of course the parties do not know the [comprehensive] doctrines of the persons they represent). The parties must then protect against the possibility that the persons each party represents might be a member of a religious, cultural, ethnic, or other minority. The veil of ignorance implies, for example, that the parties do not know whether the beliefs espoused by the persons they represent will turn out to be a majority or a minority view – once the veil is lifted – in the actual society. "They cannot take chances by permitting a lesser liberty of conscience to minority religions, say, on the possibility that those they represent espouse a majority or dominant religion and will therefore have an even greater liberty. For it may also happen that these persons belong to a minority faith and may suffer accordingly"

(PL: 311).[12] This supposition in the original position of the fact of pluralism suffices for the argument for equal basic liberties, of which liberty of conscience and religious freedom are examples, to get going.[13]

The aim of the principles of justice is to specify a fair distribution of the primary goods in the context of a democratic society. At this stage of our exposition it can hardly come as a surprise that the political principles of justice that will eventually be derived in the freestanding stage are the same ones we are already familiar with from *A Theory of Justice*.[14] But now, as is the aim of Rawls and as is expressed in the way he has set up the argument, *justice as fairness* is "freestanding" because it has not been derived and expounded from, or by accepting, any particular comprehensive doctrine. *Justice as fairness* satisfies the demands posed by a *political* conception.

It looks as if we have completed the first stage. It seems that an answer has been given to the fundamental question of whether it is at all possible that *justice as fairness* can play the role of a political conception. It looks as if we are now ready to go on to the next step in the line of reasoning: the question of whether indeed this conception will actually be accepted by all the citizens of a well-ordered democratic society, by citizens holding different conflicting, but reasonable comprehensive views. But this would, however, be too quick a step.

Let us remember that, in retrospect, Rawls now considers the basic assumption in *A Theory of Justice* to be that almost everyone accepts the same partial, liberal comprehensive moral doctrine, a general Kantian moral theory. Thus it was assumed in *A Theory of Justice* that for the *public* justification that would enable persons to accept the laws and institutions of a well-ordered society, they all accept the principles of justice and the constitution on the basis of their own reasons, that are in fact *a shared set of reasons* because they all share the same comprehensive liberal doctrine as part of the public understanding of justice (LoP: 179).[15]

The whole set-up of the argument in *Political Liberalism* is based on the idea that this presupposition of a shared set of reasons no longer holds. Thus the problem arises of sustaining agreement on the interpretation and application of the public conception of justice. To solve this problem, Rawls introduces in *Political Liberalism* "*the idea of public reason.*" It is "public reason" that has to mediate between different religious, philosophical, and moral comprehensive doctrines. Consequently this idea plays a central role in *Political Liberalism*.[16]

The idea of public reason and the criterion of reciprocity

Political Liberalism is concerned with the question how "here and now" political stability and social unity can be established when citizens are actually confronted with a situation in which society is characterized by a plurality and diversity of reasonable comprehensive doctrines. But how then is *Political Liberalism* able to explain to us, here and now, that persons who hold conflicting perspective will nevertheless publicly endorse and support the values of *justice as fairness* as the ordering principles for political and social cooperation?

The fact that people have different criteria of "Truth," different standards for assessing evidence, shows that there is a special need for *public* reason. As a basis for public justification we need a shared set of reasons and methods of inquiry and reasoning, "guidelines of inquiry" so to speak, upon which to ground our interpretations. It is in the answer to the question in the previous paragraph that Rawls, in *Political Liberalism*, in working out a political conception of justice, focuses on two kinds of political values. The first kind of political values is the set of *the values of political justice* (the principles of justice of *justice as fairness*). The second kind of political values is the set of *the values of public reason*. This second set of values is concerned with "the guidelines of public inquiry" between citizens, especially to ensure that public deliberation is free and public, as well as informed and reasonable (JaF: 91).

Here, then, there is indeed an important difference with the work the parties have to do in the original position as conceived in *A Theory of Justice*. In the freestanding perspective of "political liberalism" the parties have an additional task. For an agreement on a political conception of justice to be effective and to support a public basis of justification, there must be not only agreement on specific principles of justice as part of the political conception of justice ("the values of political justice"), but also a – companion – original agreement on the guidelines of inquiry for public reason and on the criteria as to what kind of information and knowledge is relevant in discussing political questions: it is these guidelines that express "the values of public reason" (PL: 139, 225; JaF: 89).

Rawls is of the opinion that, in a political conception of justice, these guidelines have the same basis as substantive principles of justice. Thus, the parties in the original agreement, who have to agree on a political conception of justice, must not only agree on principles of justice for the basic structure (hopefully an agreement on the principles that are contained in *justice as fairness*), they also must adopt guidelines and criteria of public reason for deriving and applying these principles. The guidelines of public reason and the principles of justice have essentially the same grounds: they belong to a particular political conception of justice. They are companion parts of one and the same original agreement (PL: 70, 139, 225–226; JaF: 91–92).

To be considered legitimate, these guidelines of public reason cannot, of course, be based on an appeal to one or another comprehensive religious, philosophical, or moral doctrine (on the whole Truth, as it were). We must also distinguish "public reason" from what is sometimes referred to as "secular reason" and "secular values." These are not the same as "public reason" because Rawls defines secular reason "as reasoning in terms of comprehensive nonreligious doctrines. Such doctrines are much too broad to serve the purpose of public reason. Political values are not moral doctrines" (LoP: 143). Secular philosophical doctrines do not provide public reason. But where then do these "guidelines for public inquiry" come from?

Discussing, in the context of *A Theory of Justice*, the set-up of the original position and the "thickness" of the veil of ignorance, we saw that the veil does allow the parties "general knowledge of social theory and human psychology." It is "we," "you and I," "here and now," in setting up the thought-experiment of the original position who specify the amount and the particulars of knowledge that the parties are to use. In *Political Liberalism* the same holds. It is "up to us to say what the parties are to know in view of the aims in working out a political conception of justice that can be, we hope, the focus of a reasonable overlapping consensus and hence a public basis of justification" (JaF: 89).

The knowledge that the parties are allowed in this companion agreement on the values of public reason is the "the general beliefs and forms of reasoning found in common sense, and the methods and conclusions of science, when these are not controversial" (PL: 224).[17] For Rawls, "the principle of legitimacy" "makes this the most appropriate and perhaps the only way to specify the companion agreement" (JaF: 90). The principles of reasoning, the fair rules of debate and argument, "are to rest on the plain truths now widely accepted, or available, to citizens generally. Otherwise, the political conception would not provide a public basis of justification" (PL: 225).

Summarizing, we see that in a political conception of justice (for example *justice as fairness*), the political values expressed in it are of two kinds, each paired with one of the two parts of the original agreement. The first part is an agreement on the values of political justice: the principles of justice for the basic structure. The second part is an agreement on the values of public reason; that is to say an agreement on "the guidelines for public inquiry" and on the rules for assessing evidence (the steps to be taken to ensure that such inquiry is free and public, as well as informed and reasonable). The political conception of justice, as developed in *Political Liberalism*, applies both sets of values of *justice as fairness* (the principles of political justice for the basic structure, and the principles of public reason) to a specific domain – the political – and citizens can affirm both these sets of values, regardless of their religious, philosophical, or moral views.

In a constitutional democratic regime the basis of social unity must come about through democratic politics. Citizens, who are aware that they cannot reach agreement on the basis of their conflicting and irreconcilable comprehensive doctrines, try to reach agreement by way of public reason, which provides a common language. Rawls understands public reason as the common reason of a political society. A society's reason is its "way of formulating its plans, of putting its ends in an order of priority and of making its decisions accordingly" (PL: 212). Public reason contrasts with the "nonpublic reasons of churches and universities and of many other associations in civil society" (PL: 213). Reasoning is something other than mere rhetoric or artifices of persuasion. We are concerned with reason, not simply with discourse (PL: 220).

Public reason imposes limits on public-political deliberation. Distinct from, but paired with, this idea of public reason is the *ideal* of public reason. It is an "ideal of democratic citizenship" in which, so to speak, these limits are internalized. The political values of public reason reflect our willingness as citizens to try to settle fundamental political matters in ways that other citizens as free and equal persons can acknowledge are reasonable and rational. At its core is "the duty of public civility," a moral, not a legal, duty by which citizens see themselves as obligated to a public use of reason in publicly discussing fundamental issues of justice (PL: 217–218; JaF: 92, 117; LoP: 55–56, 155). Being thus reasonable, in Rawls's sense of the term, they "don't appeal to the whole truth as they see it," but seek to show how their positions can be supported by the political values of public reason (PL: 219). Starting from knowledge and ways of reasoning accessible to all, citizens are able to present to one another publicly acceptable reasons for their political views (JaF: 91–92). With opinions and convictions that can also be shared by others, they try to convince one another. One starts from premises which it is reasonable to expect can be acknowledged by everyone. The public role of a generally acknowledged political conception of justice and the accompanying idea of citizenship is to specify a point of view from which *all* citizens can judge their political institutions to be, or not to be, just.

The implication of this idea of public reason is that when free and equal citizens offer one another fair terms of social cooperation according to what they consider the most reasonable conception of political justice, those proposing them must also think it reasonable for other citizens to accept them. Only a political conception of justice that all citizens might reasonably be expected to endorse can serve as a basis of public reason and justification. If it does, it satisfies "the criterion of reciprocity" (PL: xliv, li, 16, 226; LoP: 136–137).[18]

In fact "the criterion of reciprocity" is what the idea of public reason turns on. The role of (the criterion of) reciprocity, as expressed in public reason, is to specify the nature of the political relation in a constitutional democratic regime as one of "civic friendship" (PL: xliv, li, 48–50, 226; LoP: 35, 136–137, 155).[19] And, we can add here that since the criterion of reciprocity is an essential ingredient specifying public reason and its contents, "political liberalism" rejects as unreasonable all comprehensive doctrines that do not confirm to this criterion (LoP: 172–173).

Having said all of this, it should be clear what the legitimacy of the general structure of authority, with which the idea of public reason is intimately connected, requires. The "principle of political legitimacy" that is based on the criterion of reciprocity that any political conception of justice (as for instance *justice as fairness*) has to satisfy, says: "political power should as far as possible be exercised in ways that all citizens as free and equal can publicly endorse in the light of principles and ideals acceptable to their common public reason" (at least when constitutional essentials and matters of basic justice are at stake, an issue we will return to later) (PL: 137; LoP: 137; JaF: 90–91).

In this discussion of public reason we have to mention two more issues. The first concerns the content of the original agreement, which, as we have seen, has two companion parts. Recall that the political values expressed in a political conception are of two kinds, each paired with one of the two parts of the original agreement: the first part is an agreement on the principles of justice for the basic structure, the second part an agreement on "the guidelines for public inquiry." What we have not asked as of yet is whether this original agreement is fixed in the sense that it gives a definite outcome, thus for instance the political values of *justice as fairness*. Is there, indeed, an analogue to the outcome of the original position in *A Theory of Justice*, agreement on one specific political conception of justice? To jump ahead: there is not, and reasonably, so there can be several political conceptions of justice, a "family" so to speak. How is this possible?

For the answer we have to take a closer look at the second part of the agreement, the part that is concerned with the values of public reason. Rawls notes that "[t]he content of public reason is not fixed, any more than it is defined by any one reasonable political conception" (PL: liii; LoP: 142; JaF: 93). Public reason not being fixed is a consequence of the fact that it is part of a dynamic society. On the one hand there may be new views with regard to the common fund of knowledge (new scientific insights, for example). But also, as Rawls notes, "[v]iews raising new questions related to ethnicity, gender, and race are obvious examples, and the political conceptions that result from these views will debate the current conceptions" (PL: liii). The content of public reason is, then, "not specified by any one political conception of justice, certainly not by justice as fairness alone. Rather, its content – the principles, ideals, and standards that may be appealed to – are those of a family of reasonable political conceptions of justice and this family changes over time" (PL: lii–liii). We thus have to acknowledge that, since the content of public reason is not fixed, in the freestanding view reasonable agreement might be reached on a family member of a political conception of justice, and not necessarily on *justice as fairness*. It is one member of the family of political liberalisms.

Now it may well be the case that the size of this family changes over time, but what is supposed to remain unchanged is that all of these political conceptions of justice are reasonably thought to satisfy "the criterion of reciprocity." This is what limits the size of the family of political conceptions of justice. The idea of public reason which turns on the criterion of reciprocity implies that when political conceptions other than *justice as fairness* are proposed as reasonable terms of fair social cooperation between free and equal citizens, those proposing these other political conceptions (other ones than *justice as fairness*) must also think it reasonable for other citizens to accept these alternative conceptions (PL: xliv, li, 226; LoP: 136–137). Citizens will differ as to which of these political conceptions they think is the most reasonable, but they agree that all are at least reasonable. This is why we can speak of a "family" of political conceptions of justice.

Central to the idea of public reason is that no claims are formulated by citizens that are based on their own comprehensive views, views that others are bound to reject, but that claims are based on the idea of public reason, as used between reasonable people. Citizens properly consult their comprehensive views to determine whether they accept political structures and principles of justice. However, in public discussion of applications of shared principles to particular circumstances, comprehensive views have to recede in the face of public reason. Religious, philosophical, or moral comprehensive doctrines do not provide, as we noted, the content of public reason.

It should, however, be stipulated – and here we come to the second issue – that this being so does not prevent citizens from introducing into public-political discussions at any time their comprehensive doctrines, religious or nonreligious, liberal or nonliberal, provided that in due course they give *proper public reasons* that are sufficient to support whatever principles and policies their comprehensive doctrines are said to support. This requirement is called by Rawls *the proviso*. It specifies what Rawls refers to as "the wide view of public political culture" (PL: li–lii; LoP: 152–156; JaF: 90).[20]

Constitutional essentials and matters of basic justice

Public reason applies to citizens and public officials when they engage in political advocacy in a *public-political forum*. It is a particular standard for judging the appropriateness of the reasoning of legislators, executives, judges (especially of a supreme court, if there is one), and other government officials, as well as candidates for public office. It also includes, among other things, the reasoning of citizens when they take part in, for example, political campaigns, or when they vote on the fundamental political matters of constitutional essentials and matters of basic justice (PL: 382 note 13; LoP: 135).[21] In a democratic society public reason is the reason of equal citizens who, as a collective body, exercise final political and coercive power over one another in enacting laws and in amending their constitution. The basic structure and its public policies are to be justifiable to all citizens, regardless of their position in society or of their specific interests, as the liberal principle of political legitimacy requires.

But the limits imposed by public reason do not apply to all political questions. Complete agreement by public reason on each and every political issue is not required. The political values of the conception of justice have to yield reasonable answers to questions of "constitutional essentials" and "matters of basic justice": "Constitutional essentials concern questions about what political rights and liberties, say, may reasonably be included in a written constitution, when assuming the constitution may be interpreted by a supreme court, or some similar body. Matters of basic justice relate to the basic structure of society and so would concern questions of basic economic and social justice and other things not covered by a constitution" (PL: l note 23).

In the following we will have a closer look at this distinction between constitutional essentials and matters of basic justice. There is the greatest urgency for citizens to reach practical agreement in judgment, at least regarding the more divisive controversies, that is, political questions that concern "constitutional essentials." These are of two kinds:

(a) the fundamental principles that specify the general structure of government and the political process: the powers of the legislature, executive, and the judiciary; the scope of majority rule;
(b) the equal basic rights and liberties of citizenship that legislative majorities are to respect, such as the right to vote and to participate in politics, liberty of conscience, freedom of thought and of association, as well as the protection of the rule of law (PL: 227).

In a well-ordered society all citizens underwrite in a sufficient measure the same political conception of justice to solve these constitutional issues. However, constitutional essentials of the first kind (a) can be specified in various ways. Take, for instance, the difference between the majoritarian, "Westminster" model of democracy and the consensus model of democracy; or a first-past-the-post voting system versus proportional representative party lists; or presidentialism versus parliamentarism; or bicameralism versus unicameralism. The constitutional principles of the second kind (b), which specify the equal basic rights and liberties of citizens, can be specified in but one way, modulo relatively small variations, as Rawls states. In all free regimes these rights are characterized in more or less the same manner (PL: 227; JaF: 28). To this second kind of constitutional essentials belong some principles of opportunity, for example a principle requiring at least certain freedom of movement and free choice of occupation, as well as a social minimum providing the basic needs of all citizens. But fair equality of opportunity (as specified by Rawls), and the difference principle, are not constitutional essentials but matters of basic justice. Why is this so?

Principles of justice specifying the constitutional essentials, as well as those principles specifying matters of basic justice or, formulated more precisely, basic matters of *distributive* justice, such as fair equality of opportunity, and social and economic inequalities, are all certainly elements of the political conception *justice as fairness*. All express political values. That "matters of basic justice" are distinguished from "constitutional essentials" has to do with the two coordinating roles the basic structure has: the principles covering the basic freedoms specifying the first role, the principles covering social and economic inequalities specifying the second role. In the first role, the basic structure specifies and secures citizens' equal basic rights and liberties and institutes political procedures. The basic structure then establishes first of all a just constitutional regime. Its first role concerns "the acquisition and the exercise of political power. To fulfill the liberal principle of legitimacy ..., we hope to settle at least these questions by appeal to the political values that constitute the basis of free public reason" (JaF: 48).

In the second role, the basic structure sets up the background institutions regulating basic matters of social and economic justice in the form most appropriate to citizens seen as free and equal. Here the examples mentioned above, such as the principle of fair equality of opportunity and the principle that has to regulate social and economic inequalities – in the case of *justice as fairness* the difference principle – come into play. These principles "are more demanding" and are not considered constitutional essentials. But once again, and to prevent misunderstanding, political discussions of the reasons for and against fair equality of opportunity and the difference principle fall under questions of basic justice and so are also to be decided by the political values of public reason (PL: 229 note 10; JaF: 47–48).

What is important to note here is the distinction between the *aims* formulated by the principles, and the questions if these aims are in fact realized. (What are, for example, the appropriate institutional requirements to do so?) To have a difference of reasonable opinion on the question of whether the aims of principles covering social and economic inequalities have been realized, one needs in the first place agreement on those principles themselves. It is disagreement of the second kind which leads Rawls to make the distinction between constitutional essentials and matters of basic justice. It is one of the reasons why matters of basic justice are less suited to interpretation by, for instance, a supreme court. The point of the distinction is not that from the perspective of different comprehensive doctrines it would be impossible to reach reasonable consensus on a liberal political conception of justice, which, for example, would include "the difference principle." In a society characterized by plurality there need not be a difference of opinion on what the correct principles of justice are. The distinction is based on the difficulty of seeing whether the principles are achieved: it is far more difficult to ascertain whether the principles governing social and economic inequalities are realized, than to ascertain whether the basic liberties are realized. This makes principles of distributive justice less suitable candidates for constitutional essentials. They do, however, give us a framework, or a guideline, on how to deal with social and economic inequalities.

Understanding "political liberalism" in the correct way means following Rawls in thinking that the difference principle is subject to more reasonable disagreement than the first principle of justice. While he, then, still believes, again in the context of political liberalism, that the difference principle is the most reasonable principle when dealing with social and economic issues, he allows that there could be too much reasonable disagreement about it to elevate it to a status above other principled claims that get advanced in normal legislative politics.

We should note, at the same time, that there is no surprise in this issue coming to the fore here. We have of course already encountered the same source of reasonable disagreement – the burdens of judgment – in the context of *A Theory of Justice*. Debating the "four-stage sequence," we noted the problems encountered by legislators in that ideal situation in reaching agreement on "just legislation," specifically with regard to the (application of the) difference principle.

Those who favor the difference principle as a principle of basic justice can still press for it in, for instance, public-political debates about the institutions that a so-called democratic (welfare) state should contain, but they should recognize that it would be illegitimate for the Supreme

Court (or a supreme court, for that matter) to decide the matter (as it protects the Bill of Rights, or the basics of the democratic process). Of course Rawls' hope is that at some future date many of what now seem to be reasonable disagreements could prove to be unreasonable. This may eventually lead to the enshrinement of the difference principle in constitutional essentials as a legitimate step (JaF: 162).

We also have to take into account a second distinction that Rawls draws: one between constitutional essentials and matters of basic justice on the one hand, and, on the other, "ordinary" political issues. That distinction is based on discerning which issues are decided by the political values of public reason, and which are not. Whenever constitutional essentials and matters of basic justice are at stake, citizens are to reason by public reason and are to be guided by the criterion of reciprocity.

The shared political values meet the urgent political requirement to fix, once and for all, the content of basic rights and liberties, and assign them special priority. The implication of this is that raising the (political) question of whether these rights should no longer be guaranteed cannot be brought forward as an issue on the political agenda. Some rights and guarantees are no longer regarded as appropriate subjects for political decision by majority or other plurality voting. Equal basic rights determine the constitutional range of democratic government (PL: 161; JaF: 115, 194). For example, in regard to equal liberty of conscience, the separation of church and state, and the rejection of slavery and serfdom, this means that the equal basic liberties in the constitution that cover these matters are reasonably taken as fixed, as correctly settled once and for all. They are part of the public charter of a democratic constitutional regime and not a suitable topic for ongoing public debate and legislation, as if they can be changed, one way or the other, by requisite majorities (PL: 151 note 16). Would such changes or revocations be possible, every prospect of social cooperation and social unity in societies characterized by a plurality of reasonable comprehensive doctrines, as well as by multicultural and multi-ethnic diversity, would evaporate.

It should be stipulated, however, that this does not mean that, first, the list of basic rights and liberties could not, eventually, be expanded and included in the public-political charter of the democratic constitutional regime. Second, it does not mean that specific issues are precluded from being brought forward to the political forum to be subject of debate and struggle. Questions of, for instance, ethnicity, gender, and race can be debated. In fact, every issue can be brought forward to the political forum. The political agenda is not restricted, as long as it is clear that all issues, at the end of the debate in this common public-political space, have to be settled by the shared political values of a liberal democratic order, *the proviso* mentioned above. A successful appeal to public reason could, in principle, settle the case. Whether public reason, indeed, "can settle all, or almost all, political questions by a reasonable ordering of political values cannot be decided in the abstract independent of actual cases" (PL: liii).

Reflective equilibrium and *political liberalism*

Let us take stock for a moment. In developing the arguments and ideas of justification for a political conception of justice, it is important to distinguish three points of view that Rawls offers: that of the parties in the original position, that of the citizens of a well-ordered society, and finally, that of ourselves – of "you and me," "here and now" – who are elaborating *justice as fairness* and examining it as a political conception of justice.

The first two points of view belong to the conception of *justice as fairness* and are specified by reference to its fundamental ideas. As for the parties as representatives who specify the fair terms of social coop-eration by agreeing to principles of justice, they are simply parts of the original position. This position is set up by "you" and "me" in working out *justice as fairness* and so the nature of the parties is up to us. We have earlier extensively debated this.

With regard to the conception of a well-ordered society, and of citizens as free and equal persons, the revisions in *Political Liberalism*, compared to the idea of the well-ordered society in *A Theory of Justice*, revisions necessary to take into account the fact of reasonable pluralism, are such that Rawls' hope is that it might conceivably be realized in our social world, a social world that would be stable for the right reasons. In these revisions the idea of public reason as an idea of justification plays a central role.

The third point of view – that of "you and me" – is that from which *justice as fairness* (or any other political conception of justice) is to be assessed. Here the test is that of reflective equilibrium (PL: 28). This is, indeed, the same idea that was introduced in *A Theory of Justice*. Just as in *A Theory of Justice*, Rawls makes an appeal to the presupposed elements of consensus that might lie hidden under the surface of diverging opinions that we, the readers of his work, have. Justification cannot be based on a moral vacuum; a minimum of (moral) consensus has to be present.

Also recall that Rawls is of the opinion that some considered convictions, or considered judgments, may be accepted provisionally, though with confidence, as fixed points, ones that we never expect to withdraw. Thus Rawls is confident that religious intolerance and racial discrimination are unjust. These convictions are examples of provisional fixed points. We start by looking to the public culture itself as the shared fund of implicitly recognized basic ideas and principles. These shared ideas now once again play a role in *Political Liberalism*. Again, but now with regard to "political liberalism," Rawls' hope is "to formulate these ideas and principles clearly enough to be combined into a political conception of justice congenial to our most firmly held convictions. We express this by saying that a political conception of justice, to be acceptable, must accord with our considered convictions, at all levels of generality, on due reflection," once all adjustments and revisions that seem compelling have been made (PL: 8). Again this would be, just as in the case of *justice as fairness* in *A Theory of Justice*, a situation of "reflective equilibrium." But now "at all levels of generality" judgments are in line with regard to a *political* conception of justice.

This situation of "reflective equilibrium" is one in which the principles which would be chosen in the original position are identical with those that match our considered judgments and so these principles describe our sense of justice. A conception of justice that meets this criterion is the conception that is, so far as we can now ascertain, the one most reasonable to us (PL: 28). "Wide reflective equilibrium" is what I, or you, or anyone, should (try to) reach. The equilibrium is "wide" because general convictions, first principles, and particular judgments are in line. Each of us has looked not only for the conception of justice that called for the fewest revisions to achieve consistency. I, or you, or anyone, will have also taken into account alternative conceptions of justice and the force of the various arguments for those alternative conceptions. Only what Rawls calls "wide reflective equilibrium" (still in the case of one person) is reached when alternative conceptions – including views critical of the concept of justice itself, for example Karl Marx's view – have been taken into account and the force of their respective philosophical arguments, and other reasons for them, have been weighed. In this situation the reflective equilibrium is wide, given the wide-ranging reflection and possibly many changes of view that have preceded it.

In the actual situation of pluralism, a situation in which there are many views, many comprehensive religious, philosophical, and moral doctrines, it is plain that this wide reflective equilibrium, and not narrow reflective equilibrium (in which we only take note of our own judgments), is the important concept (PL: 384 note 16; JaF: 30–31).[22]

Though there is at first sight not much difference between the arguments used by Rawls in stressing the importance of "wide reflective equilibrium" in a situation where society is characterized by a plurality of comprehensive doctrines, and the importance of reaching "wide reflective equilibrium" in the situation where *justice as fairness* is characterized itself as a (liberal) comprehensive doctrine, it goes without saying that the stakes reaching "wide reflective equilibrium" are much higher in the first case, our present concern. But it is not the "wide reflective equilibrium" of just any one person we are interested in. The issue is that each citizen has to have achieved wide reflective equilibrium on the same public political conception of justice.

But how are we to imagine such a wide reflective equilibrium for each and every citizen to be possible, taking into account the plurality of comprehensive views? Let us elaborate this possibility step by step.[23] For the first step we have to return to the argument in *Political Liberalism* that the line of reasoning for the *public* justification of *justice as fairness* as it is given in *A Theory of Justice*, that would enable persons to accept the laws and institutions of a well-ordered society, no longer holds. We have to recognize that people do not all share the same comprehensive (liberal) doctrine as part of the public understanding of justice, they do not all share the same ideas of justification, and consequently they do not all accept the principles of justice and the constitution on the basis of *a shared set of reasons* as given by the liberal comprehensive doctrine. This is, of course, why Rawls has introduced in *Political Liberalism* "*the idea of public reason*," the search for "public reason" that can mediate between different philosophical, religious, and moral comprehensive doctrines that contain different ideas of justification. And in public reason, the justification of the political conception of *justice as fairness* takes into account only political values. This is of course shorthand for the freestanding view.

But will this freestanding view hold and will the political values derived in it not be overridden by citizens' comprehensive doctrines, more specifically by the non-political values of these doctrines? This brings us to the second step, the justification of the political conception of justice by an individual person as a member of civil society. The implication that society is characterized by a plurality of comprehensive doctrines is, among other things, that there is more than one idea of justification, each one specified by a certain comprehensive doctrine. People with different comprehensive moral views must justify for themselves, in their own (wide) reflective equilibria, the acceptability of a political conception of justice. Their rationales will differ according to their different comprehensive religious, philosophical, or moral beliefs.[24] Thus it is left to each citizen to say how the claims of political justice are to be ordered, or weighed against the non-political values of each citizen's comprehensive view.[25] Citizens have to see for themselves how the political conception can be embedded in various ways, or inserted, into whichever doctrine they themselves affirm. Any one person in civil society tries to achieve wide reflective equilibrium and thus a justification of the political conception (PL: 386–387).

But as we have said, it is not the "wide reflective equilibrium" of any one person that we are concerned with. We are concerned that each citizen achieves wide reflective equilibrium on the same public political conception of justice. In that case, the reflective equilibrium is also general: the same political conception is affirmed in everyone's considered judgments. Thus citizens have reached general and wide equilibrium, or what Rawls refers to as *full reflective equilibrium* in a well-ordered society (PL: 384 note 16; JaF: 31). But citizens are not concerned about how other citizens have embedded or inserted that political conception in their different comprehensive doctrines. All that is taken into account is the fact that all citizens share the political conception of justice: the fact that there exists a reasonable overlapping consensus. We have reached the third and final step in the argument, that of public justification by political society. This is the situation "when all the reasonable members of political society carry out a justification of the shared political conception by embedding it in their several reasonable comprehensive doctrines. In this case, reasonable citizens take one another into account as having reasonable comprehensive doctrines that endorse that political conception, and this mutual accounting shapes the moral quality of the public culture of political society" (PL: 387).

Imagine that a well-ordered society characterized by a plurality of comprehensive doctrines is a society effectively regulated by a public conception of justice, and thus stable for the right reasons. "In such a society, not only is there a public point of view from which all citizens can adjudicate their claims of political justice, but also this point is mutually recognized as affirmed by them all in full reflective equilibrium" (JaF: 31).

Rawls' claim is that "full reflective equilibrium" "meets the need for a basis of public justification on questions of political justice; for coherence among considered convictions at all levels of generality and in wide and general reflective equilibrium is all that is required for the practical aim of reaching reasonable agreement on matters of political justice" (JaF: 32).

Recapitulating this line of reasoning, and stressing how important it is that justification is publicly known, or at least publicly available, Rawls summarizes the argument as follows:

The basic case of public justification is one in which the shared political conception is the common ground and all reasonable citizens taken collectively (but not acting as a corporate body) are held in general and wide reflective equilibrium in affirming the political conception of justice on the basis of their several reasonable comprehensive doctrines. Only when there is a reasonable overlapping consensus can political society's political conception of justice be publicly – though never finally – justified. Granting that we should give weight to the considered convictions of other reasonable citizens, this is because general and wide reflective equilibrium with respect to a public justification gives the best justification of the political conception that we can have at any given time. There is, then, no public justification for political society without a reasonable overlapping consensus, and such a justification also connects with the ideas of stability for the right reasons as well as of legitimacy. (PL: 388–389)

As we have mentioned, there are other ideas of justification specified by certain comprehensive doctrines, and thus, presumably, coherence of the kind mentioned above does not suffice. What Rawls, however, wants to argue is that "endorsing other ideas of justification alone will not prevent such doctrines from belonging to an overlapping consensus" (JaF: 32). Thus, in short, the political conception of justice affirmed in reflective equilibrium, by reasoned reflection, makes for public justification and gives the possibility of an overlapping consensus.

Overlapping consensus, well-ordered society, and stability

We now can move on to the second stage or, better, to the second part of the argument, the issue of social unity and stability in a society that is actually characterized by a plurality of comprehensive doctrines, as well as by multicultural and multi-ethnic variety. Having explained step by step what the possibility of wide and full, and thus general reflective equilibrium demands, and thus that an overlapping consensus could exist, the question now is how we might imagine that, in a society characterized by reasonable pluralism, an overlapping consensus might actually come about. Let us recall that the idea of an overlapping consensus that plays a central role in the debate on the possibility of stability is an idea that is not to be found in *A Theory of Justice*. The reason is, of course, that the supposition there is that we are not dealing with many different comprehensive doctrines, but with only one comprehensive liberal doctrine, *justice as fairness*. The idea of an overlapping consensus is introduced in *Political Liberalism* in order to make the idea of a well-ordered society that is stable for the right reason more realistic, and to adjust it to the historical and social conditions of democratic societies, which include the fact of reasonable pluralism (PL: 388 note 21; JaF: 32, 187). To succeed in seeking agreement and stability, Rawls has to show that the political conception of justice justified in the freestanding view will actually also be endorsed and supported as the focus of an overlapping consensus among citizens with different reasonable comprehensive, religious, philosophical, and moral doctrines.

That such a consensus that is stable for the right reason would be possible at all is based on the idea that people with different reasonable comprehensive views might share similar ideas about *political* justice, and thus can agree on a specific design of the basic structure of society. It is this possibility that Rawls' theory of *Political Liberalism* exemplifies. The task Rawls has set himself is, then, to try to understand how an overlapping consensus on *justice as fairness*, a consensus that is stable for the right reasons, is not only to be conceived, but also how it actually might come about, and what concepts we would need to describe it. That is Rawls' "fundamental question about political justice in a democratic society."

The question of stability is two-fold: the issue of whether the principles or tendencies of moral psychology will indeed develop a firm sense of justice and the issue of whether the principles derived in the original agreement can gain the support of an overlapping consensus for the diversity of comprehensive doctrines that exist in a well-ordered society. Although in a well-ordered stable society the political conception of justice is affirmed by all citizens by what Rawls refers to as a "reasonable overlapping consensus," in fact all citizens need not do so, as we have seen in the preceding section, and for all the same reasons. Pluralism, after all, means that there is not one comprehensive doctrine that is shared by *all* citizens (JaF: 32). Since citizens have conflicting religious, philosophical, and moral views, they affirm the political conception of justice from *within* different and opposing comprehensive doctrines, and so, in part at least, for different reasons. As a liberal political conception of justice, *justice as fairness* is not reasonable unless it generates its own support in a suitable way by addressing each citizen's reason, as explained within its own framework. Only then is it an account of political legitimacy (JaF: 186).

The possibility of gaining the support of such a reasonable overlapping consensus is helped, or so Rawls argues, by the fact that this consensus does not require the acceptance of a specific religious, philosophical, or moral comprehensive doctrine ("political liberalism," so far as possible, neither accepts nor rejects any particular comprehensive doctrine – religious, philosophical, or moral [JaF: 28]), by the fact that its fundamental ideas are already implicit in the democratic political culture of society, and by the fact that its requirements are limited to the basic structure of society (JaF: 33). Because *justice as fairness* is a freestanding political conception that "only" articulates the constitutional essentials and matters of basic justice, endorsing it involves far less than what is contained in a complete comprehensive doctrine (JaF: 187).

In a plural democratic society with its different and even irreconcilable doctrines, and its different cultures and ethnicities, it is this overlapping consensus on *justice as fairness* that enables agreement on the ordering of political institutions. This consensus is not a political compromise between those holding different views, it is independent of changes or shifts in the distribution of power in a political order, in contrast to stability based on a *modus vivendi*. If it would depend on happenstance and a balance of relative forces, social unity would be only apparent, as it is stability contingent on circumstances remaining so as not to upset the fortunate convergence of interests (PL: 148).

The overlapping consensus is based on a moral engagement with regard to a political conception of society (itself a moral conception) and of citizens as moral persons, and is less open to the danger that it would be violated the moment it would seem advantageous for some to do so. Those who affirm the various views supporting the political conception of justice will not withdraw their support from it should the relative strength of their views in society increase and eventually become dominant (PL: 148; JaF: 195). And, in contrast with a comprehensive religious, philosophical, or moral doctrine, here only limited moral engagement is required.

For "political liberalism" to actually be possible, it was argued earlier that citizens who affirm their comprehensive doctrines have to hold that their engagement with the values of the political conception of justice will not be overridden by those comprehensive doctrines, since they themselves think that these values are related to their own religious, philosophical, or moral doctrine. But can we be sure that this is the case?

Rawls certainly does not think that there is a guarantee that *justice as fairness*, or any reasonable political conception for a democratic regime, can gain the support of an overlapping consensus and in that way generate the stability of its political institutions (JaF: 37). But of course Rawls' project as reconciliation would fail if he thought that no good reasons could be given for thinking that stability and social unity could be reached. The answer that Rawls gives to this question has two complementary parts (PL: 139; JaF: 189). The idea is that citizens in a well-ordered society affirm two distinct, although closely related, views: a political and a comprehensive perspective. The first is a view on the importance of the values of the political expressed by the principles of justice for the basic structure, and on the importance of the values of public reason. These values are not easily overridden: they specify the fundamental terms of political and social cooperation. It is left to citizens individually, as part of their liberty of conscience (be it based on religious doctrines that affirm it, or on various liberal philosophical doctrines, that likewise do so), to settle how they think the (political) values of the political domain are related to other (non-political) values of the comprehensive doctrine they accept or endorse (PL: 140; JaF: 33, 189–190).

For this to hold, Rawls needs the second, and complementary, part of the answer as to how an overlapping consensus on political liberalism could be possible. And this part says that "the history of religion and philosophy shows that there are many reasonable ways in which the wider realm of values can be understood so as to be either congruent with, or supportive of, or else not in conflict with, the values appropriate to the special domain of the political as specified by a political conception of justice. History tells of a plurality of not unreasonable comprehensive doctrines" (PL: 140; JaF: 190). It is these lessons from history that demonstrate, according to Rawls, that an overlapping consensus is possible, thus reducing the conflict between political and other values.

The idea of an overlapping consensus recognizes the conflicting and irreconcilable character of comprehensive religious, philosophical, and moral doctrines in the ethical domain, but does not want to accept that in the political–moral domain reaching consensus lies outside the range of human possibilities. It is this moral consensus with regard to the political conception of justice, and the political values it expresses, that Rawls sees contained in this idea of an overlapping consensus.

And it is the introduction in *Political Liberalism* of the idea of public reason as an idea of justification in a well-ordered society that shows that there are sufficient public reasons to be brought to the fore as to why reasonable citizens, regardless of the disunity due to their diversity of comprehensive views, can nevertheless opt for *justice as fairness* as a political conception of justice for social unity, and can defend their allegiance to it by public reasoning.

This shows once again that *justice as fairness* is not the fall-out of an individualistic, atomistic conception of a social and political order where institutions are merely instrumental in reaching individual aims, or those of associations or unions. In a well-ordered society, social unity arises through an overlapping consensus on the political conception of justice. Citizens, with their different ideas of the good life, do share the idea that there is one basic political end, an idea that there is a common priority: to uphold a just constitutional regime, and support just institutions. And in that sense a political society is a "community," social unity in it derived from *justice as fairness*, and "living together" is seen as a joint project (TJ: 522–523; TJR: 459; PL: 201; JaF: 198, 199–200).

The overlapping consensus is expressed in *the shared liberal political values* as these have, for example, been laid down in the constitution. These values are the core of liberal democratic citizenship. The stimulation of a shared identity, founded on this democratic citizenship, can perform a vital integrative function and can be the basis of social unity. It is the shared liberal political values that enable cooperation between persons with very diverse religious, philosophical, or moral comprehensive doctrines.

These arguments on democratic citizenship and shared identity do not, of course, imply that, for example, existing cultural or ethnic diversity is denied, or that people would have to give up their own specific culture, or their own specific comprehensive view, and would have to assimilate in the sense of them all sharing one and the same comprehensive doctrine. On the contrary: it leaves citizens sufficient space for their different cultural or ethnic identities. In their personal affairs or non-public life citizens have a specific idea of what their final ends and commitments are, of how to live a valuable life, and of the kind of person they want to be. Next to this "personal identity," they also have a "public" or "institutional identity" (PL: 31). Citizens have to agree that their particular personal conceptions of the good they pursue fall within the range permitted by the public political conception of justice. We have to acknowledge that even the space of the social world of a just liberal society is not without boundaries. We are, first of all, citizens. As such, we only implement those measures that we can also justify to those who do not share our personal conception of the "good life." Although, as we have said, liberal democratic citizenship does not require assimilation, it does require allegiance by all citizens to the liberal political values.

Overlapping consensus on *justice as fairness*?

But, one might wonder, are citizens in a well-ordered society actually reaching an overlapping consensus on one specific political conception of justice, to wit on *justice as fairness*? We strike here an issue in Rawls' exposition that has triggered a host of misunderstandings by critics of his project as developed in *Political Liberalism*, in particular the misunderstanding that in *Political Liberalism* Rawls, in order to reach political stability and an overlapping consensus, has abandoned his egalitarian ideals.

With respect to the "freestanding view," we have seen above that this criticism is not correct. *Justice as fairness* can be regarded as a freestanding conception of justice, and thus as satisfying the criteria of a political conception of justice. At the same time, we had to acknowledge that, since the content of public reason is not fixed, reasonable agreement might be reached on a family member of the political conceptions of justice, and so not necessarily on *justice as fairness*.

What now, we should ask, are the consequences of this for the second stage of the argument, the one where we are discussing how, in a society characterized by reasonable pluralism, an overlapping consensus might actually come about? Let us first, in answering this question, return to the first stage and to the set of political values of a specific political conception of justice, to *justice as fairness*. After presenting in *Political Liberalism* the principles of *justice as fairness*, Rawls makes a remark that, especially in light of the following argument, turns out to be important. Rawls stipulates:

[T]he two principles [of *justice as fairness*] express an *egalitarian form* of liberalism in virtue of three elements. These are

(a) the guarantee of the fair value of the political liberties, so that these are not purely formal;
(b) fair (and, again not purely formal) equality of opportunity; and finally
(c) the so-called difference principle, which says that the social and economic inequalities attached to offices and positions are to be adjusted so that, whatever the level of those inequalities, whether great or small, they are to the greatest benefit of the least advantaged members of society. (PL: 6–7; emphasis added)

Rawls notes that "[a]ll these elements are still in place, as they were in [*A Theory of Justice*]; and so is the basis of the argument for them. Hence I presuppose throughout [*Political Liberalism*] the same egalitarian conception of justice as before; and though I mention revisions from time to time, none affect this feature of it" (PL: 7). And he adds that he finds it necessary to make this comment "since some have thought that my working out the ideas of political liberalism meant giving up the egalitarian conception of [*A Theory of Justice*]. I am not aware of any revisions that imply such a change and think the surmise has no basis" (PL: 7 note 6). Thus, with regard to the family of political liberalisms, Rawls can say: "Of these liberalisms, justice as fairness is the most egalitarian" (LoP: 14 note 5).

To explore if indeed, at the second stage, an overlapping consensus is reached on *justice as fairness*, and thus on an egalitarian political conception of justice, we first have to ask what can be said about the *range* of the political conception of justice that is the focus of an overlapping consensus. In *A Theory of Justice*, in the context of discussing the original position as the preferred description of the initial situation, it had already been frequently emphasized that the objective is the practical one of proposing terms for living together that can gain the assent of all the members of society. Thus, Rawls says that it is "partly" in order to reach the greatest convergence of opinion "that we accept the constraints of a common standpoint, since we cannot reasonably expect our views to fall into line when they are affected by the contingencies of our different circumstances" (TJ: 517; TJR: 453). In *A Theory of Justice*, Rawls goes on to emphasize that "the numerous simplifications of *justice as fairness*" are justified by their role in making reasonable agreement more feasible. The hope of the parties in the original position is that, by settling for two relatively simple principles lexically ordered, they will be able to "simplify political and social questions so that the resulting balance of justice, made possible by the greater consensus, outweighs what may have been lost by ignoring certain potentially relevant aspects of moral situations" (TJ: 517; TJR: 454). The requirement that the principles of justice should form the publicly acknowledged charter of a society sets limits on how complex they can be.

Returning to *Political Liberalism* and to the second stage, the argument to accept constraints of a common standpoint is even more pressing when one acknowledges that citizens have different comprehensive doctrines, but are nevertheless supposed to reach agreement on a political conception of justice. The stakes are much higher. It can come as no surprise that Rawls now asks: "What if it turns out that the principles of justice as fairness cannot gain the support of reasonable doctrines, so that the case for stability fails?" (PL: 65). What if, in other words, the egalitarian variant of political liberalism does not gain support? Rawls' answer is that we should have to see whether "acceptable changes in the principles of justice would achieve stability; or indeed whether stability could obtain for any democratic conception" (PL: 66). Therefore, just as in *A Theory of Justice*, in *Political Liberalism* the principles of justice have to be *fine-tuned*. They are the flexible part of the theory, simplifying political and social-economic (distributive) questions.

What precisely are the implications of this "fine-tuning"? Which changes are possible if, on the one hand, one wants to keep the essence of "political liberalism" upright and, on the other, one wants to take into account the necessity to reach agreement between citizens that endorse diverse religious, philosophical, and moral comprehensive doctrines? What is the minimal core of "political liberalism"? To answer these questions, we have to bring into the discussion the issue of the burdens of judgment. They impose limits on what can reasonably be justified towards others. These burdens of judgment at several points play a role in *Political Liberalism*. (We have encountered the burdens of judgment before as an obstacle with regard to the evidence bearing on the issue of the working of the difference principle.)

The burdens of judgment lead in the present argument to the recognition that "reasonable pluralism" encompasses, among many other things, "a family of reasonable liberal political conceptions of justice" (PL: xlviii). Any conception that recognizes the burdens of judgment and meets the criterion of reciprocity viewed as applied between free and equal citizens, themselves seen as reasonable and rational, is a candidate (PL: xlix). These are the limiting conditions of all family members. And this is, of course, in line with our earlier acknowledgment that the content of public reason is not fixed.

Being members of the same family of liberalism, all family members have three characteristic principles or conditions in common.[26] These three principles that define the content of liberal political conceptions of justice are:

> first, a specification of certain basic rights, liberties, and opportunities (of a kind familiar from constitutional democratic regimes);
> second, an assignment of special priority to those rights, liberties, and opportunities, especially with respect to claims of the general good and of perfectionist values;
> third, measures assuring to all citizens adequate all-purpose means to make intelligent and effective use of their liberties and opportunities. (PL: xlviii)[27]

These characteristics formulate the constitutional essentials we have discussed earlier. They are characteristic for the many forms of "political liberalism."[28] Because these three characteristics that define the content of liberal political conceptions of justice, especially the third one, can be understood in different ways, "there are many variant liberalisms" (PL: 6). Of these, *justice as fairness*, whatever its merits, is but one.

Let us compare these three characteristics that define the general variant of liberal political conceptions of justice with one of them, with *justice as fairness*. Let us therefore repeat how Rawls himself has characterized that specific family member:

[T]he two principles of [*justice as fairness*] express an *egalitarian* form of 'political liberalism' in virtue of three elements:

(a) the guarantee of the fair value of the political liberties, so that these are not purely formal;

(b) fair (and again not purely formal) equality of opportunity; and finally
(c) the so-called difference principle, which says that the social and economic
     inequalities attached to offices and positions are to be adjusted so that,
     whatever the level of those inequalities, whether great or small, they are to
     the greatest benefit of the least advantaged members of society. (PL: 6–7;
     emphasis added)

A preliminary conclusion of the comparison is that the main difference, and the reason for calling *justice as fairness* the "egalitarian
variant," is that it includes a strong interpretation of fair equality of
opportunity as well as the difference principle; all other variants of
political liberalisms do not. What explains this difference between the
general variants of political liberalism and *justice as fairness*?

The explanation is that in fact, on the content and specification of at
least two elements of *justice as fairness* (fair equality of opportunity and
the difference principle) on admissible grounds, that is on reasonable
grounds, differences of opinion may exist between citizens. The fact
that reasonable citizens recognize that burdens of judgment limit what
we can reasonable justify towards others, brings us here – once more – to
the insight that we have to accept that there are many reasonable political
conceptions of justice. It is conceivable that *justice as fairness* as a unit is
too demanding for citizens to reach overlapping consensus on, and that
"only" an overlapping consensus will be reached on one of the other, less
demanding, family members of political liberalism. And, two of the three
egalitarian conditions of *justice as fairness*, to repeat fair (and, once again,
not merely formal) equality of opportunity and the difference principle,
are then not considered to be part of the constitutional essentials.

Although *justice as fairness* is still for Rawls the most favorable
interpretation of possible forms of political liberalism, his topic in
Political Liberalism is, "however, political liberalism and its component
ideas, so that much of our discussion concerns liberal conceptions more
generally, allowing for all variants, as for example when we consider the
idea of public reason" (PL: 7). Thus, in addition to conflicting comprehensive doctrines, *Political Liberalism* does recognize that in any actual
political society a number of differing liberal political conceptions of
justice compete with one another in society's public political debates
(PL: xlviii). In other words: in the second stage, the application of the
shared political conception of justice focuses on the general type of
political liberalism, and *justice as fairness* is used as an example of this
family of reasonable liberal political conceptions of justice.

When we take into account the different reasonable comprehensive doctrines of citizens who are seeking reasonable agreement, the range of political values that can be supported by an overlapping consensus may narrow. The consequence is that in the second stage we broaden our attention and switch from looking for agreement on only the egalitarian variant of political liberalism, *justice as fairness*, to possible reasonable consensus on any (general) variant of political liberalism, of which the egalitarian variant is still, for Rawls, the most important example. Crucial to Rawls' argument is the claim that, in seeking this overlapping consensus, all *reasonable* comprehensive doctrines in society "endorse some member of this family of reasonable [liberal] conceptions, and citizens affirming these doctrines are in an enduring majority with respect to those rejecting each of that family" (PL: xlix).

It is precisely this broadening of attention by Rawls, in which agreement is sought not only on the egalitarian variant of political liberalism, but on a possible reasonable consensus on *any* variant of political liberalism, which seems to have been overlooked by those who claim that the search for stability and overlapping consensus in *Political Liberalism* has led to the sacrifice of the egalitarian conditions of *justice as fairness*. Broadening the scope does not imply, however, that Rawls himself has abandoned the egalitarian variant of political liberalism. He has not.

Let us recapitulate: in the second stage of argumentation we are dealing with a different kind of problem than we are in the first stage, the "freestanding" one. In this second stage, societies are actually characterized by a plurality of reasonable comprehensive doctrines, and the issue is the possibility of reasonable overlapping consensus on *any* variant of political liberalism. It is this shift of focus that makes up much of *Political Liberalism*.

The overall conjecture of this stage, where we ask how a fully reasonable social unity might actually come about and where we are, when we discuss democratic institutions and the moral psychology of their citizens, dealing with "the application of common sense political sociology" and no longer with a problem of political philosophy, is the following. We can, or so it seems, provisionally conclude that it looks as if it is not *necessary* for a political conception of justice to be strongly egalitarian (more specifically, as egalitarian as *justice as fairness*).

Here it is important to note the shift in attention between the first and the second stage. Because there is a family of ways of identifying the criterion of reciprocity, the working out of the freestanding view is, in itself, not enough to lead to the reasonable overlapping consensus we are looking for in the second stage, as there will be several views. And this plurality of views is a given, not a moral opinion. Although in the second stage we are "only" looking for agreement on a political conception of justice which falls within the category of the general variants of political liberalism, Rawls is not confident that we will come to agreement on what, according to him, is (still) the most reasonable liberal political conception of justice. It is evident from the foregoing that Rawls is not sure that as things stand the reasonable overlapping consensus citizens will reach will be one on *justice as fairness*, on the egalitarian variant of political liberalism. But then Rawls would say: "How could one be sure of this?" It is more realistic and more likely that the overlapping consensus that will be achieved will be one in which the focus is on a class of liberal political conceptions of justice, and that several conceptions of justice will be political rivals, conceptions that are less "demanding" than *justice as fairness* as a unit, so to speak.

There remains, of course, Rawls' hope that, when the idea of public reason is fully realized, over time there will develop a well-ordered society with stability for the right reasons and a situation in which different liberal political conceptions of justice gather at a gradually decreasing distance around *justice as fairness* so that a fully overlapping consensus will be arrived at in which *justice as fairness* specifies the center of the focal class. Over time, then, the hope is that, first of all, a constitutional consensus (in which consensus on certain constitutional liberties that guarantee various liberties) would develop, which then eventually develops into an overlapping consensus. Next, the narrower the differences between the liberal political conceptions of justice become, the narrower becomes the range of liberal conceptions defining the focus of the consensus. And, for Rawls, eventually *justice as fairness* (including of course the difference principle) would – hopefully – specify the center of the focal class. Then a reasonable, fully overlapping consensus would be achieved (PL: 167–168).

This shows, once more, that Rawls has not given up the egalitarian dimension of political liberalism, but that he has shifted his attention to the question of how we could actually hope to reach agreement on it for the right reasons. And we should understand that from this perspective Rawls' claim that "the same egalitarian conception as before," that is as in *A Theory of Justice*, is presupposed. His hope now is that, in a well-ordered society characterized by reasonable pluralism over time, an overlapping consensus on the same liberal political conception of justice will develop, or at least on one that is a member of the family of liberal political conceptions of justice, and *in that sense* akin to the freestanding political conception of justice justified in the first stage.[29]

It should be mentioned once again, however, that in his exposition in *Political Liberalism* Rawls uses mainly the general variant of "political liberalism," especially in his considerations that are concerned with the idea of public reason. He focuses on the question of how it can be argued that people as citizens of a well-ordered society can develop allegiance to this general variant of "political liberalism" that helps to bring about consensus. It is because of this that one gets the impression that *Political Liberalism*, in contrast to *A Theory of Justice*, focuses mainly on the principle of the equal basic rights and liberties that are so central for tolerating the diversity of comprehensive doctrines in society and the different conceptions of the good that come with them. In *A Theory of Justice* the main focus, or so it seems, is on the way economic goods (income and wealth) should be distributed in a way that is fair, and is thus on the difference principle, while *Political Liberalism* focuses on what the relation should be between a modern liberal democratic state and conflicting comprehensive religious and nonreligious, liberal and nonliberal, doctrines in society. But this shift in perspective does not mean in any sense that social and economic issues have disappeared from the political agenda, or for that matter from that of Rawls. As will become clear later on, these issues are also relevant for the general variant of political liberalism, even without taking the difference principle into account.

Justification, reciprocity, and moral motivation

The basic problem that a theory of justice is designed to solve is how to take into account the circumstances of justice, that is, moderate scarcity and reasonable pluralism, whenever persons put forward conflicting claims to the division of social advantages. In short: which principles in the scheme of cooperation are those that distribute the (social and economic) benefits of cooperation in a fair way, a way acceptable to all members of a (well-ordered) society?

In Rawls' view it is "the criterion of reciprocity" as expressed in public reason that provides the justificatory yardstick to formulating a non-controversial answer to this question: in a well-ordered society the most reasonable fair terms of cooperation are expressed by the principles of *justice as fairness*, of which the difference principle – with its implicit reference to equal division as a benchmark – formulates an idea of reciprocity between citizens.

What we need, next, are arguments to explain how political allegiance, or the motivation to comply with institutional arrangements according to *justice as fairness* (or another political conception of political liberalism), is generated. The arguments on "the basis of moral motivation in the person," used by Rawls in political liberalism, are the same and serve the same function as they did in the case where Rawls was concerned with the issue of generating a sense of justice in *justice as fairness*, seen as a liberal comprehensive doctrine.

The motivation to comply, by those who have conflicting comprehensive doctrines, to institutional arrangements that are justified according to the criterion of reciprocity and expressed in a political conception of justice (hopefully in its most reasonable form, in *justice as fairness*), is generated by the "tendency to reciprocity," the most important moral psychological assumption underlying Rawls' theory of justice.[30] This tendency is, as we have seen earlier, "a deep psychological fact. Without it our nature would be very different and fruitful social cooperation fragile if not impossible" (TJ: 494–495; TJR: 433). This reasonable moral psychology is a psychology of the reasonable itself. This is so, since the idea of reciprocity appears both as a principle giving its content and as a disposition to answer in kind. The reasonable generates itself and answers itself in kind (JaF: 196). It is the disposition to act as justice requires: the psychological tendencies or principles exhibit this reciprocity of disposition.[31] It is Rawls' assumption that the principles or tendencies of moral psychology, or the reasonable moral psychology of citizens, will develop a firm sense of justice. It is these moral psychological forces that he relies on to argue that an overlapping consensus is reachable or to render it stable (should it exist) (PL: 86, 86 note 34; JaF: 196, 196 note 17). And, of course, Rawls is concerned with a well-ordered society, a society whose institutions are designed in such a way that moral sentiments can develop in conformity with *justice as fairness* (or at least in conformity with another member of the family of political liberalisms).

Now we mentioned at the start of this section that public reason plays the role of public justification for the fair terms of social cooperation that citizens offer one another. The point of the ideal of public reason is that each of us, as a citizen, conducting a public political discussion on fundamental issues, must have, and be ready to publicly explain, political principles and guidelines which, if we think other citizens may reasonably be expected to endorse them, satisfy the criterion of reciprocity.

One way to identify these political principles and guidelines, or one test for when this criterion is met, is to show that they would be agreed to in the original position. While Rawls acknowledges that others will think that other ways to identify these principles and guidelines are more reasonable, whatever ways are used to identify these principles must satisfy the criterion of reciprocity (PL: l–li, 226–227).

Following Rawls' acknowledgment that other ways of identifying the principles and guidelines of a reasonable political conception of justice are available, we can note that Rawls' ideas on contractualism bear resemblance to contractualism as it is formulated by the moral and political philosopher Thomas Scanlon. In the conception of reasonable persons from which *justice as fairness* starts, the guiding force is a "Scanlonian principle of moral motivation": the desire to find principles which others similarly motivated could not reasonably reject. That there is indeed such a Scanlonian moral motivation at play can be further corroborated. Rawls states that both aspects of the reasonable mentioned above "are closely connected with Scanlon's principle of moral motivation. ... [I]n setting out justice as fairness we rely on the kind of motivation Scanlon takes as basic" (PL: 49 note 2).[32]

Let us digress here and follow an analysis of Scanlon's contractarian moral theory of "reasonable unrejectability."[33] Scanlon formulates the core of this idea of unrejectability in the following way: "According to contractualism, the source of motivation that is directly triggered by the belief that an action is wrong is the desire to be able to justify one's action to others on grounds they could not reasonably reject."[34] The political theorist Brian Barry, who has argued that a theory of justice which turns on the terms of reasonable agreement can be called a theory of *justice as impartiality*, has noted that what Rawls is asking is "whether or not a principle could reasonably be rejected by someone aware of its impact on him. If we try to fill out the idea of reasonableness here, I believe that we shall arrive at the specification of a Scanlonian choice situation."[35] Barry has noted several reasons why the Scanlonian construction is an alternative way, and why it can be seen as a more effective realization of Rawls' objectives.[36] One reason is that in the Scanlonian choice situation, people who are arguing about principles of justice are not deprived of information. On the contrary, they are well-informed. A second, more general, reason is that theories of *justice as impartiality* which turn on the terms of reasonable agreement capture a certain kind of equality: all those affected have to be able to feel that they have done as well as they could reasonably hope to.[37]

Justice as impartiality, then, focuses attention first on those who would do worst under it, for they, more than any others, would have reasonable grounds to object. As Barry argues, "in virtue of the connection we establish between the content of justice and the terms of reasonable agreement … [i]t would be widely acknowledged as a sign of an unjust arrangement that those who do badly under it could reasonably reject it."[38] Impartiality in a natural way turns our attention to the worst off.[39] It then seems plausible to expect that all citizens, who are free and equal, may reasonably endorse a principle whose prime regard is the position of the worst off. From a Scanlonian perspective, this can be interpreted as the (moral) desire for protection, which is an important factor in determining the content of morality because it determines what can reasonably be agreed. It also means that any inequality must be accepted by all, including those who finish up with less under the proposed rule.

If indeed *justice as impartiality* calls for principles and rules that are capable of forming the basis of free agreement among people seeking agreement on reasonable terms, it seems that, assuming the fact of pluralism to obtain, the desire to protect basic rights, liberties, and opportunities (common to all variants of political liberalism) captures a principle that all will agree on. Only protection of these rights would guarantee the egalitarian premise of *justice as impartiality*, a protection of principles that are to regulate the basic structure and that cannot reasonably be rejected. How else are we to imagine that principles that are capable of forming the basis of free agreement, among all citizens who seek agreement on reasonable terms, could be justified?[40]

Returning from this digression to Rawls' contractarian theory, one could well ask why his ideas on moral motivation and acceptability, ideas that are in line with Scanlonian motivation, do not lead directly to an argument for *justice as fairness* based on a Scanlonian choice situation, as argued for in Scanlon's contractarian theory.[41]

To answer this question we have to take a closer look at the role this moral motivation plays in Rawls' contractualism, as well as at the differences between his contractualism and that of Scanlon. First of all, we have to distinguish in accounts of motivation different kinds of desires. The most important desires are, for Rawls, "conception-dependent" desires. Next there are "principle-dependent" desires. These are of two kinds, turning on whether the principle in question is rational or reasonable. The principles we desire to act from are related to, and help to articulate, the specific conception in question. In Rawls' case, the conception-dependent desire is the basic desire "to be able to justify our actions to others on grounds they could not reasonably reject"; it is the desire to act "in ways worthy of a reasonable and equal citizen." It is this desire that becomes, according to Rawls, the desire by which we are moved. And "to ascertain what answers to that desire, what it means to act in ways that can be justified to others, or in ways worthy of a reasonable and equal citizen, will call upon reasoning of many kinds. A line of thought and reasoning is needed to spell out what the conception-dependent desire requires" (PL: 85 note 33).

The starting point in this line of reasoning is the political conception of *justice as fairness*. The account of this political conception of justice connects the desire to realize a political ideal of citizenship with citizens' two moral powers: to be reasonable and to be rational (to have a sense of justice and a conception of the good). The features attributed to citizens – "their readiness to propose and to abide by fair terms of cooperation, their recognition of the burdens of judgment and affirming only reasonable comprehensive doctrines, and their wanting to be full citizens" – provide a basis for ascribing to them a reasonable moral psychology, several aspects of which are consequences of these features (PL: 86). Hence, in this line of reasoning, it is the political conception of *justice as fairness* itself from which the moral motivation of citizens is drawn.

For Rawls, as we have seen, persons are reasonable when they are ready to propose principles and guidelines as fair terms of cooperation and to abide by them willingly, and when they are ready to discuss the fair terms that others propose. We now see that to "accept the connection between these (two aspects of) the reasonable as a virtue of persons and Scanlon's principle of moral motivation is to include this form of motivation in the conception of reasonable persons from which *justice as fairness* starts" (PL: 49, 49 note 2).

We have, however, to take one more step to fully understand the role that moral motivation plays in Rawls' contractualism, as well as the differences between his contractualism and that of Scanlon. First, note the conception-dependent desire at play in Scanlon's case. It is the basic desire to act "in ways that can be justified to others." Related to this is that Scanlon formulates a general contractarian moral theory of reasonable unrejectability, in which very general claims about morality are made about "what we owe to each other." In his contractarian theory, in the first instance no claims are made about what is right and wrong in specific kinds of circumstances, for instance claims about the justice of social institutions with specific obligations.[42]

This brings us to the main difference between the contractualism of Scanlon and that of Rawls. In both contractarian theories the arguments rely on the same judgment, acceptability (or unrejectability). In Scanlon's case the judgment is part of the contractual process itself. But in Rawls' case things are more complex. Judgment of acceptability is not based "simply" on the contractual process itself, but on the contractual process as part of the rationale for its design, specifically that of the original position. In this design of "the original position argument," features are built into it that themselves already reflect substantive judgments about the subject to which it is addressed, judgments, for example, about the proper aims of social institutions.[43] And the design of the original position also *includes a specific kind of moral motivation.*

Thus, in Rawls' contract doctrine, this moral motivation has been imported right from the beginning into (the design of) the original position. It is because of this that Rawls can argue that it is the structure and content of *justice as fairness* that lays out "how, by the use of the original position, the principles and standards of justice for society's basic institutions belong to and help to articulate the conception of the reasonable and the rational citizens as free and equal" (PL: 84).

Let us recall that Rawls wants the argument from the original position to be, as far as possible, a deductive one.[44] And let us also recall that the parties in the original position are artificial persons, the characters who have a part in the play of the thought-experiment that the original position represents. Acceptance by the parties in the original position of the principles of *justice as fairness* does not depend on psychological hypotheses or social conditions in the description of the original position. The necessary psychology is included in the description of the parties as rational representatives who are moved to secure the good of those they represent (this good being specified by the primary goods) (JaF: 82–83). It is, as mentioned above, a moral psychology drawn from the political conception of *justice as fairness*. "It is not a psychology originating in the science of human nature but rather a scheme of concepts and principles for expressing a certain conception of the person and an ideal of citizenship" (PL: 86–87). Or, once again, the deliberation of the parties, and the motives we attribute to them, are badly misunderstood if they are mistaken for an account of the moral psychology, either of actual persons, or of citizens in a well-ordered society (PL: 28).

In conclusion, one can say that if this deductive original position argument is successful, that is to say if the political conception of *justice as fairness*, including its moral motivation, could be derived in the right way, this conception of justice would be justified.

In Rawls' set-up of justifications for his theory of justice, however, even if there is indeed a successful "deduction" of *justice as fairness*, we are not done yet. There remains the question of whether the moral psychology which has been included in the description of the parties can be accepted by "you" and "me," "here and now." This essentially depends on whether "we find the political conception of justice to which [this moral psychology] belongs, acceptable on due reflection" (PL: 87). The issue here is not if it can be deductively shown that the set-up of the original position justifies the principles of justice, but whether this can be confirmed by showing that the original position as designed, as well as its outcome, can be justified because it has the ability to account for our considered judgments of justice in wide reflective equilibrium. Eventually, if indeed all of us, or at least most of us, would accept on due reflection the set-up of the original position and the outcome of the choice made in it, and there would be wide and general or full reflective equilibrium, we get "much more" out of that agreement than we would get out of an agreement in a Scanlonian choice situation. But also the stakes are much higher: no agreement, unacceptability, rejectability of the design of the original position as a whole leaves us empty-handed with regard to what justice requires.

But suppose that there is indeed wide and general reflective equilibrium with regard to the political conception, and that the same conception is affirmed in everyone's considered judgments, then these justifications are provisional in the sense that it still has to be confirmed that a well-ordered society, institutionally organized in conformity with the political conception of *justice as fairness*, would be stable. After all, the wide and general reflective equilibrium on *justice as fairness*, or the inclusion of the necessary moral motivation in the description of the parties in the original position, does "not *explain* this motivation, or say how it comes about" (PL: 49 note 2; emphasis added). To be able to do this we need to return to the beginning of this section where we elaborated Rawls' assumptions that the principles and tendencies of moral psychology, the "deep psychological fact" of the tendency to reciprocity, will indeed develop a firm sense of justice. It is these "laws of moral psychology" on which Rawls relies to argue that in a well-ordered society an overlapping consensus is reachable and stable for the right reasons. And it is here that the idea of public reason that expresses the criterion of reciprocity plays its role in providing the kind of public justification citizens should offer one another. In a well-ordered society, the political conception of justice, its justification, its interpretation, are taught and learned. The political conception of justice is publicly known and becomes part of the public political culture. Put another way, in a well-ordered society the principle- and conception-dependent desires from which *justice as fairness* starts have become elements in people's motivational sets (PL: 85 note 33).

This exposition demonstrates the complexity of the process of justification in Rawls' theory. Justification rests upon the conception of justice as a whole and is a matter of the mutual support of many considerations, of everything fitting together into one coherent view. The three separate steps made above in the justification process (the derivation of principles in the original position, the method of reflective equilibrium, and the role of public reason in a well-ordered society), are intended to make a unified whole by supporting one another in roughly the following way. The first part presents the essentials of the theoretical set-up of the original position. The principles of justice are deductively argued for on the basis of reasonable stipulations concerning the choice of such a conception in the original position. In the second step, the aim is to show that the theory proposed matches the fixed points of our considered convictions better than other familiar doctrines (utilitarianism for instance), and that it leads us to revise and extrapolate our judgments in what seem on reflection to be more satisfactory ways: we reach wide reflective equilibrium. Finally, in the third step, the check is to see if *justice as fairness* is a feasible conception. Here the issue is to explain how *justice as fairness* generates its own support and that it is likely that a well-ordered society will have stability for the right reasons, since it is more in line with the principles of moral psychology. In a well-ordered society human beings might acquire a sense of justice and the other moral sentiments, whereby a person would acquire an understanding of and an attachment to the principles of justice as he grows up in this particular form of well-ordered society. These considerations do not determine the initial acknowledgment of principles in the first part of the argument, but confirm it. They show that our nature is such as to allow the choice in the original position to be carried through. Or, as Rawls formulates it: "In this sense we might say that humankind has a moral nature" (TJ: 580; TJR: 508).[45]

The ideal of public reason, political liberties, and deliberative democracy

Justice as fairness agrees with the strand of the liberal tradition of the "moderns," as formulated by Benjamin Constant in 1819 in his *De la liberté des anciens comparée à celle des modernes.*[46] It is a tradition that regards equal political liberties and the value of public life (the liberties of the ancients) as having in general less intrinsic value than, say, freedom of thought and liberty of conscience, and some basic rights of the person and (private) property, and the rule of law (the liberties of the moderns). This is also the dominant tradition today. By this is meant, among other things, that in a modern democratic society taking a continuous and active part in public life generally has a lesser place in the conceptions of the good of most citizens (JaF: 143). This does not look problematic, since citizens are not political beings whose essential nature is such that they only can fulfill their plans of life by widespread and active participation in political life. Rawls rejects a view in which political participation is seen as the privileged locus of our (complete) good. It is what Charles Taylor has described as the central notion of *"civic humanism"*: "men find the good in the public life of a citizen republic" (PL: 206). Rawls borrows this interpretation of civic humanism from Taylor. It is a view that is rejected by Rawls because it is based on a comprehensive doctrine and as such is incompatible with *justice as fairness* as a political conception of justice (PL: 206; JaF: 142–143).[47]

But even in rejecting a view like civic humanism, this "is no bar to counting certain political liberties among the basic liberties and protecting them by the priority of liberty" (PL: 299). They are, for instance, important as essential institutional means to secure the other basic liberties. The question then is to what extent, and in which way, engaging in political life is necessary for the protection of basic liberties: if we are to remain free and equal citizens, we cannot afford a complete exodus by us as citizens from politics into private life. That would lead to a loss of everybody's freedom. The safety of democratic liberties, including the liberties of non-political life (the liberties of the modern), requires the active participation of citizens who have the political virtues needed to sustain a constitutional regime (PL: 205; CP: 469; JaF: 144).

We see here the need for and the importance of the educative role of a political conception of justice. The basic institutions of a well-ordered society must educate citizens to see themselves as free and equal. The public political conception of justice formulates not only the principles for ordering the basic institutions of society, but also their wide role as educational as well. In this role they are, as mentioned before, part of the public political culture. Pointing out the importance of, for instance, public political debate through which citizens can become acquainted with their basic rights and duties, and the reasons why these need to be respected, can be typified as "*civic republicanism*" (JaF: 146).[48] This is fully compatible with political liberalism since no comprehensive doctrine is involved.

For such a debate to be possible, Rawls stresses that society should in the first place pay enough attention to the education of children: children are future citizens. That is the reason the state has to be concerned with their education. As future citizens it is essential that they acquire the capacity to understand the public political culture of society and the capacity to participate in its institutions so as to make sure they will become mature and independent citizens. It is as essential, and also a concern of the state, that they receive schooling and training, so as to guarantee their being economically independent and self-supporting members of society over a complete life. Education in the public political culture of "political liberalism," in its public spirit, encouraging the political virtues, is fundamental to generate the necessary conditions of social unity in a flourishing civil society, especially in a society characterized by a plurality of comprehensive doctrines, as well as by multicultural and multi-ethnic diversity. Note that these reasonable requirements that the state can impose for children's education, so that they can understand all the implications of the political conception of justice, are formulated entirely from within the conception of political liberalism. No comprehensive doctrine is at play here (JaF: 122, 126, 156–157).

The issues raised here are closely related to realizing the ideal of public reason. This ideal characterizes the democratic political relation itself: the duty to adopt a certain form of public discourse, a conception of democratic citizenship, and of the joint exercise by citizens of ultimate political power. The values of public reason, which govern the public debate on constitutional essentials, refer to the equal basic rights and liberties of citizenship that legislative majorities are to respect. They refer more specifically to the right to vote, to participate in politics, to liberty of conscience, and freedom of thought and of association, as well as to the protection of the rule of law.

The ideal of public reason entails a form of public political deliberation, and a belief in the importance of public deliberation is essential for a reasonable constitutional regime. The ideal of public reason underlines the importance of "*deliberative democracy*." The definitive idea for deliberative democracy is deliberation itself. It is a political and social order in which the justification of the terms of association proceeds through public reason, and where a system of ideal deliberation is mirrored in social and political institutions, especially in the constitutional essentials and matters of basic justice (PL: 430; JaF: 148; LoP: 137–139). "Democracy" is not negotiating based on self-interest and strategic behavior, it is not identical with the citizen as a *homo economicus* who sees in politics only one aspect: how to gain his advantage. Democracy stands for the necessity of deliberation and open public debate, it "limits the reasons citizens may give in supporting their political opinion to reason consistent with their seeing other citizens as equals" (LoP: 139 note 21).

The fair value of political liberties is a necessary condition to further these requirements of deliberative democracy and to set the stage for the exercise of public reason (the aim, as we noted before, that political liberalism shares with civic republicanism).

Fair value of political liberties and access to the political process

That the safety of democratic liberties requires the active participation of citizens, as noted above, means that the right to vote, to participate in politics, and to equal political liberties, are linked to *questions of access* to the political process. This is not only a formal matter, but also a substantive one. It is well known that social and economic inequalities may be such that they prevent citizens from exercising their formal political liberties. In *A Theory of Justice*, Rawls had already noted that it is the fair value of the political liberties that enables citizens to participate on an equal footing in public-political life. The worth of political liberties, whatever the social or economic position of citizens, must be approximately equal, or at least sufficiently equal, in the sense that everyone has a fair opportunity to hold public office and to influence the outcome of political decisions. All citizens ought, therefore, to have a fair chance to add alternative proposals to the agenda for political discussion. The conception of "fair value" was introduced to answer the objection that the equal liberties in modern democracies are in practice merely formal. Rawls remarks that the "liberties protected by the principle of participation lose much of their value whenever those who have greater private means are permitted to use their advantages to control the course of public debate. For eventually these inequalities will enable those better situated to exercise a larger influence over the development of legislation. In due time they are likely to acquire a preponderant weight in settling social questions, at least in regard to those matters upon which they normally agree, which is to say in regard to those things that support their favored circumstances" (TJ: 225; TJR: 198).[49]

It is the ban on inequalities of political influence that derive from unequal resources that leads to the requirement of this fair value. It necessitates a situation in which background institutions for upholding distributive justice prevent excessive accumulation of property and wealth (TJ: 225, 278; TJR: 197–198, 245). In fact, one of the conditions that guarantee the "fair value" of political liberties is that "property and wealth must be kept widely distributed and government monies provided on a regular basis to encourage free public discussion" (TJ: 225; TJR: 198).[50]

In addition, measures are to be taken such that political parties are made independent from private interests, from large concentrations of private economic and social power, by allotting them sufficient tax revenues to play their part in the constitutional scheme; that there is public financing of political campaigns and election expenditures; that there are restrictions on campaign contributions; that there are ways of ensuring the availability of public information on matters of policy; that there is the assurance of a more even access to public media.[51] In short, as Rawls later formulated it, "public deliberation must [be] set free from the curse of money" (LoP: 139).

In *Political Liberalism*, Rawls repeats these arguments on the fair value of political liberties. Again, their guarantee is a way in which political liberalism tries to meet the objection that the basic political liberties are merely formal. It enables citizens to participate in public political life. This guarantee of the fair value of the political liberties has several noteworthy features. In the first place, it "secures for each citizen a fair and roughly equal access to the use of a public facility ... which govern[s] the political process and control[s] the entry to positions of political authority." Second, "this public facility has limited space, so to speak. Hence, those with relatively greater means can combine together and exclude those who have less in the absence of the guarantee of fair value of the political liberties" (PL: 328).[52]

And, again, to guarantee that the political liberties are secured by their fair value, and that equal access to the political process is guaranteed, it means that the worth of the political liberties to all citizens, whatever their social or economic position, must be approximately equal, or at least sufficiently equal. The important role this requirement plays in Rawls' theory should not be underestimated. As he notes, "guaranteeing the fair value of the political liberties is of equal if not greater importance than making sure that markets are workably competitive. For unless the fair value of these liberties is approximately preserved, just background institutions are unlikely to be either established or maintained" (PL: 327–328). In fact, the fair value of political liberties has become an integral part of the first principle of justice. The first principle now reads: "Each person has an equal claim to a fully adequate scheme of equal basic rights and liberties, which scheme is compatible with the same scheme for all; and in this scheme the equal political liberties, and only those liberties, are to be guaranteed their fair value" (PL: 5).[53]

Now, one could well argue that the necessary condition for the "fair value" of political liberties ("property and wealth must be kept widely distributed") is taken care of in *justice as fairness*. There seems after all to be a principle in place to guarantee this: the difference principle. But it turns out that in *A Theory of Justice*, and later in *Political Liberalism*, indeed right up until *Justice as Fairness: A Restatement*, Rawls is of the same opinion: the difference principle is not sufficient to guarantee that "property and wealth are kept widely distributed." "We cannot be sure," Rawls claims, "that the inequalities permitted by the difference principle will be sufficiently small to prevent this," and thus, even with the difference principle in place, those with less means are still prevented from having fair and equal access to the political process as a public facility (PL: 328; JaF: 150). Formulated another way: the guarantee of the fair value of political liberties requires stronger restrictions on inequalities than the difference principle might allow. The difference principle is presumably not sufficient to prevent those with greater means from combining together and excluding those who have less. Other, additional measures are necessary to guarantee the fair value of liberties. And Rawls mentions here, for instance, the progressive principle of taxation to prevent accumulations of wealth that are judged to be inimical to background justice, such as to the fair value of political liberties (TJ: 277; TJR: 245; JaF: 161). (Recall that in our discussion of the design of the required background institutions, this was one aspect of the distribution branch, a branch that has to preserve an approximate justice in distributive shares by means of taxation and the necessary adjustments in the rights of property.)

It is thus arguments with regard to questions of access to the political process, as well as arguments about the actual possibility of using liberties and opportunities, that limit the acceptable level of inequalities in important ways. But there are more arguments to be given that pose limits on what is an acceptable level of inequalities.

We have already noted (discussing "deliberative democracy") that the ideal of public reason entails a form of public deliberation, and that a belief in the importance of public deliberation is essential for a reasonable constitutional regime. The argument that a fair political process should be open to everyone on a basis of sufficient equality is closely related to the ideal of public reason. In fact, in working out "political liberalism" over time, Rawls has stressed more and more that it is the ideal of public reason itself that necessitates the institutional requirements of the basic structure in order to prevent excessive social and economic inequalities from developing.

Remember that we are concerned in political liberalism with a family of reasonable political conceptions of justice, of which *justice as fairness* is just one member. Let us also recall that all family members have three characteristic principles in common that define the content of liberal political conceptions of justice:

first, a specification of certain basic rights, liberties, and opportunities (of a
   kind familiar from constitutional democratic regimes);

second, an assignment of special priority to those rights, liberties, and
   opportunities, especially with respect to claims of the general good
   and of perfectionist values;

third, measures assuring to all citizens adequate all-purpose means [pri-
   mary goods] to make intelligent and effective use of their liberties and
   opportunities. (PL: xlviii; LoP: 14, 49)

To have stability for the right reasons in which the ideal of public reason
can be realized, these three characteristics imply important requirements.
This has been further elaborated by Rawls. He gives us an indication of
the institutions that are required for stability, institutional requirements
that have to be satisfied for all variants of political liberalism.

(a) Public financing of elections and ways of assuring the availability of
    public information on matters of policy. This to ensure both that
    representatives and other officials are sufficiently independent of
    particular social and economic interests and to provide the knowl-
    edge and information upon which policies can be formed and
    intelligently assessed by citizens using public reason.

(b) A certain fair equality of opportunity, especially in education and
    training. Without these opportunities, all parts of society cannot
    take part in the debates of public reason or contribute to social and
    economic policies.

(c) A decent distribution of income and wealth, meeting the third
    characteristic of [political] liberalism: all citizens must be assured
    the all-purpose means necessary to make intelligent and effective use
    of their basic freedoms. In the absence of this characteristic, those
    with wealth and income tend to dominate those with less and
    increasingly to control political power in their own favor.

(d) Society as the employer of last resort through general or local govern-
    ment, or other social and economic policies. (The lack of a sense of
    long-term security and of the opportunity for meaningful work and
    occupation is destructive not only of citizens' self-respect, but of their
    sense that they are members of society and not simply caught in it.)

(e) Basic health care assured for all citizens. (PL: lviii–lix; LoP: 50)

Recall that these requirements are formulated to hold for all variants of
"political liberalism." The reason that these institutional requirements

are necessary is, according to Rawls, because public reason characterizes a form of public political deliberation, and for this deliberation to be possible and fruitful not only do basic liberties have to be protected, but also social and economic inequalities have to be prevented from becoming excessive. It is especially the first three institutional requirements (a, b, and c above) that should accomplish this (PL: lix; LoP: 50–51).

The argument that equal access to the political process requires, in all variants of political liberalism, a built-in guarantee that, in the basic structure of society, social and economic inequalities have to be prevented from becoming excessive, in conjunction with the argument that inequalities permitted by the difference principle will not be sufficiently small to preclude this, leads to the conclusion that, whatever member of the family of political liberalism we take, all variants require egalitarian measures.

The contention that there is no reason why the requirements for the fair value of political liberties that guarantee equal access to the political forum should be different in *any* variant of liberalism leads, at the same time, to the conclusion that the range of differences between the general variants of political liberalism, of which *justice as fairness* is a member, is substantially narrowed. Although the difference principle is not a part of the general variants of political liberalism (there are many candidates), this is irrelevant with regard to the range of social and economic inequalities that the basic structure should allow when discussing equal access to the political process. *All variants of political liberalism have an egalitarian dimension, regardless of whether they contain the difference principle or not.*

Let us add to this debate on "fair access" and on "restricting inequalities" two related issues. One may wonder whether the requirements equal access possess also have consequences for the argument that is brought forward for distinguishing "the constitutional essentials" from "matters of basic justice," such as the principles governing social and economic inequalities. Offhand, one could say that this distinction seems to become less relevant. We have just seen that the third characteristic principle of liberal political conceptions of justice requires measures that prevent social and economic inequalities from being excessive. Otherwise citizens would not have fair and equal access to public deliberation. If constitutional essentials include, as they do, the political right of freedom of speech, of voting, and of running for public office, it seems hard to uphold that measures designed to help citizens to make effective use of their basic rights should not also be a part of constitutional essentials.

Rawls' answer might be, however, that the basic principles that are worthy of being enshrined in the Constitution should also have a constitutionally enforceable scope, which is determined by how wide a range of meanings and applications can secure a consensus of reasonable views. And he might argue that, although he is sympathetic to the strong interpretation of the fair value of political liberties, he would see measures to actually accomplish this as subject to the same forms of reasonable disagreement as the difference principle, and that therefore these should not be included in the constitutional essentials.

The basis of this argument would be that, if indeed it is the case that we cannot be sure that the inequalities permitted by the difference principle will be sufficiently small to guarantee the fair value of the political liberties, we are, or so it seems, talking about strong restrictions on permissible inequalities. And there might well be as much reasonable disagreement on how to regulate these inequalities, and on the principle or principles we need to provide citizens with adequate means to make effective use of their liberties, as there would be in discussing the difference principle as the appropriate candidate to regulate this.

The problem here, however, is that if we take it as unproblematic that the default position (given reasonable disagreement about distributive principles) is to go along with what comes out of the political process, we are not to regard this as a respectable, or even legitimate, default position unless effective political rights are far more equally distributed. That is why one has to insist that, with or without the distinction between constitutional essentials and matters of basic justice, egalitarian force has to be imported into the principle of equal political rights.

A second issue that can be raised here is the following one. Fair access to political public deliberation is a necessary condition of all variants of liberalism, and consequently, as has been argued, in all variants access is an unqualified strong *equalisandum*. Without it, the outcome of the political process in determining the law and policies on, for instance, economic reform, on the difference principle, or on an alternative, would be a forgone conclusion.

If indeed fair access requires strong egalitarianism, one might argue that in the *justice as fairness* variant of political liberalism, there is nothing left for the difference principle to do. Indeed, a great amount of potential disagreement would have been cleared out of the way, were a just and stable society to turn only on fair access, with the accompanying regulation of excessive social and economic inequalities. But although fair access is a necessary condition in all variants of political liberalism, it is not a sufficient one. There are still, next to fair access, many kinds of things that have to be distributed in a fair way, such as opportunities, work, income, education, and health care. There is still work to do for the difference principle in the *justice as fairness* variant of political liberalism, as there is for principles of just distribution in other variants of political liberalism. Although the idea of reciprocity is an egalitarian one, there are many currencies of equality that give reciprocity its due.

Political liberalism, "neutrality," and respect

Since "political liberalism" recognizes the fact of reasonable pluralism, the basic constitutional principles of political society that embody the basic rights and duties of citizens have to be "neutral" with regard to different (maybe even controversial) ideas of the good life that citizens freely affirm and which typically include religion, life-styles, conceptions of the good, and cultural preferences (as long as these ideas respect the principles of justice). Thus, this idea of the neutrality of the liberal democratic state should not be confused with the idea that "anything goes," nor with the idea that the liberal democratic state is a non-interventionist state, a night-watchman state, a minimal state, or an amoral one. On the contrary, there is an active role for government to play. A democratic political order in which the political values of political liberalism are realized requires government intervention. A "strong state" is necessary to maintain a situation in which citizens can exercise their basic rights and liberties. But, and this is what will be discussed in the following, it has to do so in a "neutral" way.

As a political conception of justice for the basic structure, *justice as fairness* as a whole not only tries to provide common ground as the focus for an overlapping consensus, it also hopes to satisfy *neutrality of aim* in the sense that basic institutions and public policy are designed not to favor any particular comprehensive doctrine, or one or another specific conception of the good. After all, government cannot refer to the superiority of a specific conception of the good, or force citizens to live up to it (PL: 193).[54]

But, as Rawls notes, "it is surely impossible for the basic structure of a just constitutional regime *not* to have important *effects and influences* as to which comprehensive doctrines endure and gain adherents over time" (PL: 193; emphasis added). The basic institutions that the shared liberal political values require inevitably encourage some ways of life and discourage others, or even exclude them altogether. We must accept, as Rawls notes, the facts of common-sense political sociology (PL: 195, 193). (In parentheses, one should add that Rawls believes that the term "neutrality" is unfortunate because it has misleading connotations, or impracticable principles, and better should not be used at all [PL: 191].)

This political ideal of a "neutral" government has its parallel in the ideal of public reason that belongs with democratic citizenship. The fact that the public reason used by free and equal citizens focuses on the public charter of a democratic constitutional regime, means that public reason does not appeal to the "whole truth" of a religious, philosophical, or moral comprehensive doctrine. Doing that would show a lack of respect for the reasonable opinions of others, and would preclude any possibility of reconciliation based on the use of public reason. This reasonable sense of due respect is the outcome of democratic institutions, linked with the ideal of public reason.

This ideal formulates the ideal of a good citizen: respect for minorities and the willingness to be tolerant. It is our moral, not our legal, duty of public civility. It is on the one hand our willingness to explain to others the way in which the political values of public reason substantiate our own beliefs and claims. On the other hand, it is our willingness to not only listen to other views, but also, if this could reasonably be asked, to revise or to change our own views. Moreover, "even though we think our arguments sincere and not self-serving when we present them, we must consider what it is reasonable to expect others to think who stand to lose should our reasoning prevail" (JaF: 116).

We have to recognize, insofar as we are reasonable, that politics in a democratic society cannot be subjected to what we ourselves consider, based on our own comprehensive religious, philosophical, or moral doctrine, to be the whole truth. A livable and well-ordered society demands from its citizens a certain amount of restraint and a sympathetic attitude with respect to the views and judgments of others. These cooperative virtues of political life, the political virtues of reasonableness and a sense of fairness, of a spirit of compromise and the will to honor the duty of public civility, are necessary because we live in a society where all kinds of beliefs clash and where there are many kinds of conflicts (JaF: 116, 118).

Even more, it is at best unrealistic to presuppose that our disagreements result only from ignorance. Toleration and good citizenship demands a certain amount of relativism with regard to one's own beliefs and life-styles. It is the recognition by reasonable citizens that the burdens of judgment are a source of reasonable disagreement, and thus limit the scope of what reasonable persons think can be justified to others in cases of political judgment. It is the burdens of judgment that we are all equally subjected to that can account for the fact of reasonable pluralism (there are also, of course, Rawls notes, other reasons). They set limits to reconciliation by public reason. The burdens of judgment are of primary significance for a democratic idea of toleration, and they are why citizens endorse some form of freedom of thought and liberty of conscience (PL: 54–61; JaF: 35–37; LoP: 177).

Equal basic liberties: regulation or restriction?

Analogous to our earlier analysis of equal basic liberties in *A Theory of Justice*, it holds in political liberalism as well that since basic liberties are bound to conflict with one another, none of them is absolute. And – once again – a distinction has to be made between the restrictions of basic liberties and their regulation. Regulating means that, as it is now formulated in *Political Liberalism*, in the first principle of *justice as fairness* we are to establish the best scheme, or at least a *fully adequate scheme*, of basic liberties.[55] The basic liberties are to be adjusted to give one coherent scheme of liberties, to be secured equally for all citizens (PL: 295).

Freedom of speech, freedom of thought, liberty of conscience, freedom of movement, political liberties, and the guarantees of the rule of law, are all essential for human dignity and integrity. But how to accommodate these liberties with each other when, for example, freedom of speech comes into conflict with, for example, liberty of conscience? The solution is not to formulate a hierarchy among basic liberties and to record such an ordering in a constitution. The criterion of significance Rawls has in mind to establish the best scheme, or at least a *fully adequate scheme*, of basic liberties, is to consider which basic liberties with their priorities are essential social conditions to guarantee equally for all citizens the adequate development and full exercise of their two powers of moral personality over a complete life. In this way, basic liberties are connected with the conception of the person used in *justice as fairness* (PL: 293; JaF: 112).

Take, for instance, claims to unlimited freedom of speech, of press, and of public debates. The weight of these claims is to be assessed by this criterion. Whether indeed we can speak of an unlimited basic right depends on how far it stimulates development of one or the other of the two moral powers. Moral persons as citizens have a sense of justice about what are fair terms of social cooperation, especially with regard to the application of the principles of *justice as fairness* to the basic structure of society and their social policies. To be able to develop this power to be reasonable, equal political liberties and freedom of thought are essential. They are necessary to make possible the free use of public reason. And with regard to the power of citizens to be rational, to be able to develop their own conception of the good, maybe to revise or to change it, liberty of conscience and freedom of association are the required liberties for developing this power (PL: 332; JaF: 112–113).

With this criterion in mind, other liberties have to be assessed. How much, for example, do a free press and a public debate actually contribute in realizing the two moral powers? Rawls is of the opinion that we cannot give an answer abstracted from content, location, time, or circumstances. These all play a role here. Incitement to hate, libel, and the defamation of individuals are certainly not helpful in realizing the two moral powers. And political speech that, during a public meeting, turns into an incitement to the imminent and lawless use of force is too disruptive of democratic political procedures to be permitted by the rules of order of public debate (PL: 335–336; JaF: 113–114). Regulations, then, as to the time and place, and the means used, to express opinion are permissible. But there is no restriction on the content of speech: "the advocacy of revolutionary and even seditious doctrines is fully protected, as it should be" (PL: 336; JaF: 114).[56]

Granting all this, and keeping in mind the distinction between "regulating" and "restricting" liberties, when, then, are infringements on basic liberties justified? Rawls had earlier argued, in *A Theory of Justice* when discussing the question of when limits on liberties are justified, that "it seems ... evident, in limiting liberty by reference to the common interest in public order and security, the government acts on a principle that would be chosen in the original position. For in this position each recognizes that the disruption of these conditions is a danger for the liberty of all. ... The government's right to maintain public order and security is an enabling right, a right which the government must have if it is to carry out its duty of impartially supporting the conditions necessary for everyone's pursuit of his interests and living up to his obligations as he understands them" (TJ: 212–213; TJR: 187). As Rawls argues, this "follows once the maintenance of public order is understood as a necessary condition for everyone's achieving his ends whatever they are (provided they lie within certain limits) and for his fulfilling his interpretation of his moral and religious obligations" (TJ: 213; TJR: 187).

Take, for instance, liberty of conscience. "Everyone agrees," Rawls says, that it can be limited by the common interest in public order and security. "To restrain liberty of conscience at the boundary, however inexact, of the state's interest in public order is a limit derived from the principle of the common interest, that is, the interest of the representative equal citizen" (TJ: 213; TJR: 187).

The question, then, of tolerating the intolerant, is directly related to that of the stability of a well-ordered society. As Rawls formulates it: "Justice does not require that men must stand idly by while others destroy the basis of their existence. Since it can never be to men's advantage, from a general point of view, to forgo the right of self-protection, the only question, then, is whether the tolerant have a right to curb the intolerant when they are of no immediate danger to the equal liberties of others" (TJ: 218; TJR: 192).

Hence with regard to the right not to tolerate, for instance, an intolerant (religious) sect, and thus limit its liberty, Rawls argues "that while an intolerant sect does not itself have title to complain of intolerance, its freedom should be restricted only when the tolerant sincerely and with reason believe that their own security and that of the institutions of liberty are in danger. The tolerant should curb the intolerant only in this case" (TJ: 220; TJR: 193). The conclusion here is that the limitation of a basic liberty "is justified only when it is necessary for liberty itself, to prevent an invasion of freedom that would be still worse" (TJ: 215; TJR: 188; JaF: 111). Let us have a closer look at precisely what it means to say that liberty of conscience "can be limited by the common interest in public order and security for all citizens."

Political toleration and religion

The recognition that there are incompatible and irreconcilable differences of opinion between reasonable religious, philosophical, and moral comprehensive doctrines is also the reason that political

liberalism avoids controversies with regard to religious issues (PL: 150).
It cannot be the case that citizens have to first give up their deep
convictions before they can accept the legitimacy of the political
order. But this avoidance of religious controversies does not imply a
kind of "living-apart-together." This idea of avoidance, and the principle of toleration that goes with it, has nothing to do with a kind of
"institutionalized toleration," a society divided into separate groups,
each with its own fundamental interests (PL: 150). We would not have
stability for the right reasons, secured by a firm allegiance to a democratic society's political (moral) ideas (LoP: 150).

But what a political conception of justice does do is to set limits to the
range of religious practices. The legal order must regulate men's pursuit
of their religious interests so as to realize the principle of equal liberty. If
a religion is denied its full expression, it is presumably because it is in
violation of the equal liberties of others (TJ: 370; TJR: 325). What
Rawls had in mind in discussing avoiding religious controversies were
those that are raised by, for instance, public statements that denounce
Islam as a "backward religion." Such statements are, politically speaking, not relevant. The only relevant question here is whether this "back-
wardness" prevents those who endorse this religion – or more generally
those who endorse whatever religious, philosophical, or moral view –
from at the same time endorsing and abiding by the political values of
the liberal democratic political order. With regard to the latter, there
can be no question of avoiding controversies, and no doubt as to what is
the answer of political liberalism. Apart from that, qualifying particular
religious beliefs as "backward" of course does not show much respect,
not to speak of the public duty of civility that citizens, according to
political liberalism, should show each other.

What Rawls is concerned with is *political* toleration: toleration
expressed in terms of the rights and duties protecting religious liberty in
accordance with a reasonable political conception of justice (LoP: 152,
176). Certainly, it could well be the case that a particular religious doctrine
(or a nonreligious one) formulates from within its doctrine an idea of
toleration. Concordant judgments could be made. But political liberalism
is not concerned with toleration based on this or that religious view, and
neither with toleration based on nonreligious beliefs.[57] We are concerned
with toleration as toleration between citizens, a toleration that is based on
the political values they share, precisely without the necessity of reaching
agreement on complete final ends, or on any one or other comprehensive

value. The conjecture is that a reasonable comprehensive religious doctrine can endorse with regard to toleration some kind of political argument. Political liberalism leaves religious beliefs undisturbed as far as and as long as they are consistent with basic liberties, including freedom of religion and freedom of conscience. There is no war, or there is no necessity for one, between religion and democracy (LoP: 175–176). Noting, among others, some of the reasons for the separation of church and state, Rawls mentions that this separation protects religion from the state and the state from religion; it protects citizens from their churches and citizens from one another. The reason for the separation is certainly not primarily for the protection of secular culture. It does that, but no more than it protects all religions (LoP: 167). All of this is not to deny that controversial issues inevitably remain, as Rawls notes: "for example, how more exactly to draw the boundaries of the basic liberties when they conflict (where to set 'the wall between church and state')" (PL: 151–152).[58]

As we have noted, political liberalism leaves religious beliefs undisturbed. But can we be more precise here? It does not mean, for instance, that a religion can use as a justification for its intolerance of other religions that this is necessary for maintaining itself. Neither can the claim that the subjection of women is necessary for its survival be seen as a justification thereof. Basic human rights are involved and these rights belong to the shared institutions and practices of all liberal and democratic societies (PL: 196–197; LoP: 111). While a constitutional regime can fully guarantee basic rights and liberties for all reasonable comprehensive doctrines, "a democracy necessarily requires," argues Rawls, "that, as one equal citizen among others, each of us accept the obligations of legitimate law" (LoP: 150).

Although no one is expected to put his religious or nonreligious doctrine in danger, we must each of us give up forever, Rawls argues, "the hope of changing the constitution so as to establish our religion's hegemony, or of qualifying our obligations so as to ensure its influence and success. To retain such hopes and aims would be inconsistent with the idea of equal basic liberties for all free and equal citizens" (LoP: 150). The only possibility for those of faith, as well as the nonreligious, to endorse a constitutional regime, even when their comprehensive doctrine cannot flourish under it, indeed even may decline under it, is that they understand and accept that endorsing such a regime is the only way to ensure the liberty of its adherents consistent with the equal liberties of other reasonable free and equal citizens (LoP: 151).

The other side of the argument on political toleration is that there are limits to toleration. Unreasonable doctrines, such as fundamentalist religions or particular nonreligious (secular) doctrines can be incompatible with a tolerant democratic political order within which a civil society can flourish. Such an order is seriously threatened by a fanaticism that tries to impose its rules and beliefs on everyone and sees a compromise as treason to its own fundamental principles. There may arise situations which require political liberalism to not tolerate the intolerant. How these situations are settled is determined by the appropriate political principles and the conduct these principles permit (LoP: 178; TJ & TJR: §35). Political liberalism, then, does not take a neutral stand with regard to political liberalism itself. It does not, as previously mentioned, require that men must stand idly by while others destroy the basis of their existence.

Thus, even "though political liberalism seeks common ground and is neutral in aim [but not neutral in effects and influences, as argued earlier], it is important to emphasize that it may still affirm the superiority of certain forms of moral character and encourage certain moral virtues" (PL: 194). This encouragement is based on its minimal moral conception, which includes political virtues such as toleration, reasonableness, civic friendship, and a sense of fairness. If a liberal democratic constitutional regime takes certain steps to strengthen the virtues of toleration and mutual trust, say by discouraging various kinds of religious and racial discrimination (in ways consistent with liberty of conscience and freedom of speech), it does not thereby become a perfectionist state, and neither does it establish a particular religion, becoming therewith a theocracy. Rather, as Rawls argues, "it is taking reasonable measures to strengthen the forms of thought and feeling that sustain fair social cooperation between its citizens regarded as free and equal" (PL: 195). All of this, Rawls claims, is very different from the state's advancing a particular comprehensive doctrine in its own name, using its authority or even by exercising its powers. That after all is what political liberalism wants to avoid.

Another implication, as Rawls explains, is that "the notion of the omnicompetent laicist state is also denied, since from the principles of justice it follows that government has neither the right nor the duty to do what it or a majority (or whatever) wants to do in questions of morals and religion. Its duty is limited to underwriting the conditions of equal moral and religious liberty" (TJ: 212; TJR: 186–187).

Political liberalism and Enlightenment liberalism

The foregoing shows that political liberalism differs sharply from Enlightenment liberalism. It rejects this form of liberalism, which historically attacked orthodox Christianity (LoP: 176). Political liberalism is not comprehensive liberalism, as Enlightenment liberalism is: "a comprehensive liberal and often secular doctrine founded on reason and viewed as suitable for the modern age now that the religious authority of Christian ages is said to be no longer dominant" (PL: xl).

One can add that presently Enlightenment liberalism often shows a "religious" zeal to convert the world. Therewith it degenerates into an "Enlightenment fundamentalism" that is characterized by showing itself to have as little doubt as strong believers have, and in this way such a secular doctrine continues to have convictions, patterns of thinking, and a lack of toleration that are on a par with the way of thinking of fundamentalist religious doctrines.

This is not what political liberalism entails. Political liberalism as developed by Rawls is averse to haughtiness, to dogmatism, to messianism, and to stigmatizing dissenters; much less would it endorse a liberal *jihad*. Nobody can be forced to be "free." The kernel of political liberalism is the call to also bring one's own suppositions and prejudices into question, and to not start from a universal fundamental Truth (be it based on Reason, Allah, or God). In that sense political liberalism is itself, of course, a child of the Enlightenment: "*Sapere aude!*" "Have courage to use your own reason!"

A central characteristic of political liberalism is that it considers each religious, philosophical, or moral doctrine to be comprehensive: religious ones, but nonreligious, secular ones as well. From this perspective there is no difference between secular and religious doctrines. Secular philosophical doctrines, as we noted earlier, also do not provide public reasons, generally shared and endorsed, on which political values can be based. Let us recall that this also means that Rawls is of the opinion that even a society united on the reasonable comprehensive Enlightenment liberalisms of classical liberals such as Kant or J. S. Mill would, paradoxically, eventually require the sanctions of state power to remain so (PL: 37; JaF: 34). The problem with these Enlightenment philosophers is that while it is true that they see it as their role to emancipate individuals from the paternalism of tradition and outlived collective norms by teaching them critical thinking, it is also true that their ideals for fostering the values of autonomy, individuality, and reasonableness – in contrast to the political liberalism of Rawls – do not stop at the public political sphere of society, but permeate all spheres, including the non-public and the private spheres. Thus these ideals of autonomy and individuality can degenerate into ideals that dominate much if not all of life (PL: 199; JaF: 156). In that sense, this classical liberalism is a comprehensive doctrine, formulating a determinate conception of the good. Although a liberal philosophical and moral doctrine such as that of Kant or J. S. Mill can affirm, endorse, and support, or so one may reasonably hope, a reasonable overlapping consensus, it cannot be part of a political conception of justice (JaF: 33, 191).

Political liberalism has a different aim and requires far less. It emphasizes on the one hand the value of diversity and toleration, and on the other the value of autonomy. We should, however, be very clear about how Rawls understands the value of autonomy in the context of political liberalism. Citizens can see autonomy as a purely moral value that characterizes a certain way of life and reflection, critically examining our deepest ends and ideals, as for instance in J. S. Mill's ideas of individuality or Kant's doctrine of autonomy. Autonomy as a purely moral value, however, fails to satisfy, given reasonable pluralism, the constraint of (the criterion of) reciprocity. Given this fact of reasonable pluralism, it is not a value that can support an overlapping consensus because citizens holding certain religious doctrines may reject this kind of autonomy. Moral autonomy is not a political value. Political autonomy, on the other hand, is.[59]

For Rawls, then, autonomy does not refer to a certain way of life, but to the legal independence (guaranteed by basic rights and liberties) and assured political integrity of citizens who, in deliberation with other citizens, are exploring reasonable acceptable rules for political cooperation. In this context, autonomy is the legal and political autonomy to live a life according to self-chosen aims and beliefs, which can then also be a choice for traditionalism and heteronomy as part of a certain mode of life (PL: xliv–xlv, 98; LoP: 146). This conception of autonomy, then, does not preclude those conceptions of the good that reject the project of modernity and the culture of the modern world (PL: 200; JaF: 157).

Political liberalism emphasizes that freedom of thought and liberty of conscience do exist, and that public law does not recognize heresy and apostasy (from whichever religion or belief) as crimes, and that members of churches are always at liberty to leave their faith (JaF: 164).

Therefore "children's education [should] include such things as knowledge of their constitutional and civic rights, so that, for example, they know that liberty of conscience exists in their society and that apostasy is not a legal crime, all this to insure that their continued religious membership when they come of age is not based simply on ignorance of their basic rights or fear of punishment for offenses that are only considered offenses within their religious sect" (JaF: 156; PL: 199). Put another way, such membership should be based only on an autonomous choice, freely made, and the liberty to eventually leave a (religious, or any other kind of) sect, is part of the basic rights that are constitutionally guaranteed to each and every citizen.

Political liberalism is thus not only not indifferent to (the content of) education, but also not neutral in effects and influences. It *wants* the shared political values to be taught and encouraged, so that children are taught the importance of, for instance, tolerance of diversity, and of fighting prejudices. Children have to learn the meaning of these political principles and the historical and cultural perspective from which they have to be understood.

The fact of diversity in religious, philosophical, and moral views means that the willingness to coexist peacefully with ways of life very different from one's own is essential. A liberal democratic state is thus not neutral with regard to elements that a core, standard curriculum should contain. It should teach children the essentials of political liberalism. How else to learn the importance of its shared political values, such as tolerance for diversity, than by confronting children in school with a diversity of beliefs, for instance with regard to religious beliefs, and to explicate to them that what they consider to be "the whole truth," based on these beliefs, has to be suspended within the political domain?

Because exposure to a diversity of beliefs – without any one of them being imposed, or propagated as the only correct one – is a necessary means of teaching the basic virtues of political life (toleration, respect, reasonableness, a spirit of compromise) and the duty of public civility, political liberalism cannot allow a basic right to exemption in education. The basic question is whether parents have the right to withdraw their children from schooling that is intended to teach the values of political liberalism because such education will make it difficult for parents to convey their own specific beliefs, for instance religious ones. The answer is unequivocal: "No, parents do not have that right."[60]

These arguments also determine the position of political liberalism with regard to denominational education (private schooling), as opposed to public (state) schooling. In a private Islamic, Christian, or secular school, for instance, children can of course be taught the specifics of their own culture, religion, and language. But they also have to be taught a core, standard curriculum, analogous to the one in state schools, which teaches them the essentials of political liberalism, the importance of its shared political values such as toleration of diversity, the duty of civility, and civic friendship. Raising some awareness that there are alternative choices in life is not only a requirement of democratic citizenship, it also is a necessity to enable everyone to make these fundamental choices for themselves.

A liberal democratic state, then, is not neutral with regard to the content of the standard curriculum, regardless of whether we have in mind public, state-sponsored schooling or private, denominational schooling. The scheme of equal basic liberties for all requires limiting our own liberties, and also those liberties we would perhaps like to have in making our own choice with regard to the way our children should be educated.

The question, of course, is whether the outcome of this education in core principles of political liberalism can be reconciled with honoring non-public ethical or religious beliefs. This view on education can result, as we have just mentioned, in a clash between the content of that education and the desire of parents to pass their way of life on to their children. Schooling with the intention that children learn the values of political liberalism has the unavoidable effect that it encourages some ways of life and discourages others. In fact, the state-sponsored pursuit of liberal educational aims could threaten the future of some traditional religious and moral understandings, and thus of some diversity (PL: 199–200). In this regard, it looks as though political liberalism is wrongly hostile to certain ways of life and biased in favor of others (JaF: 157). Is this not to be considered intolerably oppressive?

Rawls' answer is that unavoidable consequences of reasonable requirements for children's education may have to be accepted. The issue of whether these requirements are permissible is answered entirely within the political conception of justice, and should remain so. As long as the political values of toleration for diversity are not widely shared and are still fragile, this is inevitable when instituting political liberal education in imperfect liberal democratic societies.

In discussing the issue of "education" from the perspective of political liberalism, we are in fact discussing the use and scope of public reason. And we can conclude from this discussion that political liberalism does not regard the political and the non-political domain as two completely separate disconnected spaces, as it were, each governed solely by its own distinct principles. In political liberalism, or so Rawls strongly believes, there is no such thing as a "private domain," or a private sphere of life that is exempt from *justice as fairness* (JaF: 166). Let us illustrate this with another example, that of the family.

The principles of justice do have an impact on what is at first sight the private sphere of the family. To be precise: the principles of a political conception of justice, it is true, are not to apply directly to the internal life of the family, but they do formulate essential constraints with regard to the family as an institution. They guarantee to each family member basic rights and liberties and fair equality of opportunity (CP: 595–601; JaF: 162–168; LoP: 156–164).[61] This is so because these principles specify the basic claims of equal citizenship, and members of a family are also, and at the same time, citizens. The institution of the "family" is part of the basic structure of society and cannot prevent these freedoms from "entering the home," so to speak. Since wives are equally citizens with their husbands, they all have the same basic rights and liberties and fair opportunities as their husbands. This should suffice, according to Rawls – together with the correct application of the other principles of justice – to secure their equality and independence. Grown-up members of a family are in the first place equal citizens: that is the fundamental starting point (JaF: 164).

Just as the principles of justice require that wives have all the rights of citizens, the principles of justice impose constraints on the family on behalf of children (constraints such as prohibition of abuse and neglect, and much else), who, as society's future citizens, have basic rights as such. The equal basic rights of women and the basic rights of children are inalienable and protect them wherever they are (JaF: 165; LoP: 160).

Let us recapitulate: the primary subject of the principles of justice is the basic structure of society, understood as the arrangement of society's main institutions into a unified system of social cooperation over time. The principles of a political conception of justice do not apply directly to the internal life of many associations within the basic structure, to for instance churches and universities, to professional and scientific associations, to business firms and labor unions, or to the internal life of families (JaF: 163–164). Associations, groups, or unions, they all have their own "sphere" or "domain," and in all cases there are particular, specific conceptions of justice appropriate to their nature and role at hand. But, just as in the example of the family, because the members of these associations, groups, and unions are also citizens, the political principles of justice do protect their rights and liberties. The principles of the political conception of justice do impose certain essential constraints on the internal governance of associations, groups, or unions within the basic structure.

From *A Theory of Justice* to *Political Liberalism*

As we have mentioned, the kernel of political liberalism is also the call to question one's own prejudices and beliefs. But political liberalism does not address this call to unreasonable persons or to unreasonable and irrational, and even mad, religious, philosophical, or moral doctrines. Rawls has no illusion about the fundamentalist being open to public reason. Nor is he of the opinion that their beliefs should be taken into account. The issue is rather how to keep the fundamentalist under control so as not to threaten the social unity and justice of society (PL: xix). Consequently political liberalism has, if necessary, to be without compromise and to take a tough stand.

Referring to Carl Schmitt's critique of parliamentary democracy and the downfall of the Weimar constitutional regime, Rawls emphasizes the importance that should be attached to formulating convincing arguments, public reasons for a just and well-ordered stable constitutional democracy. The situation in the Wilhelmine Germany of Bismarck's time that persisted into the Weimar regime with its disastrous outcome, was one of a weak political will to achieve a constitutional regime (PL: lxii note 39; LHPP: 8–9). The lessons of Weimar are not a call for a strong leader. The lessons are to formulate the requirements for strong democracy: a situation where principles of political morality are a settled part of the public political culture and presupposed and operating in the background.

This example lays out the magnitude of the role of public justification if it has to show that stability for the right reasons is at least possible for a democratic society marked by reasonable pluralism. And this "stability for the right reasons" means "stability brought about by citizens acting correctly according to the appropriate principles of their sense of justice, which they have acquired by growing up under and participating in just institutions" (LoP: 13 note 2). It explains the importance Rawls attaches to public reason in his view on justice. It is a role, it is fair to say, that over the years has become more and more central to him. As Rawls himself remarks:

> If we can make the case that there are adequate reasons for diverse reasonable people jointly to affirm justice as fairness as their working political conception, then the conditions for their legitimately exercising coercive political power over one another – something we inevitably do as citizens by voting, if in no other way – are satisfied. … The argument, if successful, would show how we can reasonably affirm and appeal to a political conception of justice as citizens' shared basis of reasons, all the while supposing that others, no less reasonable than we, may also affirm and recognize that same basis. Despite the fact of reasonable pluralism, the conditions for democratic legitimacy are fulfilled. (PL: 390)

Will public reason be successful in doing this? Rawls notes that there are limits to reconciliation by public reason. Three main kinds of conflicts set citizens at odds: those conflicts deriving from citizens' conflicting, irreconcilable comprehensive doctrines; those conflicts deriving from their different status, class position, or occupation, or those deriving from differences in ethnicity, gender, or race; and, finally, those conflicts resulting from the burdens of judgment (PL: lx; LoP: 177).

Political liberalism mitigates but cannot eliminate the first kind of conflict. Even though comprehensive religious, philosophical, and moral doctrines are irreconcilable, the intention of the project of "political liberalism" is to show that citizens share public reasons given in terms of political conceptions of justice and can thus endorse a reasonably just constitutional regime.

It is the second kind of conflicts, those deriving from differences in status, class position, or occupation, or from ethnicity, gender, or race, conflicts between citizens' fundamental interests, that can be largely removed by the principles of justice of a reasonably just constitutional regime. Once principles of justice that satisfy the criterion of reciprocity and are thus seen as reasonable (being a member of the family of political conceptions of justice) are accepted, or even accepted as the most reasonable one (*justice as fairness*), the second kind of conflict need no longer arise, or arise so forcefully.

A source of these conflicts could also be differences of nationality and culture. During our exposition on political liberalism we have argued that political liberalism takes into account the given that actual liberal democratic societies are not only not homogenous with regard to comprehensive doctrines, but also that many are characterized by multicultural and/or multi-ethnic heterogeneity. We touch here on what J.S. Mill has described as the issue of "common sympathies." Mill formulates as the requirement for "being united by common sympathies and a desire to be under the same democratic government," the idea that this is entirely dependent "upon a common language, history, and political culture, with a shared historical consciousness." But if indeed, as Rawls notes, this idea of homogeneity would be the requirement for common sympathies, "this feature would rarely, if ever, be fully satisfied. Historical conquests and immigration have caused the intermingling of groups with different cultures and historical memories who now reside within the territory of most contemporary democratic governments" (LoP: 24).[62]

We have to recognize that citizens do not all share a common language and identical historical memories, and that there is also no simple match of language and territory. However, within a reasonable just constitutional regime it is possible to accommodate the reasonable cultural interests and needs of groups with diverse ethnic and national backgrounds. The political principles of a just constitutional regime allow us to deal with a great variety of cases, if not with all (LoP: 25). Accordingly, Rawls believes that a just constitutional regime whose principles of political justice satisfy the criterion of reciprocity may also deal fairly with differences of culture and nationality (separating the idea of a nation from the idea of government or state) (PL: lx note 37; LoP: 25 note 20).

Turning to the third kind of conflicts, those arising from the burdens of judgment will always remain. This, as Rawls acknowledges, limits the extent of possible agreement (PL: lx; JaF: 35–37, 197; LoP: 177). Burdens of judgment raise problems on several levels, so to speak.

Now, one may wonder if it is realistic to hope that citizens might actually achieve agreement on *justice as fairness* by the process of public reason over time under fair and just institutions, despite the fact of reasonable pluralism? We cannot be sure. The burdens of judgment account for our uncertainty here and explain that there are, for instance, several political conceptions of justice. One reason for hope, however, lies in the central role to be played by the criterion of reciprocity.

But burdens of judgment remain haunting us. Even if, by shared public reason, agreement on *justice as fairness* has been achieved and a just constitutional regime for the right reasons is established, we encounter the burdens of judgment once again. And here lies the essential role allocated to legitimacy. As we have noted, the exercise of political power is legitimate only when it is exercised in fundamental cases in accordance with a constitution, the essentials of which all free and equal citizens might reasonably be expected to endorse. "Thus, citizens recognize the familiar distinction between accepting as (sufficiently) just and legitimate a constitution with its procedures for fair elections and legislative majorities, and accepting as legitimate (even when not just) a particular statute or a decision in a particular matter of policy" (PL: 393).[63]

Recall that this is an issue we have encountered earlier and which we have extensively debated in our exposition of the "four-stage sequence." In designing fair background institutions the issue turned out to be that even in an ideal situation a democratic constitution must include procedures of majority (or other plurality) voting to reach decisions, and that reasonable disagreement may continue to exist on questions of which specific legislation is most fit for matters of basic justice. The aim of course remained to give a sketch of background institutions that satisfy the principles of *justice as fairness*, and that would result in pure procedural justice, both with regard to the political process and with regard to distributive shares. We have, however, seen that we have to fall back on a notion of what Rawls calls "quasi-pure procedural justice": as long as the laws and policies that are chosen are ones that lie within the permitted range, they are equally just.

The shift to legitimacy rather than justice is important here. Legitimacy is a weaker idea than (political) justice and imposes weaker constraints on what can be done. This difference between legitimacy and justice points out that the outcome of a collective decision, if reached by a sufficiently just procedure (supported by a just constitution), may be legitimate but not just by a strict standard of justice. Thus the enactments and legislation of all institutional procedures should always be regarded by citizens as open to question (PL: 428–431). The burdens of judgment leave us no other choice than to come to this conclusion. But our considered judgments with their fixed points, our sense of justice, our ideas on reciprocity, are always in the background as substantive checks on the outcomes of legitimate legislative procedures.

This brings once more to the fore a shift in focus between *A Theory of Justice* and *Political Liberalism*: the shift from presenting *justice as fairness* as a liberal comprehensive doctrine to the question of how, acknowledging the fact of a plurality of reasonable comprehensive doctrines in modern democratic societies, a reasonable political conception of justice that supports a constitutional democratic society can be endorsed by citizens who also endorse one or other comprehensive doctrine. We can also note a shift in attention from the central role played in *A Theory of Justice* by the "mediating" conception of the original position, with its arguments for reasoning from shared premises, to the focus in *Political Liberalism* on another "mediating" conception: the idea of public reason with its own reasoning from shared premises. But we should be careful here: of course both *A Theory of Justice* and *Political Liberalism* have an idea of public reason. The difference is that in the first case "public reason" is given by a liberal comprehensive doctrine, while in the second case, in political liberalism, public reason is a way of reasoning about political values shared by free and equal citizens, while citizens do not share the same comprehensive doctrine.

This shift in focus to issues raised by religious, philosophical, and moral pluralism has often been interpreted as if issues of, for instance, social and economic inequality have disappeared from Rawls' agenda. Thinking this is, however, a mistake. The fact that *Political Liberalism* does not take up these types of conflicts, or does not explicitly consider them, does not mean that Rawls thinks them no longer relevant. It only means that we have to turn to *A Theory of Justice* to see how they can be settled by *justice as fairness*. This underlines once more how Rawls' work as a whole hangs together. Not mentioning or considering a specific issue in *Political Liberalism* does not mean that an earlier answer is no longer valid. And if it is not, Rawls explicitly says so.

A distinctive aspect of *Political Liberalism* stems from a concern to reconcile *social unity* and *moral pluralism*, resulting in a stable liberal, democratic, and just society. In doing this we have seen that Rawls concentrates in *Political Liberalism* on the first principle of justice. In fact how and when to tolerate religious comprehensive doctrines appears to be the main focus of his attention. There is no reason to belittle the relevance of a theory that justifies consensus on basic liberties, on freedom of expression and of association, and that proclaims a tolerant attitude to differences in general.

But, or so one may wonder, is reaching consensus on a Rawlsian first principle of justice enough to guarantee over time a stable and just society of free and equal citizens, who are not only profoundly divided by reasonable though incompatible religious, philosophical, and moral doctrines, but where there are also conflicts deriving from differences in status, class position, or occupation, or from differences in ethnicity, gender, or race?

We have seen that Rawls' concern with recasting the account of stability to bring it in line with the fact of reasonable pluralism, and removing inconsistencies from his original theory as formulated in *A Theory of Justice*, has had no consequence for his ideas on what the most reasonable political conception of justice is. The egalitarian elements of his original project are still in place.

The original intention of *justice as fairness* was to solve the disagreement about how the values of liberty, equality, and fraternity (or reciprocity) were best realized in the basic structure of society. *A Theory of Justice* had shown a possible way of solving that issue. One of the inspiring elements of *A Theory of Justice* was the permanent attention it paid to the least advantaged members of society. The essence of this idea is well captured in Rawls' own words, quoted earlier: "Justice as fairness will prove a worthwhile theory if it defines the range of justice more in accordance with our considered judgments than do existing theories, and if it singles out with greater sharpness the graver wrongs a society should avoid" (TJ: 201; TJR: 176).

This is still the underlying motivation of *Political Liberalism*. Of course, a theory that justifies a tolerant attitude is an extremely relevant one. But legitimate toleration of differences in the sphere of beliefs and ideas does not necessarily mean that unequal access to goods and services is equally to be tolerated. Toleration does not extend to all kinds of differences. Joshua Cohen has remarked that the "*acknowledgement of diversity* underscored by an overlapping consensus does not undercut the *critique of privilege* contained in the egalitarian aspects of egalitarian liberalism."[64] It does not and should not, and Rawls would certainly agree. The democratic conception of the justice of toleration should not develop into toleration of unreasonable inequalities.

The implication of "political liberalism" is not that stability, or rather social unity, can be achieved by the legitimate toleration of differences in the sphere of beliefs while negating the issue of natural and social contingencies and dealing in a fair way with undeserved advantages. Political liberalism does not lead to that conclusion. This, on due reflection, is the considered implication of Rawls' own analysis.

4 | *International justice*

The aim of Rawls

Both *A Theory of Justice* and *Political Liberalism* give a sketch of a just liberal democratic society. In both studies Rawls has formulated his ideas on democratic equality for a closed and self-contained society, isolated from other societies. The focus is on separated societies, each regulated by its own basic structure. In all countries the production of goods and services is autarkic: each country relies entirely on its own labor and resources without trade of any kind.

From the moment *A Theory of Justice* was published in 1971, criticism was formulated that by this focus on a "self-contained society" Rawls had confined himself to a theory that is applicable only to a closed political community, a nation-state that both has no contact with, and is not influenced by, the rest of the world.

However, one should immediately add in response to this criticism that it was Rawls himself who had pointed to the limits of the scope of his project. At an early stage (in 1971, in *A Theory of Justice*) he stipulated that he would "be satisfied if it is possible to formulate a reasonable conception of justice for the basic structure of society conceived for the time being as a closed system isolated from other societies" (TJ: 8; TJR: 7). The question of justice between nation-states would be postponed until he had formulated an account of justice for a well-ordered democratic society (JaF: 13).

Apart from that, Rawls had in *A Theory of Justice*, albeit not in depth, already dealt with the issue of a just cause in war (*ius ad bellum*), with the issue of regulating the means a nation may use to wage a war (*ius in bello*), and the related issues of conscientious refusal to serve in an unjust war and civil disobedience. In *A Theory of Justice* one also can find indications of how to extend the theory of justice to the law of nations. To this purpose the interpretation of the social contract idea is used once again, but in this instance the parties in the original position are seen as representatives of different *nations* who must together choose the fundamental principles for adjudicating conflicting claims among states (TJ: 363–391; TJR: 319–343). These are political principles, for they govern public policies toward other nations. The basic principle of the law of nations is a principle of equality. Independent peoples organized as states have certain fundamental equal rights. This principle is analogous to the equal rights of citizens in a constitutional regime. The consequences of this equality of nations are the principle of self-determination, the principle of the right of self-defense, and the principle that treaties are to be kept. They are part of the basic principles of "the law of nations" (TJ: 378; TJR: 331–332).

Nearly thirty years later, in 1999, with the monograph *The Law of Peoples*, Rawls now fully extends his theory of justice to the international domain. With this study we have arrived at the third phase of Rawls' development of his theory of justice. *The Law of Peoples* is concerned with the question of how an "international Society of liberal and decent *Peoples*" might be possible. With this Rawls has constructed the final, "missing" part of his theory of justice: one that applies to the principles and norms of international law and practice. The question is how to give to these principles a scope that surpasses that of the nation-state, of a closed-off political community. The procedure developed by Rawls for selecting and justifying these principles of justice for the international case has an analogy with how the principles of justice are justified in the domestic case. Again the procedure is based on the familiar idea of the social contract. The interpretation of the original position (including the idea of a veil of ignorance) is extended and now one thinks of the parties as representatives of different *peoples*.

And, once again, Kant is a source of inspiration: in this case Kant's ideas formulated in his *Perpetual Peace* (*Zum ewigen Frieden*, 1795) and his idea of *foedus pacificum* ("a league of peace").[1] In Rawls' monograph the right to war is discussed. Also, in the context of a discussion on the principles formulating the moral limits governing the conduct of democratic peoples at war, the question is raised as to how far during the Second World War the fire-bombings of Tokyo and other Japanese cities in the spring of 1945, as well as the dropping of the atomic bombs on Hiroshima and on Nagasaki, could be justified (they cannot according to Rawls: they were very grave wrongs), and until what moment during the Second World War the bombing by Great Britain of German cities was arguably justifiable, and when it could no longer be justified (the bombing of Dresden).[2]

The focus in *The Law of Peoples* is, as in the domestic case, on institutions. In the international context political, social and economic institutions are also "men made." They can be designed by us, and if necessary be adapted, changed, or recast, analogous to institutions in domestic societies. The international political and social institutional order is not fixed, as the domestic order is not.

Justice among Peoples

Crucial for understanding Rawls' ideas on international justice is that there is, according to him, a radical difference between the principles of justice for the international case and those for the domestic one. The democratic and egalitarian principles of the domestic case are not directly applicable to international relations. First of all, on the international stage the moral actors are not persons. For Rawls it is organized territorial national collectivities: *peoples*. His theory of international justice is a theory on "the international society of peoples." In Rawls' account, "liberal democratic peoples" (and, as we will see later, "decent peoples" as well) are the actors in "the Society of Peoples," just as citizens are the actors in domestic society. What counts in these relations is the moral equality of peoples: peoples have a certain moral character, and they have moral motives (as actors). Thus Rawls does not formulate a theory of an "international society of states." States are entities that strive for their basic national interest, regardless of the effects this has on non-citizens, and a state's power of sovereignty also grants it a certain autonomy in dealing with its own people. States are not moved by moral motives, but are always guided by their basic interests, and are mainly concerned with their own power, prestige, and wealth. Rawls completely and without hesitation distances himself from this dominant and typical view of the realist theory of international relations in which states are conceived as amoral, rational entities pursuing their self-interest.

For peoples, on the other hand, the traditionally conceived ideas with regard to the sovereignty of states do not hold. Peoples deny to states the traditional rights to war and to unrestricted internal sovereignty or (political) autonomy; the state's alleged right to do as it will with its own people within its own borders (LoP: 26–27). Liberal peoples have three basic features: (i) the institutions are those of a reasonably just (though not necessarily fully just) democratic government that serves their fundamental interests (these "fundamental interests" will be elaborated on later, debating the idea of the original position on an international level), and where a priority holds for basic rights to which citizens always can appeal; (ii) citizens united by the – cultural – desire for being united under the same democratic government (the issue we have discussed in the context of political liberalism as one of "common sympathies"); and (iii) peoples (as opposed to states) have a moral nature, a firm attachment to a political (moral) conception of right and justice (LoP: 23–24, 23 note 17).

The aim is to extend the Law of Peoples that is accepted by liberal democratic peoples to other societies, and to show that other peoples accept the same Law of Peoples that liberal peoples do. For this purpose Rawls introduces a typology of peoples in which respect for human rights is a major criterion. Honoring human rights is what makes the distinction between what Rawls calls "well-ordered peoples" and not-well-ordered peoples.

To "well-ordered peoples" belong, of course, "liberal democratic peoples," but also, according to Rawls, nonliberal societies that are nevertheless peaceful and do not have aggressive aims and who recognize that they must gain legitimate ends through diplomacy and trade, and other ways of peace. These are "*decent peoples.*" The basic structure of one kind of decent people has what Rawls calls a "decent consultation hierarchy" and these peoples he calls "decent hierarchical peoples." It is this kind of decent peoples Rawls discusses in *The Law of Peoples.* Each decent hierarchical people secures for all its members basic human rights and a specific form of political representation and participation ("a decent consultation hierarchy"). But decent hierarchical peoples are not completely in line with the ideal of liberal democracies. They lag for instance behind with regard to the rights of individuals. Not all members of a decent hierarchical people are regarded as free and equal citizens, nor as separate individuals deserving equal representation (according to the maxim: one citizen, one vote). But, as we have said, the legal system and social order of a decent hierarchical society does not violate human rights. The rights that are secured for each and every member of the people of decent hierarchical societies – and that of course also hold for each and every person in liberal democratic societies – are the following:

– to life (to the means of subsistence and security);
– to liberty (to freedom from slavery, serfdom, and forced occupation, and to a sufficient measure of liberty of conscience to ensure freedom of religion and thought);
– to property (personal property); and
– to formal equality as expressed by the rules of natural justice (that is, that similar cases be treated similarly) (LoP: 65).

In short, these human rights express a special class of urgent rights that, according to Rawls, cannot be rejected as peculiarly liberal or special to the Western tradition: they cannot be considered as ethnocentric. The list of human rights should be understood as universal rights, they are intrinsic to the Law of Peoples and have political (moral) effect whether or not they are supported locally. Their political (moral) force extends to all societies, and they are binding on all peoples and societies (LoP: 80–81).

All decent peoples recognize these human rights as necessary conditions of any system of social cooperation (LoP: 68). Put another way, these rights do not depend on any particular comprehensive religious doctrine, or philosophical doctrine of human nature, that a decent people may adhere to. Neither are they dependent on the way a particular comprehensive doctrine influences the way government is organized or political decisions are made. Although comprehensive religious and philosophical doctrines may have different ideas on justice, these human rights are politically uncontested. Thus, although these human rights are part of comprehensive religious or philosophical doctrines, they do not specify a political conception of justice in the Rawlsian sense (LoP: 64).

Although all persons in a decent hierarchical society are not regarded as free and equal citizens, nor as separate individuals deserving equal representation, each person is seen as a responsible and cooperating member of a specific group to which they belong, and each person engages in distinctive activities and plays a certain role in the overall scheme of cooperation (LoP: 66, 72). Each of these groups is represented in the consultation hierarchy, and in political decision making a decent consultation hierarchy allows each group to be heard. Finally, judges and other officials must have a sincere and not unreasonable belief that the legal system is guided by a "common good idea of justice," that takes into account what it sees as the fundamental interest of everyone in society (LoP: 67). The system of law (and social order) guarantees all members of a people human rights, regardless of viewing them as belonging to an "associationist social form" in which persons are seen first as members of groups – associations, corporations, and estates – and where the internal arrangements of these groups may allow basic inequalities among their members (LoP: 68).

Rawls distinguishes, along with "*liberal peoples*" and "*decent hierarchical peoples*," three other types of domestic societies. First of all, there are *outlaw states*. These are aggressive states in which the regime thinks that a sufficient reason to engage in war is that war advances, or might advance, the regime's rational (not reasonable) interests (LoP: 90). Outlaw states cannot be part of an international Society of Peoples. As Rawls conceives the list of human rights to be a list of universal rights, their reach is global and thus outlaw states should also honor them. Liberal and decent peoples should not only condemn outlaw states that violate these rights, they may pressure the outlaw regimes to change their ways (LoP: 81). In grave cases they may subject outlaw states to forceful (diplomatic and economic) sanctions. Eventually they have the right to forceful (humanitarian) intervention, if these outlaw states persist in violating human rights. Liberal and decent peoples simply do not tolerate outlaw states (LoP: 81). Regime change is what should be the objective, and outlaw states can eventually be forced to change their ways.

Next to these three types of domestic regimes (liberal peoples, decent peoples, outlaw states), there are societies whose historical, social, and economic circumstances are such that their achieving a well-ordered regime, whether liberal or decent, is difficult if not impossible. They lack the political and cultural traditions, the human capital and know-how, and often the material and technological resources needed to be well-ordered (LoP: 90, 106). These societies Rawls calls *societies burdened by unfavorable conditions*, "burdened societies" for short. Fifth, and finally, we have societies that are *benevolent absolutisms*. They honor most human rights, but because they deny their members a meaningful role in making political decisions, they are not well-ordered (LoP: 63).

Justification in *The Law of Peoples*

The theoretical framework of *The Law of Peoples* is developed and worked out of political liberalism (LoP: 7). Rawls stresses, over and over again, that it "is important to see that the Law of Peoples is developed within political liberalism and is an extension of a liberal conception of justice for a domestic regime to a Society of Peoples. I emphasize that, in developing the Law of Peoples within a liberal conception of justice, we work out the ideals and principles of the *foreign policy* of a reasonably just *liberal* people. This concern with the foreign policy of a liberal people is implicit throughout" (LoP: 9–10).[3] Put another way: international justice, or the Law of Peoples, "is developed within political liberalism" (LoP: 9). "Justice as fairness starts with domestic justice – the justice of the basic structure. From there it works outward to the Law of Peoples and inward to local justice" (JaF: 11). Or, once again, in developing the Law of Peoples, Rawls says "that liberal societies ask how they are to conduct themselves toward other societies from the point of view of their *own* political conception."

In extending political liberalism to international justice it is not surprising that, once again, "social contract," "pluralism," the issue that principles have to be "fine-tuned," "the original position," and "the idea of public reason" play a central role. But now the issue is to formulate principles of justice that can – on specific conditions – be the focus of an agreement among peoples in the Society of Peoples.

Rawls' first step is to investigate which principles should be valid as the Law of Peoples between liberal democratic peoples. For that purpose, the liberal idea of the social contract is extended to the Law of Peoples. Just as with the choice of the principles of justice in the domestic case, where all free and equal, reasonable and rational, citizens (by their representatives) are brought together behind a veil of ignorance in the (first use of) the original position to specify fair terms of cooperation regulating the basic structure of society, Rawls now brings together liberal *peoples* by their representatives (and thus not representatives of all world-inhabitants), behind a veil of ignorance – adjusted for the case at hand – in the second use of the original position on a "higher," international level, an original position among (liberal) peoples, to specify the Law of Peoples. (It is thus not a "global original position," as argued for by some "Rawlsian cosmopolitans.")[4]

It is precisely here that we no longer speak about "global citizens" or "citizens of the world," but about "peoples." The public political culture of international organizations, conventions, and treaties, is international, not interpersonal. International political institutions see peoples as free and equal, not as persons. This is the reason that peoples are the subject of Rawls' international theory of justice. As a source of claims to moral equality in the theory of international politics, "a people" is analogous to a free and equal citizen in the domestic case.

Thus it is (the representatives of) liberal peoples who, in the setting of this (second) original position, behind a veil of ignorance, and thus situated symmetrically and therefore fairly, have to specify the principles of the Law of Peoples, guided by appropriate reasons (LoP: 32). The veil of ignorance excludes in this (second) original position information on, for example, the size of the territory that each of the parties represents, and information on the size of the population. And although the representatives know that reasonable favorable conditions obtain that make constitutional democracy possible – they represent after all *liberal* societies – they do not know the extent of their natural resources, or the level of their economic development, or other such information (LoP: 32–33).

These characteristics of the second original position together model what we would regard – "you and I," "here and now," as citizens of some liberal democratic society, but not of the same one – as the fair conditions for specifying the basic terms of cooperation among peoples who, as liberal peoples, see themselves as free and equal (LoP: 32, 33). The question to be answered is: What is the outcome of this deliberation between representatives of liberal peoples in the second original position? Which principles are selected that should be designated as the reasonably just political and social rules for a "Society of Liberal Peoples"?

The use Rawls makes of the idea of the original position at this second level among liberal peoples is precisely the same as the use that was made of this idea in *Political Liberalism* in the domestic case. There it was used in a society characterized by a diversity of conflicting but reasonable comprehensive doctrines, religious and nonreligious, liberal and nonliberal. The role of a thick veil of ignorance in the domestic case was to deny to the representatives of citizens in their deliberations any knowledge of citizens' (comprehensive or non-comprehensive) conceptions of the good. On the international level, however, the veil of ignorance does not exclude or ignore the knowledge of the people's comprehensive conceptions of the good. There is no need to exclude that knowledge: a liberal society with a constitutional regime after all simply does not have *as a liberal society* a comprehensive conception of the good. A liberal society is not founded on a comprehensive religious or nonreligious, liberal or nonliberal, comprehensive doctrine. That is precisely the core idea behind a society that is regulated by political liberalism. It is only the citizens within the civic society in the domestic case who have conceptions of the good, that each and every citizen bases on either a comprehensive, or on a non-comprehensive, doctrine (LoP: 34).

Thus although the use made of the idea of the original position on this second, international, level is the same as on the domestic level, the original position has to be properly adjusted for the case at hand. In this situation the representatives are representatives of liberal peoples, and the aim is to specify principles of international justice. And liberal peoples who consider themselves as free and equal have their own fundamental interests with regard to their democratic societies, where these interests are expressed by the liberal principles of justice for a democratic society. (Just as citizens in the domestic case have their own fundamental interests.) The interests of liberal peoples are specified by their reasonable conception of political justice: they seek to protect their territory, to preserve their independence, to guarantee the well-being and security of their citizens, and to preserve their free political institutions and the liberties and free culture of their *civil society*. But Rawls adds here a significant further interest, what Rousseau calls "*amour-propre*," but now applied to peoples. This interest is "a people's proper self-respect of themselves as a people," the pride a people has, based on their common awareness of their trials during their history and of their culture with its accomplishments (LoP: 29, 34).

Altogether distinct "from their self-concern for their security and the safety of their territory, this interest shows itself," or so Rawls argues, "in a people's insisting on receiving from other peoples a proper respect and recognition of their equality" (LoP: 34–35).

Here we should note, once again, an essential distinction between "states" and "peoples": just peoples are fully prepared to grant the very same proper respect and recognition to other peoples as equals. At the same time, however, this kind of equality, equality of respect, does not mean that in various institutions in which peoples cooperate certain kinds of inequalities are not agreed to, or are not considered to be acceptable. There are inequalities that are acceptable. Note here, once more, a parallel or analogy with the domestic case: in liberal societies citizens do accept functional social and economic inequalities. Not each and every kind of inequality is "unjust," not in the domestic case, and neither in the international context (LoP: 35).

Liberal peoples have a moral character. They are, just like citizens in the domestic case, reasonable and rational. They are thus ready to offer to other peoples fair terms of political and social cooperation. These fair terms are those that a people sincerely believes other equal peoples might also accept; and there is also a sincere belief that a people will honor the terms it has proposed, even in those cases where that people might profit by violating them (LoP: 19, 35). In the international context the criterion of reciprocity applies to the Law of Peoples in the same way as it does in the domestic case to the principles of justice for a constitutional regime.

And here again there is a parallel with "the domestic case" where, when using the idea of public reason, an appeal is made to the shared public political culture between citizens to reach an overlapping consensus. But in the international case a distinction is made between the public reason of liberal peoples and the public reason of the Society of Peoples. "The first is the public reason of equal citizens of domestic society debating the constitutional essentials and matters of basic justice concerning their own government; the second is the public reason of free and equal liberal peoples debating their mutual relations as peoples. The Law of Peoples with its political concepts and principles, ideals and criteria, is the content of this latter public reason" (LoP: 55).

Thus the *role* of public reason among free and equal peoples is analogous to its role in a constitutional democratic regime among free and equal citizens. Also, remember that in the domestic case the content of public reason is given by the family of liberal political conceptions of justice for a constitutional democratic regime, and not by a single one. There are, as we have discussed, many political liberalisms and therefore many forms of public reason specified by the family of reasonable political conceptions.

In this second original position, the one among liberal peoples, an appeal is made to shared *international* public reason, which contains ideals, principles, and standards that could sensibly be accepted by all (liberal) peoples. Although there is an analogy with regard to the role of public reason, the *content* of the public reasons is not the same: domestically shared political culture differs from internationally shared political culture. "If a reasonable pluralism of comprehensive doctrines is a basic feature of a constitutional democracy with its free institutions, we may assume that there is an even greater diversity in the comprehensive doctrines affirmed among the members of the Society of Peoples with its many different cultures and traditions" (LoP: 40).

It will be much more difficult to uncover by due reflection public reason that is shared between different peoples and that can be the basis of the justification of principles that are to regulate cooperation in the international realm. In fact, according to Rawls, there simply is not a shared international (or for that matter global) political culture that formulates the idea that peoples see themselves united as "free and equal" in an international Society of Peoples that is "a cooperative venture for mutual advantage." The fair terms of cooperation offered to other peoples are not analogous to the fair terms offered in the domestic case. More than that, there is no shared international political culture that formulates the idea that the distribution of, for instance, natural resources ought to be based on circumstances that are not morally arbitrary. There is, on the international level, simply no point of convergence that is comparable, or even similar, to the basic ideas of the "domestic" public political culture of liberal democracies, or that prescribes that citizens are to be seen as free and equal, regardless of the arbitrariness of their specific natural endowments, or of their social contingencies.

Which principles – initially only among liberal democratic peoples – would be selected? Which "Law of Peoples" would representatives of liberal peoples in the second original position adopt, guided by appropriate shared "international" public reason and based on a people's fundamental interests? The representatives of well-ordered liberal peoples will, as a first principle, insist on one that expresses equality among themselves as peoples. The selection, then, of the principles for the Law of Peoples – based on a liberal people's fundamental interests, fundamental interests that are the same for all liberal peoples – will be those principles of which the importance is evident: that aggressive wars that extend territory are unacceptable; that there is a right of self-defense; and that treaties are to be kept. On these principles representatives of liberal peoples will quickly reach agreement. These principles take the baseline of equality as a starting point: the equality and equal rights of all (for the case at hand, liberal) peoples.

Next in this second original position among liberal peoples, attention can be directed to issues of just international distribution. And once again the analogy with political liberalism in the domestic case is important. Also, on the international level, that of "the society of liberal peoples," egalitarian liberal aspirations have to be downgraded if peoples want to reach agreement. It is unlikely, Rawls surmises, that, taking into account the difficulty of uncovering by due reflection public reason that is shared between different liberal peoples and that can be the basis for the justification of principles that are to regulate cooperation in the international realm, in the setting of the original position among representatives of liberal peoples, agreement will be reached on a principle that is analogous to the difference principle for the domestic case. In this setting, agreement will be reached on the best possible minimum of a plurality of shared ideas between (the representatives of) liberal peoples when issues of economic distribution among peoples are debated. What the content of these ideas will precisely be, which substantive principle will be agreed on, is difficult to say. But taking the analogy of the domestic case into account, the lower boundaries are in principle fixed.

At the domestic level, political liberalism formulates that excessive economic inequalities that prevent citizens from having the means of subsistence and minimum economic security, and thereby infringe the rights of free and equal citizens, should be avoided. The parallel condition in the international case is the guarantee that a people's basic needs should be fulfilled such that a people can stand on its own. This leads to agreement on the *duty of assistance* for peoples that are confronted with unfavorable conditions. The goal of assistance is to reach a situation in which each people is able to develop into a just liberal democratic society (or, as we will see later, into a decent society). The duty of assistance assures the political autonomy of free and equal liberal peoples in the Society of Peoples.

The outcome of the deliberation in the second original position is that an international political society of "well-ordered peoples" can develop, and in which the following eight principles hold:

(1) Peoples are free and independent, and their freedom and independence are to be respected by other peoples.
(2) Peoples are to observe treaties and undertakings.
(3) Peoples are equal and are parties to the agreements that bind them.
(4) Peoples are to observe a duty of non-intervention.

(5) Peoples have the right of self-defense but no right to instigate war for reasons other than self-defense.
(6) Peoples are to honor human rights.
(7) Peoples are to observe certain specified restrictions in the conduct of war.
(8) Peoples have a duty to assist other peoples living under unfavorable conditions that prevent their having a just or decent political and social regime (LoP: 37).

These principles constitute the basic charter of "*the Law of Peoples.*" In the argument in the original position at the second level, Rawls considers the merits of only these eight principles, which are taken by him from the history and usages of international law and practice (LoP: 57, 37).[5] Thus the parties in the original position are not given a menu of alternative principles and ideals from which to select, as they are in *Political Liberalism*, or as they are in *A Theory of Justice* (LoP: 41). In this (second) original position the representatives of well-ordered liberal peoples agree that these eight principles express equality among peoples and they see, according to Rawls, no reason to depart from them or to propose alternatives. Of course the principles must also satisfy the criterion of reciprocity: reciprocity holds at both levels, between citizens as citizens and between peoples as peoples (LoP: 41, 57). Having made this choice of eight principles that specify the basic terms of cooperation between peoples and that satisfy the criterion of reciprocity, the conjecture now is that the just society of liberal peoples would be stable "for the right reasons," and not a mere *modus vivendi*. Stability rests in part on allegiance to the Law of Peoples itself.

This statement of the principles of just international cooperation is, as Rawls admits, incomplete. After having agreed to these principles that formulate basic equality between (in the first instance) liberal peoples, the parties as representatives of peoples, still situated behind the veil of ignorance, will formulate principles for forming and regulating federations (associations) of peoples, will agree to standards of fairness of trade, and will formulate guidelines for setting up other cooperative organizations, as well as certain provisions for mutual assistance (LoP: 38).

Suppose that there are three such cooperative institutions: one framed to ensure fair trade between peoples (an organization in some ways analogous to GATT [the General Agreement on Tariffs and Trade]);

another to allow a people to borrow from a cooperative banking system (analogous to the World Bank); and the third an organization with a role similar to that of the United Nations (referred to by Rawls as a "Confederation of Peoples," not one of states), or a cooperative organization analogous to the European Union (LoP: 42–43). (Or a cooperative association consisting of two liberal democratic societies in Europe [say Belgium and The Netherlands] who have decided they want to join and form a single society, or a single federal union.)[6]

Consider fair trade. If free trade is regulated by a fair background framework, a free competitive market trading scheme is to everyone's mutual advantage, at least in the longer term. A further assumption here is that there will be no attempt by larger nations with wealthier economies to monopolize the market, or to conspire to form a cartel, or to act as an oligopoly. Thus the market is kept free and competitive. Rawls' assumption is that unless there exist fair background institutions which are maintained over time from one generation to the next, (international) market transactions will not remain fair, and unjustified inequalities among peoples will gradually develop. These unjustified distributive effects would have to be corrected and taken into account by the duty of assistance. Parenthetically note here once more the analogy with the domestic case, where the background conditions and all that they involve have a similar role: to prevent the accumulation of excessive inequalities within a society over time, and to keep (internal) markets free from monopoly and the forming of cartels (JaF: 42–43, 115).

We have now completed the extension of the liberal political ideas of right and justice to the Law of Peoples of liberal societies. Our next step is to extend the principles for international justice to decent (hierarchical) societies and to eventually show that these societies accept the same Law of Peoples as liberal societies do.

Decent hierarchical peoples and the Law of Peoples

Representatives of decent hierarchical peoples deliberate among themselves, in a separate, third, original position (thus the second original position on the international level), to work out international principles of justice. They also come to a choice of the Law of Peoples, and thus a society of "well-ordered *decent* peoples" is established. Decent peoples (or rather their representatives) are moved in their deliberation by appropriate shared reasons: in the first place they share the idea that decent hierarchical peoples do not engage in aggressive war; they do not present a threat to liberal peoples (or for that matter to anyone else). Therefore the representatives of decent peoples respect the civic order and integrity of other peoples and accept the symmetrical situation of the original position (that of equality in which the representatives of decent peoples deliberate with each other) (LoP: 69). Next, "in view of the common good ideas of justice held in decent hierarchical societies, the representatives [of decent peoples] strive both to protect the human rights and the good of the people they represent and to maintain their security and independence. The representatives care about the benefits of trade and also accept the idea of assistance among peoples in time of need" (LoP: 69). Hence, representatives of hierarchical societies are decent and rational. The core of the argument turns on *the representatives* of decent hierarchical societies, situated in the appropriate original position, adopting the same eight principles of the Law of Peoples as those that are adopted by the parties representing liberal societies, including respect for everyone's human rights (LoP: 63–64, 69). Taking this reasoning into account, *the members* of decent hierarchical societies would accept – "as you and I would accept, as members of a decent hierarchical society, but not the same one" – the original position as fair among peoples, and thus would endorse the Law of Peoples adopted by their representatives as specifying fair terms of political cooperation with other peoples (LoP: 69).

The outcome of the choice of the principles of international cooperation and justice in each of the original positions among peoples is that now a situation has been reached in which each people is able to manage its own affairs, has stabilized its domestic institutions in line with (the respect of) human rights and principles of decent and effective government, and is also able to honor the other principles of the Law of Peoples, or to develop into a just liberal democratic society. We now can speak of an international political "Society of well-ordered Peoples" that consists of decent peoples and liberal peoples together (LoP: 23).

Earlier, we have seen that the principles of the Law of Peoples among liberal peoples satisfy the criterion of reciprocity. The same holds among decent peoples. The Law of Peoples requires that, in proposing a principle to regulate the mutual relations among peoples, a people or their representatives must think that it is not only reasonable for them to propose it, but also that it is reasonable for other people to accept it.

Recall: although the ideas of justice of decent hierarchical nonliberal societies allow basic inequalities among their members, and although not all persons in these societies are regarded as free and equal citizens, nor as separate individuals deserving equal representation, the *representatives* of decent peoples are to be situated equally in the original position, just as the representatives of liberal peoples are. There is no inconsistency here: although a decent hierarchical society is not as reasonable and just as a liberal society, a people affirming a nonliberal idea of justice may still reasonably think its society should be treated equally in a reasonable and just Law of Peoples. A decent society honors a reasonable and just Law of Peoples, the same Law of Peoples that is honored by liberal peoples.

The Law of Peoples applies to how peoples treat each other as *peoples* (LoP: 83, 70). The Law of Peoples does not ask of decent societies to submit themselves to a position of inferiority or domination. Neither does the Law of Peoples require decent societies to abandon or modify their religious institutions and adopt other ones, replacing them by, for example, liberal ones (LoP: 121). The basic question is what "we," "you and I," think can reasonably be asked of the other, in this case of another people. There has to exist a willingness to look at one's own position, one's own ideas, one's own political conception of justice, from the point of view of the other. It is the Law of Peoples that provides such a perspective. Decent peoples can affirm the same Law of Peoples as liberal peoples do. This enables that law to be universal in reach. The Law of Peoples asks of other societies only what they can reasonably endorse once they are prepared to stand in a relation of fair equality with all other societies (LoP: 121–122). Rawls adds that other societies "cannot argue that being in a relation of equality with other peoples is a western idea! In what other relation can a people and its regime reasonably expect to stand?" (LoP: 122).

Let us here take stock for a moment. We should remember that Rawls' intention is to show how the content of the Law of Peoples might be developed out of a liberal idea of political justice. Once the principles of a political conception of justice are in place for the domestic case, as they are, and not before, we have to elaborate the foreign policy for the international political world as "we," a liberal people, see it. The Law of Peoples is developed *within* political liberalism and is an extension of a liberal political conception of justice for a domestic regime to a Society of Peoples. In working out the Law of Peoples in this way, we, a liberal people, want to assure ourselves that the ideals and principles of our foreign policy secure conditions for us, as a liberal people. But we also want to assure ourselves that these principles of foreign policy (the Law of Peoples) are also reasonable from the point of view of a decent nonliberal people. But what we, as a liberal people, do not do is to prescribe principles of justice for *them*, for decent hierarchical peoples (LoP: 10, 83).

The idea of justice is based on the idea of the social contract, and the procedure which is followed before the principles of right and justice are selected and agreed upon is in some ways the same in both the domestic and the international case. An essential role in this procedure is played by the original position. The flexibility of the idea of the original position is shown in each step of the procedure by being modifiable to fit the subject in question (LoP: 86). Part of the versatility of the original position is displayed in how it is used in the two cases: the domestic one and the international one (LoP: 40). As we have seen, it plays its role first in the domestic case, a closed and self-contained liberal society. Next we have seen that it plays a parallel role in the international case. Both (representatives of) liberal peoples as well as (representatives of) decent peoples use the device of the original position to agree upon principles of international justice. But having recapitulated all this, one may still wonder why the idea of the original position is not used *four* times, instead of "only" three times. The answer is that the social contract idea, as used by Rawls, is a *liberal* idea (LoP: 70).

The choice of the principles of ordering a society, with the help of the argument of the original position, is only possible if the parties are symmetrically situated in the original position: only *equal* parties can be symmetrically situated. Therefore, the original position argument can be used for deriving the principles of domestic justice to regulate the basic structure of a liberal society. But it cannot be used for deriving the principles of, and does not apply to, the domestic case of a decent hierarchical regime. Although in decent societies human rights are respected, not all members of a decent society are regarded as free and equal citizens, nor as separate individuals deserving equal representation. Consequently the original position argument cannot be used for the domestic case of a decent hierarchical regime. In the international case, however, it is not only the representatives of liberal peoples who, as equal parties, are symmetrically situated in a (second) original position among each other, but also the representatives of decent peoples are, as equal parties, symmetrically situated among each other in a (third) original position, even though – once again – *within* each decent society basic inequalities among their members exist. These societies lack the liberal idea of citizenship (LoP: 83). It should be recognized, according to Rawls, that how peoples treat each other and how they treat their own members are two different things. The Law of Peoples applies to how peoples treat each other as *peoples* (LoP: 83). There is, however, no inconsistency here because a decent people "may still reasonably think its society should be treated equally in a reasonably just Law of Peoples. Although full equality may be lacking within a society, equality may be reasonably put forward in making claims against other societies" (LoP: 70).

The fact that full equality is lacking within a decent society, while at the same time such a society can be a member of the international well-ordered Society of Peoples, makes it relevant to explore further how Rawls describes the basic institutions and the political virtues of a decent hierarchical people. This will enable us to illustrate and to elaborate precisely how "toleration" is to be understood in the context of the "international society of well-ordered peoples" that consists of liberal peoples, as well as of decent peoples.

Kazanistan: a decent hierarchical people

The Law of Peoples does not presuppose the existence of actual decent hierarchical peoples (any more, it should be added, than Rawls presupposes the existence of actual reasonably just constitutional democratic peoples). Rawls' question is whether we can imagine a decent society that, although lacking full democratic and liberal rights, nevertheless honors human rights. And, should it exist, whether we would judge that it should be tolerated politically. With the example of "Kazanistan," Rawls gives a description of such a concrete, albeit hypothetical, decent hierarchical society (LoP: 75).

Kazanistan is an idealized Islamic people whose system of law does not institute the separation of church and state. Islam is the favored religion, and only Muslims can hold the upper positions of political authority and influence the government's main decisions and policies, including foreign affairs. Yet other religions are tolerated and can be practiced without fear or the loss of most civic rights. Non-Islamic religions and other minorities have been over time loyal subjects of society, and they are not subjected to arbitrary discrimination, or treated as inferior by Muslims in public or social relations. Also – unlike most Muslim rulers, as Rawls adds – the rulers of Kazanistan have not sought empire and territory, because its theologians have interpreted *jihad* in a spiritual and moral sense, and not in military terms.[7]

This idealized image of the Islamic people of Kazanistan is based on an interpretation of the Ottoman Empire some centuries ago.[8] It is a society in which each member belongs to a group, and in which the many different groups are represented by legal bodies in the procedure of consultation, while not all the groups have the same rights. The groups are represented in a "consultation hierarchy," where they participate in debate and political decision making. In the assemblies, where the bodies in the consultation hierarchy can meet, representatives can raise their objections to government policies, and members of the government can express their replies, which the government is required to do. Members of the government have to spell out how they think their policies are in line with its common good idea of justice. And Rawls also imagines that dissent in Kazanistan has led to important reforms in, for example, the rights of woman and their role in society, reforms that have been successfully implemented because the judiciary has agreed that existing norms (such as, for example, discriminating against women) could not be squared with society's common good idea of justice (LoP: 78).

Why is Rawls now paying all this attention to "decent hierarchical peoples," and even working out a hypothetical example of one such society? It is because one of his central aims in extending the Law of Peoples is to specify how far liberal peoples are to tolerate nonliberal peoples. And "to tolerate" means, among other things, to recognize these nonliberal societies as equal participating members in good standing of the Society of Peoples (LoP: 59). The example of Kazanistan shows that Rawls is inspired by the unacceptability, for liberals, of the internal basic institutions of (Muslim) states that do not recognize the separation of state and religion. And Rawls is looking for certain specified conditions in these basic institutions that would make such a regime acceptable for liberals.

Kazanistan is a thought-experiment, but not baseless utopianism. It is an enlightened society in its treatment of religious minorities. It should be stressed that Rawls certainly does not claim that, from the perspective of political liberalism (or of liberalism generally), such a society is perfectly just, or as reasonable and just as a liberal society (LoP: 83). Not at all. But we have to make a distinction between a legitimate regime and a just one. Decent societies have a legitimate political order that deserves respect, even if their institutions as a whole are not sufficiently reasonable from the point of view of political liberalism or liberalism generally.

In the international society of liberal peoples are tolerated liberal societies that differ widely in many ways: for example, depending on which variant of political liberalism is adopted, some are far more egalitarian than others. Yet these differences are tolerated. Each liberal people has, in any case, a legitimate regime. "Might not," Rawls asks, "the institutions of some kinds of hierarchical societies also be similarly tolerable," if these institutions honor human rights? Rawls' answer is: "I believe this to be so" (LoP: 84).

The situation in the domestic case where, in liberal democratic societies, there is a pluralism of religious and nonreligious, liberal and nonliberal comprehensive doctrines, and where liberalism is only one of these comprehensive doctrines, forces us to recognize that affirming (one of the variants of) political liberalism is the most reasonable and deepest basis of social unity available to us. The Law of Peoples expresses the same ideas and gives a parallel reasoning with regard to the limits and reach of liberalism in the international case. It is our "enlightened" insight into these limits of liberalism that, according to Rawls, requires that we design a reasonably just "Law of Peoples" that can be endorsed by liberal peoples as well as by nonliberal but decent peoples.

Liberal democratic peoples have to respect other societies that are ordered along nonliberal, non-democratic comprehensive doctrines as long as their political and social institutions honor the conditions of decency. In such a case, decent peoples ought to be regarded by liberal peoples as *bona fide* and equal members of a reasonable Society of Peoples. This is the crucial issue when we ask what "toleration" means (LoP: 84). Also, among peoples, just as among citizens, there exists the duty of civility. Mutual respect among peoples constitutes an essential part of the Society of Peoples.[9]

This, of course, does not mean that critical objections cannot be raised against decent societies. Criticism can be based on political liberalism, but it can also be based on comprehensive doctrines, religious and nonreligious, liberal and nonliberal. Raising objections is, for example, the right of liberal peoples. But liberal peoples, represented by their governments, have to cooperate with nonliberal decent peoples in the international society of peoples. The territorial integrity, political independence, and autonomy of decent nonliberal peoples have to be respected. Respect for other opinions, for other comprehensive religious or nonreligious doctrines, is, as has been argued earlier, a core element of political liberalism in the domestic case. The same holds for the international case. Leaving aside the question of whether some forms of culture and ways of life are good in themselves, a particular culture of a people deserves due respect by other peoples. Withholding respect from decent peoples might impede their willingness to participate in the Society of Peoples and would prevent any hope for gradual changes and reform within decent societies. Due respect consistent with the equality of all peoples is what peoples want to receive and what they want to give to other peoples. It is this type of equality that is important, and on which turns the "Equality of Peoples."

As we have seen, human rights is a class of special rights: they restrict the justifying reasons for war and its conduct, and they specify the limits to a regime's internal autonomy and sovereignty. Their fulfillment is sufficient to exclude justified and forceful intervention by other peoples, for example by diplomatic and economic sanctions, or in grave cases by military force (LoP: 80).

Next and even more so: if human rights are indeed the basic rights of persons, rights that are binding on all peoples and societies, including outlaw states, and if as a criterion of minimal decency an outlaw state may be subjected to forceful sanctions and even to intervention when it violates these rights, then there are good reasons why we should not consider each and every right to belong to the class of human rights. After all, the broader we define this set of special rights, the wider its scope, the more frequent would be the possibility for (liberal) peoples to justify action against outlaw states, but also to make other peoples change their ways, and to force on them changes in their internal institutions and practices. And once peoples start permanently intervening in the internal affairs of other peoples or states, there will be no stability or peace in the world. From Rawls' perspective it is not merely "western" or ethnocentric liberal imperialism to want to "export" human rights. It would, however, be a form of liberal imperialism to force, for example, *justice as fairness* on other peoples. Not all peoples can reasonably be required to be liberal, even if those holding a liberal view might think the world would be a better place if indeed all societies were to be so (LoP: 122).

Territorial boundaries and responsibility

In the foregoing we have always spoken of "peoples" and not of "states." But using the concept "peoples" instead of "states" does not, of course, alter the fact that a people lives on a specific territory, delimited by a "border." It is important to have a closer look at the role boundaries play in *The Law of Peoples*.

A people has a specific responsibility, especially with regard to the least advantaged members of its own people (in this case we speak of a liberal society), in caring for their territory and the size of its population, as well as for maintaining the land's environmental integrity (LoP: 8, 38). This responsibility is not the result of some psychological principle which formulates that feelings for one's own people are stronger than feelings for humanity as a whole, or that a people identifies more closely with its "own" least advantaged than with the least advantaged of other peoples. The argument is based on the psychological principles or tendencies "that social learning of moral attitudes supporting political institutions works most effectively through society-wide shared institutions and practices" of a well-ordered society (LoP: 112 note 44).

Rawls here repeats the argument that we already discussed in our exposition of *A Theory of Justice* and *Political Liberalism*. It is these moral psychological principles that we now also have to take into account in the international context. A shared (just) basic structure to stimulate and develop, across borders, these moral feelings and affinities is precisely what is missing among peoples. It is these principles of moral psychology which set limits for us when we reflect on what can sensibly be proposed as principles of the Law of Peoples (LoP: 112).

But there is also another element that shows us the important role of a boundary. Only with a boundary is it clear who bears responsibility for what. An important role of a government is to be the effective agent of a people as it takes the responsibility for their – border-delimited – territory, for its environmental integrity, and for the size of their population (LoP: 38–39, 8). And, as Rawls notes: "Unless a definitive agent is given responsibility for maintaining an asset and bears the responsibility and loss for not doing so, that asset tends to deteriorate. On my account the role of the institution of property is to prevent the deterioration from occurring" (LoP: 8). The government is the definitive agent that is responsible for the loss of territory, and/or the deterioration of the environment. But "the agent" is not an abstract entity. It is a people itself, as politically organized.

The territory of a people has the potential capacity to support a people *in perpetuity*, as Rawls claims. A people itself bears the responsibility for the capacity to support itself. "People must recognize that they cannot make up for failing to regulate their numbers or to care for their land by conquest in war, or by migrating into another people's territory without their consent" (LoP: 8, 39). Irresponsible behavior, non-renewable resources badly husbanded, cannot be compensated for in such a way. Peoples have to know what their own responsibilities are and they have to act accordingly.

The point Rawls wants to drive home is that in a reasonable just Society of Peoples, the inequalities in power and wealth are to be decided by all peoples for themselves. If inequalities eventually exist, these are based on decisions a people has made itself, managing its own affairs within its own territory. A people can be held accountable for the (favorable or unfavorable) condition it is in. And it is in following this line of reasoning that we arrive at "the duty of assistance" that reasonable liberal peoples and decent peoples, thus well-ordered peoples, have for burdened societies that are victims of unfavorable conditions. The claim that a people is itself responsible for the decisions it makes is, of course, no more than a hollow phrase if the possibility of making decisions is not available at all. Burdened societies then, or so it seems at first sight, cannot be held accountable for the unfavorable conditions they encounter. They can claim assistance from well-ordered peoples. But directly linked to this claim of assistance is their "own responsibility": poverty, and failing or corrupt governments in poor developing countries are, according to Rawls, attributable mainly to faults within their political and social structure. It is their political and social culture that needs to be changed. (Recall that we encountered this argument earlier in discussing the distinction between "the general conception of justice" and "the special conception of justice," and in working out which "requisite circumstances" or "favorable conditions" would allow "the special conception of justice" to hold, and hence what the appropriate favorable conditions for the principles of *justice as fairness* with their priority rules are.)

Before we have a closer look at this duty of assistance, another issue should be raised. Why, in the Law of Peoples, is there "only" a duty of assistance, and why, for example, should not a "global principle of distributive justice" play a role? We have already hinted several times in the text that it would be unlikely that the difference principle would be the principle on which an agreement would be reached in the original position among representatives of liberal peoples (or in the original position among the representatives of decent peoples): there is no shared international public political culture that would support the choice of such a principle. But here, in the context of the role that boundaries play among peoples, this issue can be further elaborated.

Territorial boundaries and social cooperation

In order to analyze Rawls' rejection of a "global principle of distributive justice," such as, for example, the difference principle that would be global in reach, let us first of all recall Rawls' aim in *The Law of Peoples*: to develop a Law of Peoples out of political liberalism. The Law of Peoples is an extension of a liberal conception of justice for a domestic regime to a Society of Peoples, and in developing the Law of Peoples in that way Rawls works out the ideals and principles of the foreign policy of a reasonably just liberal people.

The starting point in this line of reasoning is the domestic case: a liberal society, ordered by its basic structure. It is "we," "you and I," citizens of such a society, who have to justify for our own domestic society the principles of justice that regulate social cooperation among us, as free and equal citizens; principles that define the division of the benefits and burdens of our social cooperation in our domestic society. It means, among other things, that the point of reference for assessing a principle of distributive justice (for example the difference principle) is the basic structure of our own society, and especially how the benefits and burdens of social cooperation are distributed among *us*, citizens of that domestic society, within the confinement of *that* basic structure.

Social cooperation then – a core idea in Rawls' account of social justice – is regulated by the institutions of the basic structure. Under the terms of a political constitution, the basic structure also regulates the legal system, for example the institution of property (largely being a legal institution) that is presupposed by economic cooperation. Put another way: social cooperation is regulated by principles of social justice, principles that "design" the institutions of the basic structure and that are enforced by political authority. This has all been explained and elaborated before, in the context of the domestic case. There is nothing new here.

As Rawls makes clear in *The Law of Peoples*, and as we have seen in the section on "Territorial boundaries and responsibility," it is the government that is the definitive effective agent that is given responsibility for maintaining, in this example, the (legal) institution of property, within the boundaries of a specific territory. The presence of a government, of "political authority," is crucial for that purpose. But this, of course, holds not only for the institution of property: the presence of political authority is necessary to guarantee the enforcement of all of the (legal) institutions of the basic structure of a society. The issue Rawls wants to convince us of, is that we don't have much choice if we ask ourselves where, on what "level," such a political authority is to be found. It is certainly not to be found on a global level. A world-state which could play this role of (global) political authority and which could enforce globally legal institutions is clearly not available. And thus, according to Rawls, in "the absence of a world-state, there must be boundaries of some kind" (LoP: 39).[10] Only within the boundaries of a determined political space (the borders of, for example, a nation-state) can political authority be enforced. Only "within boundaries" can the legal institutions of the basic structure be recognized and enforced by the existing political regime of that bordered territory. And it is only within these boundaries that "social cooperation," in Rawls' sense, can exist: social cooperation is regulated and "bounded" by the – specific – basic structure of that society. There are specific terms of social cooperation (the principles of *justice as fairness*, or other reasonable terms of fair cooperation) that apply to the members of that society and that regulate how the result of social cooperation, "output," has to be distributed. These specific terms do not apply to those who are not members, to those who fall outside the borders of that society, and thus outside the basic structure of that society. And this is the reason why Rawls argues that by having boundaries it becomes clear who is responsible for what, and it is also the reason why he can add that inequalities of power and wealth are to be decided by all peoples for themselves, within their own system of social cooperation. Social and political cooperation *within* the basic structure is special, and one aspect of this special relation is expressed by the difference principle and the idea of reciprocity it entails. Thus "political authority," "basic structure," and a specific form of "social cooperation" according to the principles of the political justice of political liberalism, go hand in hand.

Once again we have here an example that the understanding of Rawls' line of reasoning with regard to international justice, or with regard to "global principles of distributive justice," rests on a willingness to see that his arguments are based on "political liberalism" as developed for the domestic case; not only in the sense that the Law of Peoples is a working out of the principles of the foreign policy of a reasonably just liberal people, but in a much more fundamental sense. The idea of political justice on which the Law of Peoples is based is the same as that of the "political liberalism" out of which it is developed, that is to say it is part and parcel of Rawls' ideas on "political constructivism."

In addition to what has been said above on "borders," "basic structure," and "social cooperation," the following holds, according to Rawls. Although we have to recognize the fact that there is presently no world-state, no political agent with authority on a global level, no global legal system (and thus no *global* basic structure), and although Rawls is of the opinion that the adoption of principles for equality among peoples will make room for various forms of cooperative associations and federations among peoples, they will not affirm a world-state. Here Rawls follows Kant's lead in *Perpetual Peace* "in thinking that a world government – by which I mean a unified political regime with the legal powers normally exercised by central governments – would either be a global despotism or else would rule over a fragile empire torn by frequent civil strife as various regions and peoples tried to gain their political freedom and autonomy" (LoP: 36; JaF: 13). For Rawls, it is clear then that nothing comparable to the basic structure of a domestic society exists on the international (or the global) level. And the associational cooperation that does exist among peoples is of a qualitatively different kind from the social cooperation that exists within the basic structure of a democratic society. Certainly, different kinds of cooperative organizations among peoples are subject to the judgment of "fair principles," to wit the Law of Peoples. But the Society of Peoples is not a political society, and there is no effective political regime with effective political power. There is, to repeat, no "social cooperation" in a "global basic structure" in a "Rawlsian" meaning of these terms. In the Law of Peoples there is, contrary to what cosmopolitans want to argue, no place for an international principle of *distributive* justice.[11]

And, of course, this "institutional" argument about bounded social cooperation is completely in line with earlier arguments for the impossibility of a global, or an international, principle of distributive justice. The weakness of "cross-border" common sympathies and lack of desire of liberal peoples (as well as that of decent peoples) to be under the same – democratic – government, the lack of affinity among different peoples and the absence of a shared public political culture, all of these closely connected arguments explain Rawls' rejection of a global or international principle of distributive justice.

Duty of assistance

The account by Rawls of the extension of a general social contract idea to the society of liberal democratic peoples, and the extension of the same idea to the society of decent peoples, showing that both kinds of societies, liberal and decent, would agree to the same Law of Peoples, is part of what Rawls has called "ideal theory" (LoP: 4–5). It is nonideal theory that takes up the issue of "unfavorable conditions," and that deals with the question of how far liberal and decent peoples owe a duty of assistance to societies in unfavorable conditions. What, then, are the precise implications of this duty, a duty formulated in the last principle (the eighth) of the Law of Peoples?

First of all, and most important in the specification of the situations when the duty of assistance holds, is the following. The unfavorable conditions are, according to Rawls, the consequence of national, historical, social, and economic circumstances.[12] And a failing political culture is the main culprit. There is domestic incompetence or an unwillingness to set the record straight. Rawls believes "that the causes of wealth of a people and the form it takes lie in their political culture and in the religious, philosophical, and moral traditions that support the basic structure of their political and social institutions, as well as in the industriousness and cooperative talents of its members, all supported by their political virtues" (LoP: 108).

Burdened societies lack the political and cultural traditions, the human capital and know-how, and often the material and technological resources to realize and preserve an internal just, or decent, political regime. Burdened societies are unable to preserve and realize a just or decent regime on their own: they need help to change their political culture. The aim of the duty of assistance is to help burdened societies to manage their own affairs so that they are able to comply with the minimal requirements of each *bona fide* member of the international Society of well-ordered Peoples. The duty of assistance should mean that they themselves can also become members of this Society of well-ordered Peoples. But the duty of assistance is conditioned and subject to important guidelines. From this duty it does not follow that the only way, or the best way, to carry out this duty is by following a global principle of distributive justice, for example a "resource redistribution principle" or a "global difference principle among peoples" that could be applied to bring burdened societies into the Society of well-ordered Peoples.

It is in this context that Rawls critically discusses a proposal of the political theorist Charles Beitz to regulate inequalities among peoples and to prevent their becoming excessive. It is Beitz who formulates "a resource redistribution principle." Beitz views this principle as giving each society a fair chance to establish just political institutions and an economy that can fulfill its members' basic needs by redistributing from countries with sufficient resources to resource-poor countries, as Rawls himself summarizes this principle of Beitz in *The Law of Peoples* (LoP: 116). But, or so Rawls argues, Beitz overlooks a crucial factor. How a country fares is not dependent on the level of its resources. Rawls conjectures, for example, "that there is no society anywhere in the world – except for marginal cases – with resources so scarce that it could not, were it reasonably and rationally organized and governed, become well-ordered. Historical examples seem to indicate that resource-poor countries may do very well (e.g., Japan), while resource-rich countries may have serious difficulties (e.g., Argentina)" (LoP: 108). So why is the one doing so well, although poor in resources, while the other – rich in resources – is doing badly? It is not the level of its resources.[13] It is the political culture of a country, its members' political and civic virtues, that is Rawls' answer. Certainly, there is no easy recipe to help to change this culture, but "*the arbitrariness of the distribution of natural resources causes no difficulty*" (LoP: 117; emphasis added). Accordingly, Rawls rejects the "resource redistribution principle."

The same shortcomings hold, according to Rawls, with regard to another principle that Beitz proposes, a "global difference principle" (a principle analogous to the difference principle for the domestic case). In a situation where there exists a global system of cooperation, applying this principle gives a principle of distributive justice between societies. Since Beitz believes, as in the case of the "resource distribution principle," "that the wealthier countries are so because of the greater resources available to them, presumably the global principle (with its scheme of taxation, say) redistributes the benefits of greater resources to resource-poor peoples," Rawls rejects this principle on the same grounds as he rejects the "resource redistribution principle" (LoP: 116).[14]

There is a second important specification of situations when the duty of assistance in the international situation holds. This specification shows once again a parallel with the domestic case, as discussed in both *A Theory of Justice* and in *Political Liberalism*. In the domestic case social and economic inequalities are not always unjust. In *The Law of Peoples* the same holds for inequalities among peoples; they are not always unjust if they are designed to serve the many ends that peoples share. As in the domestic case, peoples think it reasonable to accept various functional inequalities once the basic equality of all peoples, defined by the Law of Peoples, is firmly established (LoP: 113, 115).

When these inequalities are unjust it is because they have unjust effects on the relations among peoples and among their members. And we have already mentioned that the reason why parties as representatives of liberal peoples and parties as representatives of decent peoples would agree – in the original positions on the second, international, level – to the duty of assistance, is because they share the argument used on the domestic level. There it is argued that the excessive economic inequalities that prevent citizens from having the means of subsistence and minimum economic security, and that thereby infringe on the rights of free and equal citizens, should be avoided. The least advantaged should have sufficient all-purpose means to make intelligent and effective use of their freedoms and to lead a reasonable and worthwhile life. For example, the range of inequalities between the most and the least favored is determined by the idea of reciprocity and the (application of the) difference principle. If inequalities are still there under these conditions, they are nevertheless permissible and not unjust.

The parallel condition in the international case is the guarantee that a people's basic needs should be fulfilled such that a people can stand on its own. This leads to agreement on the *duty of assistance*. Once "the duty of assistance is satisfied and all peoples have a working liberal or decent government, there is again [analogous to the domestic case] no reason to narrow the gap between the average wealth of different peoples" (LoP: 114).

These elaborations of situations in which an appeal to the duty of assistance to correct "unjustified distributive effects" could be justified, already point in the direction of the duty of assistance being a principle of *transition*. And once again there is a similarity here with the domestic case, to wit with the duty of just savings discussed in *A Theory of Justice*. In each instance the aim is to realize and preserve just (or decent) institutions (LoP: 107). In the Society of well-ordered Peoples, the duty of assistance holds until all societies have achieved just liberal or decent basic institutions. "Both the duty of real saving and the duty of assistance are defined by a *target* beyond which they no longer hold. They assure the essentials of *political autonomy*" (LoP: 118). In the domestic case, political autonomy is a situation in which we can speak of free and equal citizens; and in the international case political autonomy stands for free and equal liberal and decent peoples in the Society of Peoples.

The duty of assistance in the international case guarantees burdened societies "only" the minimum material (economic) conditions sufficient for them to be able to manage their own affairs, to change their political and social culture, to stabilize their domestic institutions in line with the principles of decent governance, to affirm human rights, or to reach a situation that is in line with the requirements of a liberal society. Once this is accomplished, further assistance is not required (LoP: 111). This defines, in Rawls' words, the "target" of assistance, or *the cut-off point*. The assistance given has enabled burdened societies to be able to henceforth determine the path of their future by themselves. They are now "on their own," and are free and fully responsible for the decisions they make domestically, and for the consequences that these decisions have (LoP: 118).

As previously mentioned, Rawls believes that the causes of the unfavorable conditions of burdened societies lie mainly in their political culture (as – at the other extreme – do the causes of wealth). It means there is no easy recipe for well-ordered peoples to help a burdened society to change its political culture. Throwing funds at it is usually undesirable and is anyway not sufficient to end basic political and social injustices. But certain kinds of advice may be helpful, as well as exerting (external) pressure in the direction of effective government and insisting that concern for human rights can contribute to changing ineffective regimes, and to changing the conduct of rulers who have been callous about the well-being of their own people (LoP: 109). For example, the main cause of famine, or even a minor cause, may not be a decline in food, but the failure of governments to distribute (and supplement) the food that is available. Ineffective and corrupt government is the problem here. And, as for example Amartya Sen has convincingly shown in his study on famines, it is precisely the democratic regimes that are successful in coping with poverty and hunger.[15] (Indeed, we are already familiar with Sen's argument, because it was discussed in the context of the – favorable – circumstances in which "the special conception of justice" would hold.)

Respecting human rights could also relieve population pressure within a burdened society, relative to what the economy of the society can decently sustain (LoP: 109). Rawls points here to what appears to be a decisive factor: the status of women. He reminds us of the draconian Chinese measures of imposing harsh restrictions on the size of families, while adding that there are other ways to deal with this issue. "The simplest, most effective, most acceptable policy is to establish the elements of equal justice for women" (LoP: 110). Empowering women, giving them the right to vote, the right to participate in politics, to receive and to use education, and to own and manage wealth and property, all of this results in a decline in the birth rate, without invoking the coercive powers of the state. Of course, this is not the only reason to grant these rights to women. Rawls' advice is that burdened societies would do well "to pay particular attention to the fundamental interests of women. The fact that women's status is often founded on religion, or bears a close relation to religious views, is not itself the cause of their subjection, since other causes are usually present" (LoP: 110).[16]

Assistance that is offered can, then, be conditioned by the idea that measures should be adopted that prevent the violation of human rights, especially those of women. Rawls adds that this condition cannot be subject to the charge of improperly undermining a society's religion and culture. "The principle here is similar to one that is always followed in regard to the claims of religion. Thus, a religion cannot claim as a justification that its intolerance of other religions is necessary for it to maintain itself. In the same way a religion cannot claim as a justification for its subjection of women that it is necessary for its survival. Basic human rights are involved, and these belong to the common institutions and practices of all liberal and decent societies" (LoP: 111). If burdened societies do indeed want their claim to assistance to be honored, and if they want to become members in the good standing of the well-ordered

Society of liberal and decent Peoples, then they must, Rawls argues, affirm and honor these basic human rights.

Cosmopolitanism and *The Law of Peoples*

As we have seen, Rawls rejects a "global egalitarian principle of distributive justice," and more specifically the (application of the) difference principle in the case of international justice. Agreement on it – even in an ideal situation – will not be reached. And in the nonideal situation Rawls' idea is that peoples will not recognize trans-national principles of distribution to adjust for varying levels of wealth and welfare, once the duty of assistance is fulfilled and the "target" has been reached: to raise the standard of living to what is necessary to sustain a reasonably just and stable, or a decent, society. There is no justifiable reason for any society asking for more than is necessary to sustain just institutions, or for the further reduction of material inequalities among societies (LoP: 119).

These ideas clearly show the contrast between Rawls' view on international justice and the cosmopolitan perspective, the contrast between the Law of Peoples and the idea of "global justice for all persons." The core difference between the two views is, as Rawls stipulates, that the "ultimate concern of a cosmopolitan view is the well-being of individuals and not the justice of societies" (LoP: 119). Even after each domestic society has achieved internally just institutions, even after the duty of assistance has reached its target, there is for cosmopolitans still a question about the need for further global distribution (LoP: 119). The cosmopolitan view "is concerned with the well-being of individuals, and hence with whether the well-being of the globally worst-off person can be improved" (LoP: 120).

Certainly, Rawls concedes, the appeal of a "global principle of distributive justice" that "is meant to apply to our world as it is with its extreme injustices, crippling poverty, and inequalities … is understandable." He adds, however, that "if it is meant to apply continuously without end – without a target, as one might say – in the hypothetical world arrived at after the duty of assistance is fully satisfied, its appeal is questionable" (LoP: 117). It is not only questionable, and it is not only not required by Rawls, but this continuous global (re-)distribution will in the end lead to unjust and even unacceptable results. Recall that in the domestic case the end of social justice is not equal individual welfare, but the freedom and equality of citizens. The same holds for the international case: the end of the Law of Peoples is not the total welfare of a people or the well-being of the least-advantaged individuals, but, as stated earlier, equal political autonomy among peoples.

The problem with applying a global principle of distributive justice is that one does not pose the question as to what lies at the base of the inequalities one wants to reduce, or even to eliminate. And this is what Rawls objects to. What is the consequence of continuously applying a global redistribution principle? It prevents us, once the duty of assistance is fully satisfied, and consequently peoples have been able to join "the Society of well-ordered liberal and decent Peoples," from making a distinction between those societies that with foresight and prudence have increased their wealth, and those societies that have squandered their wealth through irresponsible and careless behavior. Or between societies that, for example, have stressed equal justices for women and where its women flourish in the political and economic world and where, as a consequence, these societies have gradually reached zero population growth, which allows for an increasing level of wealth over time, and those societies that have not reduced the rate of population growth, it remaining rather high (LoP: 117–118).

Nevertheless, cosmopolitan egalitarianism is of the opinion that in all cases redistribution is necessary from the wealthier societies to the poorer societies. And this even in a situation where two liberal or decent countries some decades earlier would have been at the same level of wealth and natural resources (and could also have had the same size population). The application of a global principle of distributive justice, Rawls strongly believes, would be unacceptable in these cases. It would mean that some societies would be punished for their considered domestic policy, since other societies would have to be compensated for their carelessness.

And thus we have come full circle, back to the earlier discussion of the responsibility a people has for its own deeds, for inequalities that are the result of decisions that a people itself has made, and for those inequalities that are the result of unfavorable conditions. The duty of assistance focuses on the second kind of inequalities, with the purpose of bringing these societies into the Society of well-ordered Peoples. A global principle of distributive justice, however, and that is what Rawls is worrying about, does not make a distinction between "choice" and "circumstances." Consequently, citizens of societies that act responsibly and make considered policy choices are unfairly

treated by the application of a global principle of justice that demands
continuous redistribution.

Parenthetically note here that Rawls' argument that the cosmopolitan
egalitarian principles of distributive justice do not take into account the
distinction between the responsibility a people has for those inequalities
that are the result of decisions they themselves have made, and for those
inequalities that are the result of unfavorable conditions – a distinction
between "choice" and "circumstances" – and his argument that the end
of the Law of Peoples is not the total welfare of a people or the well-
being of the least-advantaged individuals, are both analogous to the
arguments formulated by Rawls in the domestic case, where the distinction is made between "circumstances" (natural endowments and social
contingencies) and "choice," and where the end of social justice is not
equal individual welfare, but the freedom and equality of citizens. They
are the core aspects of *justice as fairness*, aspects that play a major role
in understanding the distinction between "the principle of redress" and
"the difference principle." In the domestic case we noted the analogy
between the principle of redress and "luck egalitarian principles" such
as "equal opportunity for welfare" and "equal access to advantage."
Here, in the international context, one could well argue that cosmopolitans such as Charles Beitz and Thomas Pogge are "luck egalitarians" who, with their principles of global distributive justice, apply
"luck egalitarianism" to the global domain. And thus, consistently,
Rawls now formulates the same objections that he has against applying
such principles in the domestic case, to the analogous "global luck
egalitarian principles."

But there is more: the duty of assistance, although not a principle of
distributive justice, for this duty extends no further and establishes no
further claims once the target has been reached, can itself be problematic, as Rawls himself argues (LoP: 112). After all, assistance is
based not only on a "duty," it also needs motivational support for
following it. And there is legitimate concern if this motivational support does not "[presuppose] a degree of affinity among peoples, that is,
a sense of social cohesion and closeness, that cannot be expected, even
in a society of liberal peoples – not to mention in a society of all well-
ordered peoples – with their separate languages, religions, and cultures" (LoP: 112).

Note here, once again, an important aspect of Rawls' argument and
the analogy it has with his long-standing argument in the domestic case.

It is an argument that has already been developed and extensively elaborated in the third part of *A Theory of Justice*. Remember that *justice as fairness* is an institutional project: "justice is the first virtue of social institutions." It is in the context of society-wide political, and social and economic institutions of a single domestic society that members share a common central government and (political) culture, and it is here that the moral learning of political concepts and principles of justice works most effectively, and where the tendency to reciprocity will indeed develop a firm sense of justice.

It is within this "environment" that a common base for social cooperation exists and that political conflicts, if such there are, can be resolved, in terms of – shared – public reason. It is in the context of a domestic well-ordered society that a sense of justice develops.

Now in the international realm, Rawls' project is of course also an institutional one. And in this context Rawls, as we have noted before, draws on the same psychological principles that the social learning of moral attitudes works most effectively through society-wide shared institutions and practices that are widely and publicly considered to be just. And, although we may regret this, this learning weakens in the international context, and even more so where shared "cross-border" institutions are missing. The sense of social unity and allegiance, the affinity among different peoples, is naturally weaker (as a matter of human psychology) than in a domestic society, and may even be totally lacking. Rawls sees it as "the task of the statesman to struggle against the potential lack of affinity among different peoples": the statesman must continually combat these short-sighted tendencies (LoP: 112). What encourages the statesman's work, as Rawls notes, is "that relations of affinity among peoples are not a fixed thing, but may continually grow stronger over time as peoples come to work together in cooperative institutions they have developed" (LoP: 112–113). If in the first instance peoples can be moved by self-interest to cooperate, to honor treaties, and to guarantee human rights, as peaceful cooperation proceeds this can develop over time into mutual caring, and eventually the psychological conditions for mutual cross-border solidarity may become the ideals and principles of liberal and decent civilizations, and the principles of the Law of all civilized Peoples (LoP: 113).

The full argument of *The Law of Peoples* turns on the relation among peoples. In domestic societies it is persons viewed as citizens who are to be considered as free and equal; in the international society it is peoples who are seen as free and equal. But having said this, it should be stressed that Rawls also incorporates a basic premise of cosmopolitanism. Just like Kant's *Perpetual Peace*, *The Law of Peoples* has a principle that formulates the moral rights of the individual: "Peoples are to honor human rights." And it is this duty to respect human rights that highly limits a government's internal sovereignty. Striving for mutual respect among peoples, for a reasonably just and well-ordered Society of Peoples, and for the universal reach of human rights, that is the focus of *The Law of Peoples*.

5 | Justice as Fairness *in practice*

Justice as fairness on the political spectrum

In the following, *justice as fairness* will be applied to practical political issues. In doing so, it should be kept in mind from the outset that the examples are given to explicate and illustrate *justice as fairness* itself. *Justice as fairness* remains the point of reference.

In applying *justice as fairness* to practical political issues, it should be noted that what is important to Rawls are the central aims and ideas of *justice as fairness* as a philosophical conception for a constitutional democracy. His hope is that *justice as fairness* will seem reasonable and useful "to a wide range of thoughtful political opinion and thereby express an essential part of the common core of the democratic tradition" (CP: 416). At the same time, he acknowledges that readers of his work are likely to see *justice as fairness*, as with any political conception, as having a specific location on the political spectrum. But "the terms used to describe these locations are different in different countries. In the United States this conception has been referred to as liberal, sometimes as left-liberal; in England it has been seen as social democratic, and in some ways as Labour" (CP: 415–416). Be that as it may, Rawls underlines that it is for others to make these descriptions.

With regard to these descriptions of *justice as fairness*, we should keep in mind the moment in time that Rawls is referring to them. He does so in 1987, in his introduction to the French translation of *A Theory of Justice*.[1] With regard to England, where *justice as fairness* "has been seen as social democratic, and in some ways as Labour" this description refers – as far as "social democratic" is concerned – to David Owen and Shirley Williams, who had invoked *A Theory of Justice*. (They founded, in March 1981, [with Roy Jenkins and Bill Rodgers, the so-called "Gang of Four" who left the Labour Party] the Social Democratic Party [SDP], a party that existed until 1988, when it merged with the Liberal Party to form the Social and Liberal Democrats [SLD], now known as the Liberal Democrats.)

With regard to the remark that *justice as fairness* in England "has been seen in some ways as Labour," one can think of Anthony Crosland's "democratic socialism," as formulated by him in 1974, in his *Socialism Now and Other Essays*.[2] As Crosland wrote (referring to earlier positions taken by him in his *The Future of Socialism*, published in 1956), socialism is basically about equality: "By equality, we meant more than a meritocratic society of equal opportunities in which greatest rewards would go to those with the most fortunate genetic endowment and family background; we adopted the 'strong' definition of equality – what Rawls has subsequently called the 'democratic' as opposed to the 'liberal' conception [Crosland refers here to *A Theory of Justice*]. We also meant more than a simple (not that it has proved simple in practice) redistribution of income. We wanted a wider social equality embracing also the distribution of property, the educational system, social-class relationships, power and privilege in industry – indeed all that was enshrined in the age-old socialist dream of a more 'classless' society."[3] The question for Crosland was not "how much equality?" but rather the issue that there are plenty of "harsh, specific and unmerited inequalities to combat."[4]

In 1956, in his *The Future of Socialism*, Crosland had already noted that from a socialist point of view the limited goal of equality of opportunity and social mobility is not enough.[5] "They need ... to be combined with measures, above all in the educational field, to equalise the distribution of rewards and privileges so as to diminish the degree of class stratification, the injustice of large inequalities, and the collective discontents which come from too great dispersion of rewards."[6] Being sensitive to the fact that there may be the need to pay differential rewards, the issue is on what criterion unequal rewards and privileges are to be distributed. If, Crosland argued, this distribution would be based on, for example, "intelligence," the question is why this trait should be singled out for unequal rewards and privileges. "One might hold this to be palpably unjust on the grounds that superior intelligence is largely due to parental status, through a combination of heredity and beneficial upbringing: and that no one deserves either so generous a reward or so severe a penalty for a quality implanted from the outside, for which he himself can claim only a limited responsibility."[7] It is this "Croslandite" egalitarian legacy to which the current prime minister,

Gordon Brown, is a self-proclaimed disciple, as his foreword to the new edition of *The Future of Socialism* attests.

Another member of the Labour Party who invokes Rawls is Roy Hattersley.[8] A returning issue here is that "meritocracy only offers shifting patterns of inequality." It is argued that the "meritocratic" foundations of New Labour's philosophy and program of social justice are alien to the tradition and wider egalitarian prospects evoked by the likes of Tawney, Crosland, and Hattersley himself.

Let us add two points: invoking Rawls' idea on "democratic equality," as Crosland does, would mean that justifiable inequalities exist only if they work to the benefit of the least advantaged. Second, Crosland remarked in *The Future of Socialism* that what constitutes a "just" distribution of privileges and rewards is "in essence a simple moral judgment, it is not susceptible of proof or disproof; it must be accepted or rejected according to the moral predilections of the reader."[9] But there are better ways of founding these ideas than on "the moral predilections of the reader." Simply put, what Crosland's ideas on socialism lacked was a theory of justice to ground his ideas on. In this context it is noteworthy that Stuart Hampshire, in his review of *A Theory of Justice*, remarked in 1972: "[*A Theory of Justice*] is a noble, coherent, highly abstract picture of the fair society, as social democrats see it. In England, books about the Labour Party's aims – for example, those written by Douglas Jay and Anthony Crosland since the war – needed just such a theory of justice as this, stated in its full philosophical generality. This is certainly the model of social justice that has governed the advocacy of R. H. Tawney and Richard Titmuss and that holds the Labour Party together. Society must repair the cruelties of nature, and it exists not only to preserve law and order but also to correct the natural differentials between the strong and the weak, and to give institutional support to self-respect, which is for Rawls a primary value."[10]

And Brian Barry noted in his obituary on John Rawls, with regard to the location of *justice as fairness* on the political spectrum: "Politically, the significance of Rawls is that, though he never appeared to be much interested in any country except the US, he produced the philosophical basis for European social democracy that it had always lacked. Rawls showed that strong concern for the worst-off class within a market economy was not a half-baked dilution of Marxism but a natural extension of basic liberal commitments."[11]

Justice as fairness: implications for public policy

We have seen that Rawls has a broad perspective on what are to count as distributive issues. The benefits arising from social cooperation are not only a material product (income and wealth), but also basic rights and liberties, diverse opportunities, the powers and prerogatives of offices and positions of responsibility, and the social bases of self-respect. It is these scarce "resources" that have to be distributed in a fair way. And it is the principles of justice that, in specifying the fair terms of social cooperation, regulate the division of benefits and allot the burdens necessary to sustain it.

This broad perspective on distributive issues is in line with, or so one could argue, ideas that since the Second World War have been formulated in the context of the development of so-called welfare states. Granting the rather imprecise use of the term "welfare state" made in the following, the essence of the welfare state will be understood as "government-protected minimum standards of income, nutrition, health, housing, and education, assured to every citizen as a political right, not as charity."[12]

A welfare state has an obligation to provide all its members with a decent level of means of subsistence, and a government should be able to account for inequalities in life prospects. The upshot of these ideas is that total societal distribution is more and more subjected to decisions taken in the democratic political process. This is expressed in the size of the public sector and the economic–political goal of an acceptable distribution of income and wealth.

From the perspective of these central ideas of what a welfare state entails, the three characteristic principles that Rawls formulates for the family of political liberalisms can be interpreted as also describing the institutional requirements of welfare states. Let us recapitulate these characteristics:

> first, a specification of certain basic rights, liberties, and opportunities (of a kind familiar from constitutional democratic regimes);
> second, an assignment of special priority to those rights, liberties, and opportunities, especially with respect to claims of the general good and of perfectionist values;
> third, measures assuring to all citizens adequate all-purpose means [primary goods] to make intelligent and effective use of their liberties and opportunities (PL: xlviii; LoP: 14, 49).

Taking into account the institutions required by these three characteristics, a further parallel with the institutions and arrangements of welfare states can be discerned. Recall that Rawls gave the following indication of these institutions:

(a) Public financing of elections and ways of assuring the availability of public information on matters of policy;
(b) A certain fair equality of opportunity, especially in education and training;
(c) A decent distribution of income and wealth meeting the third characteristic of [political] liberalism;
(d) Society as employer of last resort through general or local government, or other social and economic policies; and
(e) Basic health care assured for all citizens (PL: lviii–lix; LoP: 50).

In the following we will first ask what in practice the public-policy implications would be when in the "daily politics" of an actual welfare state it is claimed that one is applying *justice as fairness* and that, in doing so, one is giving a "Rawlsian" dimension to that welfare state. How to substantiate such claims?

Just income distribution

As mentioned, the three characteristic principles that Rawls formulates for the family of political liberalisms entail a basic structure that can be interpreted as also describing the institutional requirements of welfare states. To be able to discuss the "applicability" of "political liberalism" in an actual welfare state, then, there ought to be reasonable agreement on one of these variants. Let us go one step further and suppose that within an actual welfare state there is an overlapping consensus on the egalitarian variant of political liberalism, thus on *justice as fairness* as the appropriate political conception of justice. Presuming that agreement on the aims of these principles of justice is indeed widely shared in this welfare state, agreement is next needed on the institutional requirements to actually realize these principles. We noted earlier that institutional requirements which specify the equal basic rights and liberties of citizens can be specified in but one way, modulo relatively small variations, and that it is easy to see for each and every citizen whether these requirements are indeed met. A broad consensus in society being available on *justice as fairness* means, next, that there is a shared idea that social and economic inequalities, and let us take income as the main concern here, should contribute in an effective way to the benefit of the least advantaged members of society. There is in this society also widespread agreement, or so we suppose, that it is the difference principle that formulates this requirement.

The issue now is how, in a practical way, the institutions of the basic structure must be designed and regulated so that a fair, efficient, and productive system of social cooperation can indeed be maintained: What (policy) measures have to be actually institutionalized (say, what forms of taxation) so as to guarantee that the difference principle, that applies to institutions as a public system of rules, has the required effect? The difference principle applies to the institutional background, and thus there are no unannounced and unpredictable interferences with citizens' expectations and acquisitions. Thus citizens, "you and I," who have correctly understood Rawls' intentions, could not object "that the difference principle enjoins continuous corrections of particular distributions and capricious interference with private transactions" (PL: 283). The difference principle does not do such things. Thinking that it does is based on a misunderstanding. Thus the search should be for policy measures that do not involve unpredictable or unannounced interferences with our plans and actions but that are foreseeable (such as expected forms of taxation).

Let us now suppose that the political agenda in the parliament of our imaginary welfare state turns to the issue of "just income distribution." In the parliamentary debate on this issue only two political parties participate, say one located on the "left" of the political spectrum (let us call this a traditional "social democratic party"[13]), and one on the "right" of the political spectrum (let us call this a "liberal party" in the continental European sense). Let us also assume that both political parties are of the opinion that ideas on just income distribution would be more legitimate, or more acceptable, if they could be based on a respected and influential political theory: on that of Rawls. Both agree that implementing the difference principle would be the way to reach a just income distribution.

Both parties agree then, in line with the difference principle, on the idea that inequalities are justified only when they improve the long-term expectations of the least advantaged. Agreeing on this normative starting point, they agree that the search should be for the appropriate institutional requirements, the appropriate policy measures, to make this happen. It seems, then, that the question of how a welfare state ought to treat the least advantaged members of its society has shifted from being a political ideological issue to a technical one; to a question of what, for example, should be the optimal tax structure to raise the long-term prospects of the least advantaged.

However, and here we come to the kernel of the issue at hand, it turns out that in our imaginary parliamentary debate no agreement on this technical question can be reached. Political disagreement turns on different interpretations of the empirical effects of a specific income policy. Our politician on the "right" argues that *more* inequality, a greater distance between the least advantaged and the more and most advantaged would be necessary to improve the position of the least advantaged. Our politician on the "left" argues that inequalities are already too extensive. Both of these arguments are concerned with the same issue. Recall that it is the dilemma on which the difference principle turns: the trade-off between how much is produced and the way it is distributed, the given that a large product goes hand in hand with an unequal distribution, and that a small(er) product does so with a (more) equal distribution. By varying wages and salaries, to be paid out of output, more may be produced. Under these circumstances, and assuming that we can measure the extent to which particular arrangements of the basic structure determine this trade-off, one could strive for reforms of the existing social and economic institutions such that a greater product would be available for distribution, while the unequal distribution that accompanies it is such that the position of persons in the lowest positions – compared to their actual situation – would improve. From the perspective of the difference principle, this kind of reform of institutions would be considered just.

It is this kind of reform that lies behind the policy proposal of our politician on the "right": to strive for more inequality, for a greater distance between the least advantaged and the more and most advantaged. But crucial here is the assumption mentioned above that "we can measure the extent to which particular arrangements of the basic structure determine this trade-off." "More" inequality, generated say by specific incentive effects (different tax rates, for example, for earned income, particularly in the upper brackets) has to be shown empirically to improve the position of the least advantaged. From the perspective of *justice as fairness* it is only then that we can speak of reciprocity in the distribution of the burdens and benefits of social cooperation.

Thus the real issue now is the practical empirical question of whether indeed the inequalities are already too large, or as of yet not large enough. Remember how this dilemma was illustrated with the help of the contribution curve (see Figure 2.1). The curve indicates the returns of the most and least favored, when only (schedules of) wages and salaries are changed. It demonstrates that the less favored gain (although not equally) from the greater expectations of the better off (and thus from increasing inequalities) only on the upward rising part of the contribution curve. On this segment of the curve the expectations of both the better off, and those of the worse off, increase. Total production increases and both groups gain: the idea of reciprocity, which is a principle of mutual benefit, is fulfilled (TJ: 102; TJR: 88). These (increasing) inequalities can be justified; they are "permissible" inequalities. Now, if a political party wants to defend that not only existing social and economic inequalities are necessary for stimulating and enlarging productivity, but that those inequalities have to be enlarged so as to improve everybody's position, it has to be shown that the increasing inequalities are situated on the upward rising part of the contribution curve.

The empirical question is thus: Where are we actually situated on this curve? Are existing inequalities in fact still located on the upward rising part? That is the claim of our politician "on the right," who proposes that more inequality is necessary. But his political opponent could argue that inequalities are already too extensive, claiming that we have in fact already passed the maximum and are actually on the downward slope of the contribution curve. In short, our politician "on the left" argues that existing inequalities are already unjust. Increasing them, then, would make an unjust situation even more unjust.

But since it has to be acknowledged that reasonable disagreement can exist on these issues because too little is known about the relation between (the level of) taxation of wage incomes and the magnitude of the (negative) incentive effects, the answer to whether inequalities between the least and the most advantaged are too large, or should be considered too small, will turn out to be a "political" issue, tainted by political opportunism rather than by complex empirical verification. And this also explains that in proposing a just income policy, both politicians, the one on the "left" of the political spectrum and the one on the "right," try to justify their specific proposals by each claiming that they are making the correct appeal to what *justice as fairness*, and more particularly what the difference principle, requires.

This imaginary political debate illustrates Rawls' own point that one has to be careful about the different ways in which distributive principles, for example the difference principle, might be subjected to a rather broad range of more or less reasonable disagreements, not only in its very justification, but also in the way it is to be applied. The disagreement is presumably about how best to deal with the worst off, from a position that really improves their lot. Much depends on what one takes to be, in Rawls' terminology, the burdens of judgment, and differences of opinion on these issues can be reasonable.

Recall that it is these kinds of disagreement which led Rawls to make the distinction between constitutional essentials and matters of basic justice, a distinction based on the difficulty of seeing whether social and economic distributive principles have achieved their aim. We encountered this issue *in ideal theory*, in the four-stage sequence, in the process of designing the background institutions of the basic structure of a well-ordered society. In the legislative stage, reasonable questions about whether legislation is "just," or at least not "unjust," could be raised, especially with regard to the difference principle.

The situation we are presently concerned with is not one of an ideal legislative procedure, neither is it one in a well-ordered society. We are now confronted in a non-ideal situation with a reasonable difference of opinion on just policies. That is, on the question of what would really favor the position of the least advantaged: What are the "necessary" incentive mechanisms that the (working of the) difference principle compels us to implement? How to ascertain and to evaluate its effects? In fact, they are problems that we, or for that matter our politicians, should have expected to encounter. One can add that in a dynamic, democratic political order it is not a "problem" but rather a "natural," given that differences of opinion exist with regard to what a principle such as the difference principle requires.

In our imaginary parliamentary debate, competing political parties are trying, with the help of the majority rule, to get their own specific ideas accepted. And the outcome of the parliamentary debate will be in the best of cases a compromise, a bargain struck between opposing parties trying to advance their ends. Now this of course is how political practices work. Generally speaking, it is precisely the partial and self-interested views or group-interests that are decisive. No wonder that we are now squarely confronted with these issues when debating adequate policy measures with regard to the difference principle, issues that basically turn on the range of "permissible" inequality between rich and poor, between wealth and poverty.

But the fact that there can be a difference of opinion on the question of how – and if, empirically speaking – the difference principle is actually accomplishing its task, that of raising the long-term expectations of the least advantaged, does not in any way alter the fact that it makes sense to come to a political choice in favor of this principle. It gives us a framework and a guideline on how to deal with social and economic inequalities. It is a choice that expresses the idea that society should be concerned with its least advantaged, and especially how best to really favor their lot. It also brings to expression the idea that efficiency is not prior to justice, and that inequalities have to be shown to express the idea of reciprocity.

Let us add a couple of points from this perspective. When in an actual political debate the difference principle is brought forward as the principle to follow in a just income policy, more often than not it is interpreted as the "maximin criterion." It is not unlikely that it is our politician on the "right" of the political spectrum, the one who argues that "more" inequality is necessary to improve the position of the least advantaged, who is interpreting the difference principle in this way. In that case the issues raised by the contribution curve do not arise. The argument of our politician on the "right" would be that *any* rise in the position of the least advantaged would be a satisfactory outcome of policy measures taken, if this would be the happy consequence of raising the position of the more and the most favored, and regardless of how much the range of inequality between them and the least advantaged would increase. But, as has been argued before, the maximin criterion does not express the idea of reciprocity and does not represent in any way the core of the idea of what, in a Rawlsian sense, a "just distribution" entails. As we have explained, in contrast to the (application of the) difference principle, the maximin criterion has nothing to say about on what grounds differences could be justified, or about what the permissible range of inequalities should be, as long as the position of the least advantaged is the highest possible one. On the question of whether there should be any limits at all, or a maximum to earned income, maximin remains silent. Let us be aware that we are not presently debating theoretical differences between the difference principle and the maximin criterion. We are now concerned with an actual political debate on income policy. And a political choice made in favor of maximin, claiming that such a choice is analogous to a choice in favor of the difference principle, can result in outcomes that are far away from anything required or justified by Rawls' theory.

Also, let us remember there is another important reason why limits should be posed on the accumulation of income and wealth, limitations on social and economic inequalities that are not directly related to the permissible inequalities of earned income that the difference principle would allow. They are restrictions required by the fair value of political liberties. It is difficult to see how a political plea for increasing inequalities between the least, the more, and the most favored of society could contribute to fair and equal access to the political process by the least advantaged.

The most important problem with the plea for a greater distance between the least and the most favored could be that the implicit argument that lies behind it is one based on efficiency and on capital accumulation, not one based on justice. A focus on efficiency, *replacing* one on justice, would of course be in flat contradiction to the priority rules *justice as fairness* formulates: its principles, including the difference principle, have priority over efficiency and welfare.

But even if it would be the difference principle that is taken as the guiding principle for a just distribution of income and wealth, a further feature of it should not be overlooked. That is that continual economic growth over generations to indefinitely maximize upward the expectations of the least advantaged (expressed in terms of income and wealth) is not required by the difference principle. Rawls himself does not consider that to be a reasonable conception of justice. In general, it can be said that great wealth is not necessary to establish a just society, as shown earlier in the exposition on the distinction between the general conception of justice and the special conception of justice. Rawls is of the opinion that it "is a mistake to believe that a just and good society must wait upon a high material standard of life. What men want is meaningful work in free association with others, these associations regulating their relations to one another within a framework of just basic institutions. To achieve this state of things great wealth is not necessary. In fact, beyond some point it is more likely to be a positive hindrance, a meaningless distraction at best if not a temptation to indulgence and emptiness" (TJ: 290; TJR: 257–258). Rawls does not rule out J. S. Mill's idea of a society in a just stationary state where (real) capital accumulation may cease (PL: 7 note 5; JaF: 63–64, 159). "The thought that real saving and economic growth are to go on indefinitely, upwards and onwards, with no specified goal in sight, is the idea of the business class of a capitalist society" (LoP: 107 note 33). Their goal is simply larger profit, and the "long-term result of this – which we already have in the United States – is a civil society awash in a meaningless consumerism of some kind."[14] "Is this what we want?" Rawls rhetorically wonders.

Parenthetically, it should be noted that Rawls had already, in an earlier and different context, taken a stand against "meaningless consumerism." In formulating his ideas on the right to the advertising of products by firms, he noted that "advertising tries to influence consumers' preferences by presenting the firms as trustworthy through the use of slogans, eye-catching photographs, and so on, all designed to form or strengthen the habit of buying the firm's products. Much of this advertising is socially wasteful, and a well-ordered society that tries to preserve competition and remove market imperfection would seek reasonable ways to limit it" (PL: 365).[15]

Returning to our imaginary parliamentary debate, the difference principle is taken in this debate as a principle of distributive justice in a narrow sense, regulating primary income (wages and salaries) that is received in exchange for the efforts of individual labor. Of course, the difference principle is certainly an important aspect of the principle of distributive justice. But it certainly is also not the only aspect of it, nor the only role it plays in *justice as fairness* as a whole. In actual politics, making the choice in favor of (using) the difference principle (and hopefully a correct interpretation thereof!) as the principle to be applied in a welfare state, and next drawing the conclusion that in doing so a welfare state could be considered to have moved in a "Rawlsian" direction, would be a huge simplification. It narrows down Rawls' theory of justice to a theory of just income policy.[16] Consequently, his broad conception of social justice and the richness of ideas that accompany it remain out of sight. To be able to speak of a just society in a Rawlsian sense, any form of "reductionism" has to be avoided. Only an analysis of the theory of *justice as fairness* in its entirety gives us a clear insight into the choices to be made if we actually want to strive for a just society.

Between fate and freedom of choice: personal responsibility

Freedom of choice, fair equality of opportunity, and relative priority for the position of the least advantaged, are not only core elements of a (political) conception of justice, they are also characteristics of modern welfare states. Pointing to the importance of freedom of choice means that, in actual social economic policies in welfare states, more than has been the case in the past, a distinction is being made between the positions that people are in, and for which they themselves bear responsibility, and the positions that they are in for which they are not to blame, positions that are a consequence of the "Rawlsian" "contingencies of social life," so to speak. Freedom of choice, in this line of reasoning, goes together with stressing personal responsibility, provided that conditions are fulfilled such that people can actually take responsibility for their choices.

As we have noted before, *justice as fairness* is not concerned with those inequalities that are a consequence of making a personal choice (for example a choice not to develop one's abilities and talents, or of showing no willingness to do so). These choices fall under one's own responsibility. Pointing out the issues of "choice" and "circumstances," Rawls has triggered a debate on "personal responsibility" with regard to issues of distributive justice. It has become a starting point for theorizing on "choice-sensitive" egalitarianism: inequalities that are the consequence of circumstances we cannot be held responsible for are unjust; inequalities that are the consequence of "circumstances" we are ourselves responsible for are just, or at least not unjust.

What we are concerned with here is the way these issues play a role in debates on reforming, by retrenching or revitalizing, actual welfare states. In these debates, issues of a just income distribution have receded into the background and are replaced by debates on how far citizens themselves bear "responsibility" for the position they are actually in. In the context of a reorientation of the welfare state there is a search for a new interpretation of "solidarity." In this debate Rawls' ideas also play a role. An "ethics of social responsibility" proclaims that people should not be discriminated against on the basis of personal characteristics and circumstances for which they cannot be held responsible, and which are beyond their control, a basic notion borrowed from Rawls (antecedent privilege) and Dworkin. But at the same time, it is now argued that we should recognize that there are further choices here as well, to wit those between "equality," "responsibility," and "financial incentives."

Let us recall that Rawls' idea of "citizens viewed as free" means that they are "viewed as capable of taking responsibility for their choices"

(PL: 33, 185). This has led to a debate on whether Rawls' ideas on "personal responsibility" are consistent with his ideas on social contingencies and natural endowments. Is there indeed, as Rawls claims, such a thing as genuine personal responsibility for choices made? Does, in fact, "hard determinism" leave any space for choices? If it does not leave any space, the idea of personal responsibility would never apply to any human choices. In the context of our debate on the retrenchment and reorientation of the welfare state and a search for a new interpretation of "solidarity," it would, however, as Richard Arneson has argued, "still leave personal responsibility as most people understand it highly relevant to what social justice requires. In a host of institutional and informal practices central to social life, personal responsibility is important instrumentally as a tool to achieve the goals the practices are set up to achieve. Holding people responsible for their conduct means attaching rewards and penalties to it depending on its quality. We seek to adjust institutions and practices so that people acting within them have incentives to behave in socially desirable ways."[17]

In this context it is argued by Brian Barry that of course "it can still be accepted that we shall have to have incentives to get people to do things and punishments to prevent them from doing others, but these arise from purely pragmatic considerations. In fact, the same issue arises (or may well be thought to arise) in relation to the conclusions about social justice that I draw from a principle of social justice that includes the principle of personal responsibility: how far must we sacrifice social justice to provide incentives, produce an efficient labour market, and so on?"[18] In other words, personal responsibility might matter instrumentally even if it should turn out that it does not matter intrinsically for its own sake.

The Belgian politician and political theorist Frank Vandenbroucke has pointed out that it is from the perspective of these issues that the agenda of the welfare state should be broadened.[19] In fact these issues turn out to be ones on which many social democrats seem to agree. Taking a sample of the European literature on the welfare state published since say the mid-1990s by center-left policy institutes, parties, and scholars, Vandenbroucke notes that there is a broad convergence on these issues. Despite important national differences there is a recurrence of the following "fixed points."[20]

In a welfare state not only should the traditional social risks be covered (unemployment, illness and disability, old age, child benefit).

A welfare state should also cover new social risks (lack of skills causing long-term unemployment or poor employment, single parenthood) and new social needs (namely, the need to reconcile work, family life, and education, and the need to be able to negotiate changes within both family and workplace, over one's entire life cycle).

Next, there is the point that the "intelligent welfare state" should respond to those old and new risks and needs in an active and preventive way. The welfare state should engage not only in "social spending," but also in "social investment" (training and education). Also, active labor market policies should be higher on the agenda and upgraded, both in quantity and quality, by tailoring them more effectively to individual needs and situations. Active labor market policies presuppose a correct balance between incentives, opportunities, and obligations. One can characterize this as "opportunity solidarity." Persons that are under-privileged in the opportunities of choice have to be helped in acquiring skills to compensate for the inequalities of result. Ideas on a fundamental moral equality between persons are combined with an obligation to put effort into acquiring and training skills, so as to minimize as far as possible claims on society for welfare provisions.

An example of the literature in which these "fixed points," on which many social democrats seem to agree, are worked out is the report *Social Justice; Strategies for National Renewal*, published in 1994 by The Commission on Social Justice in the UK. This commission was set up in 1992 by the then leader of the Labour Party, John Smith, fifty years after the Beveridge Report *Social Insurance and Allied Services* was published, a report which became the foundation of the welfare state in the UK. The Commission was charged with formulating a fundamental reappraisal of the welfare state. The report stipulates that the values of social justice comprise "the equal worth of all citizens; their equal right to be able to meet their basic needs; the need to spread opportunities and life chances as widely as possible; and finally the requirement that we reduce and where possible eliminate unjustified inequalities. Social justice stands against fanatics of the free market economy; but it also demands and promotes economic success. The two go together." It includes "the belief not only that we owe something to each other, but that we gain from giving to each other. This is the heart of a moral community."[21] In working out these ideas we find in this report many of the "fixed points" mentioned by Vandenbroucke, including an implicit critique of Rawls' approach on social justice and personal responsibility. The report contains a comprehensive vision on the key issue of the relationship between rights and responsibilities. The egalitarianism of "old Labour" is criticized by The Commission for being unduly focused on material redistribution and for downplaying the individual's responsibilities. A more active approach to social welfare is recommended in which paid work is not the antithesis of welfare, but its partner. The report expresses a social investment approach in which investment in children and families is viewed as fundamental both to the achievement of social justice and to prudent government – reducing defensive public expenditure in the long run. The report articulated the thinking behind the social and economic policies of "New Labour." As the cover of the report tells us, Tony Blair hailed it as "essential reading for everyone who wants a new way forward for our country."[22]

In the public political debate on the range of social risks that should be covered in a welfare state, the claim is that traditional political philosophy (of which Rawls is considered the prime example) points more to the "rights" that citizens have than to their "obligations." While it is recognized that people should not be penalized for things they cannot control (as argued by Rawls), growing emphasis is placed on the responsibility of the relevant individuals to do whatever is in their might to minimize claims on society, and on an incentive structure that brings income and substitution effects in line with the goals of the policies pursued.

Rawls' difference principle mitigates natural and social contingencies, and is an effort to deal in a fair way with undeserved advantages (by mitigating them and *not* by trying to eliminate these contingencies, or by insisting that the actual distribution of, for example, income conforms at any given time [or over time] to any observable pattern, say equality. Recall that the difference principle is not the same as the principle of redress, or for that matter a "luck egalitarian principle.").

Now, or so it is argued, the problem with (the application of) the difference principle is this: it is based on a denial that people can be responsible (if only in part) for the outcomes of their actions. It seems to deny any *desert* or personal responsibility. Once the difference principle is implemented, anyone in a disadvantaged situation can claim that it is natural or social contingencies, or both, that are to blame for the situation they are in. These contingencies lie outside one's personal control and thus one does not bear any personal responsibility for them, or for the situation one is in. Accordingly, so the argument continues, a claim on society is formulated by saying that this claim can be justified by making an appeal to Rawls' theory.

The core of this line of reasoning against (the application of) the difference principle is that the principle, by focusing on "natural and social contingencies," does not take sufficiently into account the responsibility that people themselves have for the wide range of choices they make. Instead of mitigating conflict of interests over the distribution of benefits and burdens of social cooperation, the difference principle may have the unintended effect of creating instability, fueling resentment, and threatening social unity.

We touch here on what, for example, Samuel Scheffler has suggested is the reason a theory like that of Rawls lacks resonance outside academia, namely that it doesn't run with the grain of popular ideas of personal responsibility: "the reason various liberal programs may appear incompatible with ordinary thinking about responsibility is that they assign important benefits and burdens on the basis of considerations other than individual desert."[23]

Consequently, a search for an "ethics of responsibility" that would generate widespread legitimacy in actual welfare states should be more focused on the possibility of considering both issues: that of unfortunate contingencies and that of personal responsibility. Social justice should be about the reconciliation of two apparently conflicting principles, to wit the principle of compensation and the principle of responsibility, and about attempts to find room for responsibility within the larger approach to justice.

One reason why specific retrenchment policies in welfare states could be acceptable is, or so it is argued, because those measures would (re-) establish a link between entitlement to social welfare and personal responsibility, or choice-based inequalities. For example, the reciprocal duty in which, on the one hand, the unemployed look for work and, on the other, (local) government institutions give support in finding it (by, for example, providing supplementary education and thus creating a "reasonable expectation" for a job), is not only an actual example of linking compensation and responsibility, but also one that would widely be considered legitimate. There has to be at least an effort on the side of the recipient of welfare benefits towards a contributive activity while, at the same time, a "productive handicap" will be taken into account. This reciprocal duty could guarantee that people are prepared in the long run to be (or to remain) contributors to social insurance schemes that provide welfare provision, collectively organized and implemented by a welfare state.

But regardless of the search for a new interpretation of solidarity, the issue still holds that unequal access to goods and services, or unreasonable inequalities, should not be tolerated. This is implied not only by Rawls' own analysis. Refashioning the welfare state by establishing a clear link between compensation and responsibility within a larger approach to justice will only be considered reciprocal, and thus legitimate, if problems of unequal access are also taken into account. The political community as a whole has a shared responsibility to guarantee that conditions exist in which every person can actually bear responsibility for the choices he makes.

The difference principle and the problem of envy

We noted in the preceding paragraph that in debates on reconstructing actual welfare states, aspects of the difference principle which are considered to be problematic are brought forward. These aspects are used to explain why, once this principle would actually be applied, it would not generate a distribution of income and wealth which would generally be considered to be fair. On the contrary, or so the argument goes, the difference principle negates each form of desert and would only generate envy and resentment. Its application does not, for example, make enough of a distinction between unjust (because "unchosen") inequality of income, and just, choice-based inequalities of income. It does not take sufficiently into account, or so it is claimed, the responsibility citizens themselves have for choices they make.

We have as of yet not questioned the correctness of this view on (the effects of) the application of the difference principle. How to judge this interpretation of it, as well as the related interpretation of "desert" from within *justice as fairness* itself? Is it indeed correct to suggest that it is possible that the difference principle would engender in practice too much destructive general envy (TJ: 531–532; TJR: 466)? Or can it, contrary to this suggestion, generate envy-free distribution? What does it mean, in discussing the fair distribution of income, to appeal to desert?

First of all, it should be remembered that the difference principle does allow inequality of income, if this works out to the advantage of the least advantaged. The analysis of the contribution curve has illustrated this idea. Second, and relevant in our present discussion, is that the difference principle does in fact allow inequalities of income and of leisure time as well, if these inequalities are actually the outcome of preferences and choices people themselves make.

An "expensive taste" is, as far as Rawls is concerned, everybody's own responsibility. Thus the personal choice not to develop one's talents and abilities, of showing no willingness to do so if the opportunity to do so is available, falls under one's own responsibility, and *justice as fairness* is not concerned with inequalities that are a consequence of this choice. Also, according to Rawls, it holds that those who prefer not to work under conditions where there is much work that needs to be done (positions and jobs are not scarce or rationed), for example those who prefer to surf all day off Malibu in California, must find support for themselves and would not be entitled to public funds. They do not "deserve" a reward or assistance (PL: 181 note 9; CP: 455 note 7; JaF: 179).[24] *Justice as fairness* is not concerned with inequalities that are the consequence of choices in personal *life-style*, and if there is such a one, it is surfing all day off Malibu.

To substantiate these claims by Rawls, we have to have a closer look at the concept of "desert." A permanent element in Rawls' theory (we have noted it many times) is that there can never be a relation between any native endowments that persons have and their (moral) desert. We do not *deserve* our place in the distribution of native endowments, any more than we deserve our initial starting place in society (TJ: 104; TJR: 89; JaF: 74–75). It also should by now be clear that this idea has nothing to do with interpreting the conception of *justice as fairness* as a liberal comprehensive doctrine, or with focusing on *justice as fairness* in the context of political liberalism. "Moral desert" is a concept that cannot be incorporated in the theory of justice, neither conceived as a liberal comprehensive doctrine, nor as a political conception of justice. Since citizens have different, conflicting conceptions of the good, it is impossible for them to agree on a comprehensive doctrine to specify an idea of moral desert for political purposes. Distribution in accordance with "moral desert" is not a feasible political and social aim (JaF: 73; LoP: 147).

But having said this, it does not mean that there is no place for "desert" in *justice as fairness*. In a (political) conception of justice, "desert" is replaced by the idea of "legitimate expectations" (with which is connected the idea of entitlements). It is this idea that expresses "desert."[25]

Legitimate expectations and entitlements are specified by the public rules of the scheme of social cooperation, in short by *justice as fairness* itself.

Earlier we explained that the difference principle can be interpreted as an agreement to regard the distribution of native endowments (the differences among persons) as a common asset. All members of society can benefit from these differences, but especially the least advantaged. That is the core of the idea of reciprocity that the difference principle entails. The difference principle does not reward people for the native endowments they have, but for the efforts they invest in training and developing their native endowments and using them in such a way that they not only contribute to their own good, but also to the good of the less endowed (whose less fortunate place in the distribution they also do not morally deserve) (TJ: 101, 104–105; TJR: 87, 89–90; JaF: 74–77, 124).

When people act in this way they act "deservingly," as specified by the principle of legitimate expectations, which is just the other side of the coin of the principle of *justice as fairness*. And the idea of entitlement presupposes – just like ideas of moral desert do – a conscientious effort, or acts intentionally done. These acts provide the basis of legitimate expectations and earned entitlements. This can be formulated much more briefly: it is the difference principle itself that expresses "desert." *Justice as fairness* holds that the idea of "desert as entitlement" is fully adequate for a (political) conception of justice. And this is, of course, a moral idea (though not the idea of moral desert defined by a comprehensive doctrine), because the political conception of justice to which it belongs is itself a moral conception.

This all looks like a rather cumbersome way of answering the simple question posed at the beginning of this exposition: Would the application of the difference principle not generate envy and resentment? There can be little doubt about the answer Rawls himself would give: no, it would not. But we also have to realize the context in which he would give this answer. It is not the context of an actual welfare state. Rawls concentrates in his work on *ideal theory*, a theory meant for "favorable circumstances": a well-ordered society where the principles of *justice as fairness* are at work, with the related rights and duties of free and equal citizens. In such a society citizens have a sense of justice, one knows that everybody abides by the principles of justice and that mutually advantageous social cooperation is based on reciprocity. It is against this background that the difference principle expresses democratic equality. In this ideal situation, then, there is no place for fear that the application of this principle could have a destabilizing effect. And here we get to the issue of the kind of regime that Rawls argues would ideally best fit *justice as fairness*. As he explicitly makes clear, to "see the full force of the difference principle it should be taken in the context of property-owning democracy (or of a liberal socialist regime) and not a welfare state: it is a principle of reciprocity, or mutuality, for society seen as a fair system of cooperation among free and equal citizens from one generation to the next" (TJR: xv).

However, the context in which the application of the difference principle (or for that matter, *justice as fairness* as a whole) is usually debated is not ideal theory, and certainly not a "property-owning democracy." Its consequences are, more often than not, debated in the non-ideal situation of actually existing welfare states. In the practice of actual welfare states, we can conclude, the issue is not so much that the difference principle when applied would be a destabilizing force and would generate envy and resentment, nor that of whether we can empirically verify that its application "correctly" works out the distribution of income and wealth in a fair way. Neither is the issue to evaluate "real existing welfare states" from the perspective of *justice as fairness* and to propose changes in their basic institutions. This does not pose the issue in the right way. The real issue is that it is the concept of "welfare-state capitalism" in its entirety that raises a fundamental problem. It is a kind of regime that conflicts with *justice as fairness*, and the design of whose basic institutions makes it impossible to realize *justice as fairness*.

This conclusion forces us to reconsider what we have been doing so far. We were analyzing whether in actual welfare states, in debates on a just income policy, or on the personal responsibility of citizens for the choices they make, we could discern "Rawlsian" elements. In doing so we claimed that the three characteristics of political liberalism in fact describe so-called welfare-state-like institutions and arrangements. However, the exposition above on the difference principle, on envy, and on desert, shows we have not posed the question in the right way. The question ought to have been: How far does Rawls himself share the opinion that his theory of justice can be associated with the so-called welfare state?

Justice as fairness and the welfare state

In none of his publications over time has Rawls been concerned with the question of which actual model of a welfare state, for example the specific

"Anglo-Saxon model," the "Rhineland-model," or the "Scandinavian model," ought to be preferred. To substantiate his claim that a "property-owning democracy" would best realize *justice as fairness*, he does, however, analyze the contrast between different kinds of regime.

Rawls distinguishes five kinds of regime: *laissez-faire capitalism*; *welfare-state capitalism*; *state socialism with a command economy*; *liberal (democratic) socialism*; and a *property-owning democracy* (JaF: 135–138). We have already mentioned that Rawls notes that there is in fact no inconsistency of market arrangements with socialist institutions: market institutions are common to both private-property and liberal democratic socialist regimes.[26] However, *justice as fairness* leaves open the question of whether its principles are best realized by some form of "property-owning democracy," or by a "liberal socialist market regime." In theory, a liberal socialist regime can also answer to the two principles of justice. The decision as to which system is best for a given people depends upon their historical circumstances, institutions, and historical traditions, and the social forces of each country.[27]

Here, we are specifically concerned with the way Rawls compares a "*property-owning democracy*" with a welfare state, or "*welfare-state capitalism*." This comparison illustrates that Rawls' ideal of a stable, social, cohesive liberal political democratic society contains a fundamental critique of the idea of "welfare-state capitalism." This kind of regime does not satisfy the demands posed by *justice as fairness*. Contrasting "welfare-state capitalism" with "property-owning democracy" will make clear why this is so.[28]

To start with, let us remember that in the ideal sketch of the supporting or "surrounding" background institutions of *justice as fairness*, not only is considerable use made of market arrangements, but Rawls also assumes that the kind of regime is that of a "property-owning democracy." We have already discussed these issues extensively, in the section "Fair background institutions and market arrangements" in Chapter 2. Let us repeat that the role of the background institutions of a "property-owning democracy" is "the steady dispersal over time of the ownership of capital and resources by the laws of inheritance and bequest, on fair equality of opportunity secured by provisions for education and training, and the like, as well as on institutions that support the fair value of the political liberties" (TJR: xv). Thus a small part of society is prevented from controlling the economy and, indirectly, political life as well (TJR: xiv–xv; JaF: 139).[29]

Now the first important difference between "welfare-state capitalism" and a "property-owning democracy" is that "welfare-state capitalism" permits a small class to have a near monopoly of the means of production. Second, the main concern in a capitalist welfare state is the pursuit of self-interest by each citizen, individually and separately. This, or so the claim goes, would have for each and every member of society a positive effect: the general level of wealth in society would be enlarged or even maximized. Here the political morality of utility reigns, personified by the competitive ethos of the calculating citizen, maximizing his material possessions. It is a "private society" writ large, a society "not held together by a public conviction that its basic arrangements are just and good in themselves, but by the calculations of everyone, or of sufficiently many to maintain the scheme, that any practicable changes would reduce the stock of means whereby they pursue their personal ends" (TJ: 522; TJR: 458).

Turning to the welfare provisions in a capitalist welfare state, it should be noted that these may be very generous and guarantee a decent social minimum covering basic needs. Be that as it may, it is important to look at the aim of a welfare state. This is that "none should fall below a decent standard of life, and that all should receive certain protections against accident and misfortune – for example, unemployment compensation and medical care. The redistribution of income serves this purpose when, at *the end of each period*, those who need assistance can be identified. Such a system may allow large and inheritable inequities of wealth incompatible with the fair value of the political liberties ... as well as large disparities of income that violate the difference principle. While some effort is made to secure fair equality of opportunity, it is either insufficient or else ineffective given the disparities of wealth and the political influence they permit" (TJR: xv; JaF: 139–140; emphasis added).

This conception of the aim of the adjustments over time by background institutions is illustrative of the basic shortcomings of "welfare-state capitalism." The issue should not be, according to Rawls, to help people once they are struck by accident and misfortune. Because of the lack of background justice and because of inequalities in income and wealth, "there may develop a discouraged and depressed underclass many of whose members are chronically dependent on welfare. This underclass feels left out and does not participate in the public political culture" (JaF: 140). Formulated another way: "welfare-state capitalism" does not recognize an idea of reciprocity to regulate social and economic inequalities.

Now compare this with a "property-owning democracy." There "the aim is to carry out the idea of society as a fair system of cooperation over time among citizens as free and equal persons. Thus, basic institutions must *from the outset* put in the hands of citizens generally, and not only of a few, sufficient productive means to be fully cooperating members of a society [on a footing of equality]" (TJR: xv; JaF: 140; emphasis added). The intent of a "property-owning democracy" is not simply to assist those who lose out through accident or misfortune, but rather that all citizens should be brought into a position where they are able to manage their own affairs on a footing of a suitable degree of social and economic equality. Rawls' hope is that under these conditions the least fortunate will also participate in the public political culture. In this situation one can prevent an underclass from coming into existence. The least advantaged will realize that they also "belong to society." They are thus not "the unfortunate and unlucky – objects of our charity and compassion, much less our pity – but those whom reciprocity is owed as a matter of political justice among those who are free and equal citizens along with everyone else" (JaF: 139).

Having contrasted these two kinds of regimes to illustrate what Rawls has in mind with a society designed according to the aims and principles of *justice as fairness*, we should note, once again, that in fact in this respect nothing has changed over the years, and that it is all fully in line with what Rawls had already stated in 1971 in *A Theory of Justice*.[30] Regardless of whether we consider *justice as fairness* to be a liberal comprehensive doctrine, or whether we see it as a political conception of justice, Rawls' opinion has remained the same: the kind of regime that best fits *justice as fairness* is still a "property-owning democracy." Its ideal institutional description satisfies what is necessary to realize all of the main political values expressed by the principles of *justice as fairness*.

Let us recall here that the idea of *justice as fairness* is to use the notion of pure procedural justice: the social system is to be designed so that the resulting distribution is just, however things turn out. In order to apply the notion of pure procedural justice to distributive shares it is necessary to set up and to impartially administer the social and economic process within the surroundings of suitable political and legal institutions. Only against the background of a just basic structure, including a just political constitution and a just arrangement of economic and social institutions, can one say that the requisite just procedure exists. And this ideal scheme makes considerable use of market arrangements. It is only in this way, Rawls believes, that the problem of distribution can be handled as a case of pure procedural justice. Further, we also gain the advantages of efficiency and protect the important liberty of free choice of occupation. If idealized market arrangements are reasonably competitive and open, the notion of pure procedural justice is a feasible one to follow.

Right from the beginning it has been Rawls' conviction that it is the basic structure of a "property-owning democracy" that will realize – as far as possible – the notion central to *justice as fairness*: pure background procedural justice, from one generation to the next.

We have also, however, noted that there are impediments that prevent this ideal from being fully reached, and that on many questions of social and economic policy we must fall back upon a notion of quasi-pure procedural justice: laws and policies are just provided that they lie within the allowed range, and that the legislature, in ways authorized by a just constitution, has in fact enacted them. It is here that the (status of the) majority rule comes in. If the law actually voted is, so far as one can ascertain, within the range of those that could reasonably be favored by rational legislators conscientiously trying to follow the principles of justice, then the decision of the majority is practically authoritative, though not definitive. We must rely on the actual course of discussion at the legislative stage to select a policy within the allowed bounds. These cases are not instances of pure procedural justice because the outcome does not literally define the right result. It is simply that those who disagree with the decision made cannot convincingly establish their point within the framework of the public conception of justice. The question is one that cannot be sharply defined. This is what underlies the situation of quasi-pure procedural justice.

Recall that here we have the shift from justice to legitimacy debated earlier. Legitimacy is a weaker idea than (political) justice and imposes weaker constraints on what can be done. It points out that the outcome of a collective decision, if reached by a sufficiently just procedure (supported by a just constitution), may be legitimate but not just by a strict standard of justice. Thus the enactments and legislation of all institutional procedures should always be regarded by citizens as open to question.[31] This having been said should not, however, prevent us – and certainly not in the context of discussing the "applicability" of *justice as fairness* – from using the ideal conception to appraise existing arrangements, and as a framework for identifying the changes that should be undertaken.

But there is more. One aspect that has not until now been considered, neither in the earlier exposition on Rawls' theory of justice, nor in the discussion of debates on the (reorientation of the) welfare state, is the issue of "the social bases of self-respect," one of the primary goods. It is to that issue we now turn.

The social bases of self-respect

We have noted earlier that the primary good "the social bases of self-respect" is not as such part of any of the principles of *justice as fairness*. It is, however, for Rawls an important, perhaps even the most important, primary good. Without the presence of self-respect, life looks valueless and the zest to pursue one's plan of life, whatever it may be, with pleasure and to delight in its fulfillment is lacking; without it nothing seems worth doing. Self-respect is rooted in one's "confident conviction of the sense of one's own value, a firm assurance that what one does and plans to do is worth doing" (CP: 158). Thus self-respect presupposes the development and exercise of both moral powers, and therefore of an effective sense of justice.

The self-respect of moral persons is determined by circumstances in society. "The social bases of self-respect are those aspects of basic institutions that are normally essential if citizens are to have a lively sense of their own worth as moral persons and to be able to realize their highest-order interests and advance their ends with [zest and] self-confidence" (CP: 366, 314; JaF: 59). The idea is that a just basic structure as a whole, regulated by all the principles of justice, guarantees its realization. No single feature works alone in doing so.[32] No wonder that the parties in the original position are highly motivated that the principles of justice they choose for a well-ordered society should be able to realize this primary good. The parties want "at almost any cost" to prevent a situation in which the well-ordered society could hinder the development of self-respect.

A desirable feature of a conception of justice is, then, that it should publicly express men's respect for one another. In this way they ensure a sense of their own value. It is, according to Rawls, the two principles of *justice as fairness* that achieve this end (TJ: 179; TJR: 156). They do this in two ways. Let us explain.

The content of the public principles of justice for the basic structure, the principles of *justice as fairness*, has two aspects, each paired with one of the two elements of self-respect. Recall that the first element of self-respect is our self-confidence as a fully cooperating member of society rooted in the development and exercise of the two moral powers (and so as possessing an effective sense of justice); the second element is our secure sense of our own value rooted in the conviction that we can carry out a worthwhile plan of life.

The first element is supported by the basic liberties which guarantee the full and informed exercise of the two moral powers. The second element is supported by the public nature of this guarantee and the affirmation of it by citizens generally, all in conjunction with the fair value of political liberties and the difference principle. Our sense of our own value, as well as our self-confidence, depends on the respect and mutuality shown us by others (PL: 319). The public recognition of the first principle of justice, and thus of the basic liberties, confirms for the citizens of a well-ordered society their mutual respect as reasonable and trustworthy citizens, and it also expresses that each citizen can formulate his own conception of the good. Self-respect is reciprocally self-supporting.

Rawls, however, is not of the opinion that each and every plan of life is worth carrying out and deserves to be respected. A plan of life, or a conception of the good, that moral persons have chosen in realizing their two moral powers has to satisfy what Rawls calls "the Aristotelian Principle." This principle is a principle of motivation and is a consequence of the moral psychology used in *justice as fairness*. A plan of life has to formulate a challenge, it should bring someone to realize his capacities. Human beings "enjoy the exercise of their realized capacities (their innate or trained abilities), and this enjoyment increases the more the capacity is realized, or the greater its complexity" (TJ: 426; TJR: 374). Activities undertaken by someone that do not fulfill this Aristotelian Principle of motivation are a tiresome routine, become dull, uninspiring, and empty, and do not stimulate self-respect. The more someone can develop and realize his capacities, the better it is. The place where this can be given substance is of course in the well-ordered society.[33]

And here an important idea of Rawls' comes into play. It is an idea we have already noted, one that is related to the meaning of "social cooperation." Rawls is of the opinion that the social nature of our human relationships points to a situation of dependence on each other. People need each other because only by actively cooperating with others can the capacities everyone has actually be realized. Therefore Rawls can remark: "Only in the activities of social union can the individual be complete" (PL: 321). It is the principles of justice that reflect this "human sociability."

Rawls contrasts the social nature of mankind with the conception of *"private society."* The chief features of a "private society" "are first that the persons comprising it, whether they are human individuals or associations, have their own private ends which are either competing or independent, but not in any case complementary. And second, institutions are not thought to have any value in themselves, the activity of engaging in them not being counted as a good but if anything as a burden. Thus each person assesses social arrangements solely as a means to his private aims. No one takes account of the good of others, or of what they possess; rather everyone prefers the most efficient scheme that gives him the largest share of assets" (TJ: 521; TJR: 457).

This is, needless to say, not the notion of a well-ordered society. Human beings do in fact have shared final ends and they value their common institutions and activities as good in themselves (TJ: 522–523; TJR: 458; JaF: 199–200). It is the well-ordered society itself that is a form of "social union." In fact it is, as noted earlier, a social union that encompasses all associations and communities in society, it is "a social union of social unions" (TJ: 527; TJR: 462; PL: 320–323; JaF: 142, 201). In a "social union," a community or association, the members can fully realize the sense of their own value. For each and every member of the well-ordered society there must be at least one such association or community of shared ends where he feels at home, where his activities are valued by the other members of that association, and where he can develop a sense of self-respect.

Although the Aristotelian Principle formulates a plea to develop and to realize the widest range of diversity of capacities as possible, there remains in "a social union of social unions" a division of labor. As Rawls remarks: "[A] well-ordered society does not do away with the division of labor in the most general sense. To be sure, the worst aspects of this division can be surmounted: no one need be servilely dependent on others and made to choose between monotonous and routine occupations which are deadening to human thought and sensibility. Each can be offered a variety of tasks so that the different elements of his nature find a suitable expression" (TJ: 529; TJR: 463–464). In a well-ordered society there has to be meaningful work available for all, such that those who wish to perform such work can do so (TJ: 529; TJR: 463–464).

Taking all this into account, it is not surprising that Rawls considers the primary good of the social bases of self-respect to be of fundamental importance. It is also abundantly clear why a capitalist welfare state with the pursuit of self-interest by each citizen, individually and separately, where the political morality of utility reigns, personified by the calculating citizen, a "private society" that is not held together by a public conviction that its basic arrangements are just and good in themselves, can in no way be aligned with the requirements that *justice as fairness* poses.

Also, it now is clear why not one single principle of *justice as fairness* is sufficient to accomplish self-respect, but that all the principles of justice that order the basic structure working in tandem, do so. Summing up, one could say that realizing self-respect is proof of accomplishing *justice as fairness*.

An evaluation

Evaluating this exposition on "applying" *justice as fairness*, we note that a so-called "Rawlsian perspective" is mainly concerned with issues of the social and economic order, without taking into account the fundamental critique Rawls formulates with regard to so-called "welfare states."

But there is more. Discussions on "*justice as fairness* in practice" tend to ignore that Rawls' work also pays extensive attention to actual, contemporary societies characterized by a plurality of religious, philosophical, and moral, comprehensive beliefs and opinions, to issues of toleration in liberal democratic societies, societies that are also multicultural and multi-ethnic, to issues of a "neutral" state, to issues of the separation of state and church, to issues of the role of education and schooling, to issues of the level of political participation of citizens and of how to cope with the curse of money in politics, to the issue of the problematic character of the calculating citizen behaving as a *homo economicus* and the related issue of a "private society," and most of all to the issue of how to realize, or maintain, social unity in a plural society. These are topical issues, but they are issues that in actual debates on "*justice as fairness* in practice" to this day play hardly any role.

The working-out Rawls gives to his theory of political liberalism does not result in any overall blueprint for a well-ordered society. What it does do is to formulate a coherent set of general principles and arguments that stress that society should be considered a "social union of social unions," characterized by the criterion of reciprocity. The theory gives us a normative framework that in actual processes of legislation could provide guidelines on how to formulate public policies so as to realize *justice as fairness* in the best possible way. In this process, weighing alternative policy options, and the eventual choice of a particular one, should be based on democratic deliberation, not on (political) self- or group-interest, or on the whim of the day.

In actual public-political debates on questions of the general aims and means of a liberal, plural, democratic political, and social and economic order, the theory of Rawls can be a helpful guide. It provides criteria to evaluate what today should count as legitimate public policy, and what as a just society. In so doing, political philosophy fulfills one of its roles, that of orientation: "political philosophy may contribute to how a people think of their political and social institutions as a whole, and their basic aims and purposes as a society with a history – a nation – as opposed to their aims and purposes as individuals, or as members of families and associations" (JaF: 2).

Rawls' theory also provides the opportunity for established political parties to reflect on the philosophical background of their own thinking. Certainly, it should be stressed once again that Rawls himself does not take a stand in party-political debates. But this of course in no way precludes that political parties, or for that matter any citizen really interested in realizing a more just society, can take *justice as fairness* as a guideline, and its principles as yardsticks in formulating ideas on social justice in their efforts to bring the institutional frameworks of our actual societies more in line with what is required by *justice as fairness*.

6 | Justice as Fairness: *a realistic utopia*

With regard to the reception of the *magnum opus* of Rawls, one can ascertain without much ado that *A Theory of Justice* is generally considered to be the most influential philosophical work since the Second World War. It is hailed as a milestone in the development of political philosophy, an opinion shared by those who take a critical stand on it.

Reactions to *Political Liberalism* have been more diverse. From the perspective "if it is not broken, don't fix it," the question has been raised as to whether the recasting and revision that account for the nature and extent of the differences between *Political Liberalism* and *A Theory of Justice* were necessary at all and, if so, whether they were successful. Illustrative here is the reaction of Brian Barry. He believes "that, as time goes on, *A Theory of Justice* will stand out with increasing clarity as by far the most significant contribution to political philosophy produced in [the twentieth] century." But having said this, Barry argues with regard to *Political Liberalism* that "Rawls's sweeping recantation is uncalled-for," and that Rawls' "earlier self should be defended against his latter self." Barry first takes a stand against Rawls' own claim in later days that the liberal doctrine in *A Theory of Justice* is a (liberal) comprehensive one.[1] After all, as Barry notes, "the whole point of *A Theory of Justice* was that it left people to form, revise, and pursue their own conceptions of the good."[2] It formulates the fair conditions under which persons having different conceptions of the good could live together. Rawls' own account of what was in this regard wrong with *A Theory of Justice* does not stand up, according to Barry. This does not mean that *A Theory of Justice* is without problems, in particular with the issue of the stability of justice turning on the appropriate motivation for doing what justice requires. Barry agrees with Rawls that there are, indeed, problems here but *Political Liberalism* does not, or so Barry argues, succeed in fulfilling its stated task of solving them.

In formulating the principles of international justice, Rawls completed his design of just institutions. With regard to the monograph

The Law of Peoples, one can note that the reception thereof seems to be tainted by disappointment: disappointment that Rawls did not regard especially the difference principle as the appropriate principle to be extended to the international domain; in addition, that Rawls applies his theory of justice to "peoples" and not to "citizens of the world" has encountered many misgivings; and Rawls' idea that non-liberal but decent peoples should be tolerated is seen as an unacceptable subversion of what liberal toleration ought to encompass.

What is especially striking in these critical reactions to *The Law of Peoples* is not the rejection of Rawls' conclusions in themselves, but rather that the line of reasoning that led Rawls to reach his conclusions, especially his argument that "the Law of Peoples" rises within political liberalism, is usually negated. This holds first and foremost for Rawls' argument that there is no "global basic structure" where one can speak of "social cooperation for mutual advantage" in a "Rawlsian" meaning of the term, and that accordingly there is in "the Law of Peoples," contrary to what cosmopolitans want to argue, no place for an international principle of *distributive* justice.

What, finally, is also hardly debated is Rawls' position that, although the time of the absolute sovereignty of peoples (or if one prefers in this context that of "the sovereign nation state") is over, there are nevertheless good reasons to take a critical stand on the idea of exporting or even globally enforcing *justice as fairness* (or, more generally, any form of "liberalism"). Evidently, and contrary to Rawls' arguments, liberal imperialism is not seen by his critics as problematic. That Rawls, at the same time, holds a plea for the possibility of intervention when fundamental human rights are violated, is seen by the same critics as offering too "thin" a kind of universalism of what is required by a liberal theory of international justice.

Rawls himself always has been very selective in responding to criticism of his work. First of all, the sheer insurmountable and seemingly never-ending flow of publications made this impossible as a practical matter. But a more important reason to be selective was that Rawls considered it meaningful to react only if he had the feeling that the critique was serious. As he once said: "One has to learn to accept criticisms. Often they are not well founded and based on misunderstanding. Those I try to ignore. But there are criticisms that are very good. While I'm not overjoyed by those, I do appreciate them, eventually, and I try to incorporate them into what I write later."[3] A famous example here is the fundamental criticism raised by H. L. A. Hart in 1973 on Rawls' views on basic liberties as formulated in *A Theory of Justice*.[4] With regard to this critique Rawls noted in an interview in 1991 that Hart "was absolutely right. I was stuck about what to reply but eight years later I decided what the answer should be. I wrote it out and it was published in 1982. That was of enormous value to me. It caused some pain, certainly, but now I can state the view in a much stronger form."[5]

Also, already mentioned, the main reason for Rawls not to move on to a new topic after the publication in 1971 of *A Theory of Justice*, was because he thought "the way things have turned out, that it would be better if I spent my time trying to state justice as fairness more convincingly and to reply to people and remove their objections."[6]

One of the explanations for the enormous influence of Rawls' work, and also for the interest it has raised outside the circle of academic political philosophers, is the fact that, by demonstrating that it was possible to produce a powerful and coherent piece of theorizing, it provided a tool for reflecting in a systematic way on the basic choices that have to be made when debating the requirements for a just political order. Rawls shows us in a penetrating and convincing way how we can reflect on the fundamental interests of citizens, especially those of the worst-off members of society, from a perspective that really favors their lot. In so doing, he has provided us with an unprecedented refined insight into the moral and the social. What makes Rawls a major philosopher is not the broad scope of his ambition, but rather the depth of his perception. It is his ability to bring to the fore the difficulties and complexities of (political) philosophical questions.

Accordingly, in *Political Liberalism* Rawls needs some four hundred and sixty pages to show us the practical possibility that citizens with their plurality of conflicting reasonable comprehensive doctrines, religious and nonreligious, liberal and nonliberal, could nevertheless reach agreement on just and stable social cooperation in a democratic political order. His exposition demonstrates the central role "public reason" has to play in this search for fair terms of cooperation and in reaching an overlapping consensus on a political conception of justice. The point to note is that Rawls is conscious of the fact, much more so than most defenders of liberal democracy, that it is not self-evident that agreement will be the outcome of deeply disputed questions. He demonstrates that the search for terms of fair cooperation that are reasonable for all to accept, is quite a task, even if we confine ourselves to reasonable citizens.

Mentioning the magnitude of the task of public justification is not, however, to say that we, following Rawls, should not work hard (in the name of justice properly understood) to convince enough people of the importance of adhering to a family member of a political conception of liberalism. But is it realistic to suppose that the outcome will indeed be that "you and I," "here and now," will be convinced of the importance of adhering to such a conception of justice?

We touch here upon Rawls' idea that one of the tasks of political philosophy is to extend "what are ordinarily thought to be the limits of practicable political possibility and, in so doing, reconciles us to our political and social condition" (LoP: 11). The nature and content of justice are discussed by Rawls in the context of a well-ordered society, as ideal theory, in which (nearly) everyone abides by the principles of justice. For this idea of a well-ordered society to be suitably realistic, it is assumed to exist under "circumstances of justice." Recall that these are of two kinds: first, there are the *objective* circumstances which make human cooperation both possible and necessary, the condition of moderate scarcity. In addition, the circumstances include the fact of reasonable pluralism. This condition is permanent as it persists indefinitely under free democratic institutions. This fact of reasonable pluralism limits what is practicably possible under the conditions of our (actual) world (JaF: 4, 84). Next, there are the *subjective* circumstances, the relevant aspects of the persons working together, with their own plans of life, putting forward conflicting claims on the division of social advantages (TJ: 126–127; TJR: 109–110).

Taking these circumstances of justice into account, political philosophy asks: "What ideals and principles would a just democratic society try to realize given the circumstances of justice in a democratic culture as we know them?" "What would a reasonably just democratic society be like under reasonably favorable but still possible historical conditions, conditions allowed by the laws and tendencies of the social world?" "How do these conditions relate to laws and tendencies bearing on the relations between peoples?" (LoP: 11; JaF: 4, 84).

The answer given to these questions is not only what a just, or nearly just, constitutional regime might be like, taking the circumstances of justice into account. Rawls conceives of the task of political philosophy more broadly. The question is also whether it may come about and be made stable under the circumstances of justice, and so under realistic, though reasonable, favorable conditions (JaF: 13). When political philosophy, in answering these questions, is indeed extending what we ordinarily think the limits of the possible to be, it is *realistically utopian*. And for Rawls it is a specific political philosophy, *justice as fairness*, that "probes the limits of the realistically practicable, that is, how far in our world (given its laws and tendencies) a democratic regime can attain complete realization of its appropriate political values – democratic perfection, if you like" (JaF: 13).

A liberal political conception of justice (including of course the family member *justice as fairness*) is "*realistic*" because it "takes people as they are (by the laws of nature), and constitutional and civil laws as they might be, that is, as they would be in a reasonably just and well-ordered democratic society" (LoP: 13). It is "realistic" because it does not require us to become "new men," new types of human beings. It is "realistic" because realizable by us, here and now, notwithstanding the fact of a plurality of reasonable comprehensive doctrines. And a liberal political conception of justice is "*utopian*" because of its use of political (moral) ideals, principles, and concepts to specify an (institutional) sketch of a reasonable and just society that for free and equal citizens is reasonable to accept, satisfying the criterion of reciprocity.

To summarize: the aim of the family of reasonable liberal political conceptions of justice is to provide a sketch of the practical political possibility of a reasonable just constitutional democratic society: of a "*realistic utopia*."[7] And the aim of political philosophy being realistically utopian is also to extend that conception of political liberalism outward, in showing that a reasonable just liberal and decent Society of Peoples is possible as well, and thus that the Law of Peoples is also a realistic utopia. The "idea of a realistic utopia doesn't settle for a compromise between power and political right and justice, but sets limits to the reasonable exercise of power" (LoP: 6 note 8).

By formulating the outlines of a just political order for the domestic, as well as for the international, case, political philosophy gives us a perspective on what it is worthwhile to strive for in politics. Convincing arguments, deliberation, good reasons, all are essential to accomplish this and to convince us of the plausibility that this utopia is indeed realistic. An appeal to a shared fund of ideas, to a common forum, is crucial for us to be successful in changing prevailing convictions in existing political orders on what is reciprocal, acceptable, and fair, and to be able to make a successful appeal to the political and socio-logical imagination of citizens. The thinkable all too often is condi-tioned by what seems possible. Many issues are not, however, out of our reach, but have disappeared out of our sight. The theory of justice as formulated by Rawls provides an example on how to broaden our perspective: "The problem here is that the limits of the possible are not given by the actual, for we can to a greater or to a lesser extent change political and social institutions, and much else. Hence we have to rely on conjecture and speculations, arguing as best we can that the social world we envision is feasible and might actually exist, if not now then at some future time under happier circumstances" (LoP: 12).

It goes without saying that the idea of a "realistic utopia" is an institutional idea. It is also not an idea newly introduced by Rawls.[8] All along he has sought to work out a *realistic* ideal of justice. This is in fact the permanent motivation underlying Rawls' works, and the idea of a realistic utopia envisions the culmination of his institutional project. With this idea we have come full circle, right back to the start of the project as formulated in *A Theory of Justice*: the idea that "justice is the first virtue of social institutions." Rawls' theorizing turns on formulat-ing an answer to how to design political, and social and economic institutions such that citizens would act correctly according to the appro-priate principles of their sense of justice, which they have acquired by growing up under and participating in just institutions (LoP: 13 note 2).

A central motivation throughout Rawls' works, one that has been present from the beginning but that has become more and more out-spoken in later years, especially in *The Law of Peoples*, is to find ways to eliminate the great evils of human history so as that they will eventually disappear. We must not allow these great evils (such as the Inquisition and the Holocaust, unjust war, oppression, religious persecution, slav-ery), evils that are essentially man-made, to "undermine our hope for the future of our society as belonging to a Society of liberal and decent Peoples around the world" (LoP: 22). This is the core of Rawls' lifelong project of reconciliation, our shared responsibility to explore the possi-bility – in ways existing circumstances allow – of a just social world. It is in this context we have to understand *justice as fairness*: it should help us to identify which wrongs it is urgent to correct.

Although there is no guarantee that a just Society of Peoples must come into existence or that it will – how could one guarantee such a thing? – the possibility that it could is important. "By showing how the social world may realize the features of a realistic utopia, political philosophy provides a long-term goal of political endeavor, and in working toward it gives meaning to what we can do today" (LoP: 128). There is an alternative. That is to reject the idea of the possibility of ever achieving a liberal and decent political and social order. Rawls, however, asks us to contemplate the costs of such an alternative: "If a reasonably just Society of Peoples whose members subordinate their power to reasonable aims is not possible, and human beings are largely amoral, if not incurably cynical and self-centered, one might ask, with Kant, whether it is worthwhile for human beings to live on the earth" (LoP: 128; PL: lxii).

Notes

Preface

1. John Rawls, 2000, "A Reminiscence: Burton Dreben," in Juliet Floyd and Sanford Shieh, eds, *Future Pasts: Perspectives on the Place of Analytical Tradition in Twentieth-Century Philosophy*, 417–430, 417, New York: Oxford University Press; John Rawls, 2000, *Lectures on the History of Moral Philosophy*, xvi, Cambridge, MA: Harvard University Press. See also John Rawls, 2007, *Lectures on the History of Political Philosophy*, xii–xv, Cambridge, MA and London: The Belknap Press of Harvard University Press.
2. John Rawls, 1996, *Political Liberalism*, xxxvii, New York: Columbia University Press.

1. Life and work

1. Norman Malcolm, 1958, *Ludwig Wittgenstein: A Memoir*, Oxford: Oxford University Press, revised 1984.
2. "Fifty years later," in an issue of *Dissent* dealing with reflections on Hiroshima: *Dissent*, 1995, 42(3): 323–327. Also in CP: 565–572; see also LoP: 95.
3. It is not necessary to know the biography of Rawls to get an insight into his philosophical work, in which "unmerited contingencies" and "arbitrariness of fortune" play such an important role. It does, however, provide insight into what brought Rawls to pose the question of "under which circumstances it can be just that someone like me is so much better off and fortunate."
4. Rawls resumed his studies with the help of the so-called "GI Bill of Rights." Signed into law on June 22, 1944 by President Franklin D. Roosevelt, the GI Bill related to the eleven million American soldiers in World War II, with the intention of enabling them to return from the war with more opportunities. With regard to education this law turned out to be especially important. It provided, among other things, financial assistance for those veterans who wanted to resume their schooling (at university or otherwise), or for those who wanted to start college – settling their families, paying tuition, buying books. The GI Bill covered living

expenses for half the nation's college students by 1947. Between 1944 and 1951, almost eight million ex-soldiers received free job training or higher education under two GI Bill programs. Of these, 2.3 million went to high school and university. An important effect was that this new student population changed the idea that higher education was a privilege for the elite. The GI Bill added nearly three years to the average veteran's education. See Taylor Branch, 2007, "Justice for Soldiers," *The New York Review of Books*, 54(6), April 12.

5. It is Rawls himself speaking here in, "On My Religion," composed in the 1990s; an essay in which he lays bare the reasons why it was in particular his experiences during the war that made him change his religious beliefs, and eventually led him to abandon being a "believing orthodox Episcopalian Christian." Some pages of this essay are published in Thomas W. Pogge, 2007, *John Rawls: His Life and Theory of Justice*, 13–14, Oxford: Oxford University Press. Together with Rawls's senior thesis this essay is published in John Rawls, 2009, *A Brief Inquiry into the Meaning of Sin and Faith*, with "On My Religion", edited by Thomas Nagel, Cambridge, MA: Harvard University Press, 259–270.

6. Walter Kaufmann, 1950, *Nietzsche: Philosopher, Psychologist and Antichrist*, Princeton, NJ: Princeton University Press.

7. John Rawls, 1950, "A Study on the Grounds of Ethical Knowledge: Considered with Reference to Judgments on the Moral Worth of Character." Unpublished PhD dissertation, Princeton University.

8. As it is called by J. Feinberg, 1972, "Justice, Fairness and Rationality," *The Yale Law Journal*, 81: 1004–1031, 1018–1021.

9. Pogge, *John Rawls*, pp. 20–21; see also Ben Rogers, 1999, "Portrait of John Rawls," *Prospect*, 42, June: "According to Rogers Albritton, 'Both of us thought that it was wrong that the sons of the privileged should be allowed to stay out and accumulate grades, while someone who wanted to start a filling-station was sent off.' In retrospect, Albritton saw the irony in their position: 'There was something a bit bizarre about saying we were against the war, but our students should go to fight in it.'" It was with Albritton, former Princeton classmate, one-time colleague at the Harvard Department of Philosophy, and lifelong friend, that Rawls in those years discussed issues of conscription and when it could be justified; see TJ: 380; TJR: 333.

10. "John Rawls: For the Record," interview with John Rawls, *The Harvard Review of Philosophy*, 1991(1): 38–47, 42.

11. The brief, "Assisted Suicide: The Philosophers' Brief. By John Rawls, Judith Jarvis Thomson, Robert Nozick, Ronald Dworkin, T. M. Scanlon, Thomas Nagel," was published with an introduction by Ronald Dworkin in 1997, *The New York Review of Books*, 44(5), March 27. See also

Rawls on the brief in CP: 616–619. The Court eventually unanimously upheld the laws and rejected the notion of a constitutional right to physician-assisted suicide.

12. Rawls received innumerable invitations to participate in conferences. Only in exceptional cases did he accept one or another. One of these cases was a conference about his work in Santa Clara (CA) at the end of October 1995, organized by his former students on the occasion of the twenty-fifth anniversary of *A Theory of Justice*. Rawls did not want to disappoint them, and participated in the conference. After the conference, on his way to the airport to fly home, Rawls was struck by the first of a succession of severe strokes.

13. To those whom Rawls has over the years trained and/or supervised the dissertations of, and who are now well-known philosophers in their own right, belong Thomas Nagel, Tim Scanlon, Onora O'Neill, Sisila Bok, Norman Daniels, Barbara Herman, Joshua Cohen, Christine Korsgaard, Jean Hampton (who died in 1996), Thomas Pogge, Samuel Freeman, Susan Neiman, Elizabeth Anderson, Henry Richardson, Peter de Marneffe, Erin Kelly, and Alyssa Bernstein.

14. Because the Nobel Prizes do not include the category "logic and philosophy," the Swedish philosopher Rolf Schock, who died in 1986, specified in his will that half of his estate should be used to fund four prizes in the fields of "logic and philosophy," "mathematics," "the visual arts," and "music." Starting in 1993, the prizes are awarded every three years.

15. John Rawls, 1951, "Outline of a Decision Procedure for Ethics," *Philosophical Review*, 60: 177–197.

16. "John Rawls: For the Record": 43, 44.

17. Rawls himself was reluctant to permit the publication of his collected papers in book form. After all, as Rawls used to say, these papers are to be seen as experimental works, opportunities to try out ideas that later may be developed or revised in his books, but which may also be abandoned. When it was explained to him that students and academics had to spend hours tracing his articles, he was finally persuaded to have them published in one volume.

18. The German translation, published in 1975, did not contain a "Preface for the German Edition" by Rawls. It is only mentioned by the publisher that: "Der Übersetzung liegt ein vom Autor anlässlich der deutschen Ausgabe revidierter Text zugrunde." That may explain why the revisions went unnoticed for a long time. Only with the French translation of *A Theory of Justice*, published in 1987 (*Théorie de la justice*, Paris: éditions du Seuil), did Rawls include a "Preface for the French Edition of *A Theory of Justice*." It is also part of CP: 415–420. The introduction

that opens the *Revised Edition* of *A Theory of Justice*, published in 1999, is 95 percent identical with the introduction to the French edition.

19. John Rawls, 2000, "A Reminiscence: Burton Dreben," in Juliet Floyd and Sanford Shieh, eds, *Future Pasts: Perspectives on the Place of Analytical Tradition in Twentieth-Century Philosophy*, 417–430, 427, New York: Oxford University Press; LHMP: xvi; see also LHPP: xii.
20. Samuel Freeman, in his "Editor's Foreword" to LHPP: x.
21. Arnold Brecht, 1959, *Political Theory. The Foundations of Twentieth-Century Political Thought*, Princeton, NJ: Princeton University Press.
22. T. D. Weldon, 1960 [1953], *The Vocabulary of Politics*, Harmondsworth: Penguin Books Ltd.
23. A. De Crespigny and K. Minogue, eds, 1975, *Contemporary Political Philosophers*, x, London: Methuen & Co.
24. John Plamenatz, 1960, "The Use of Political Theory," *Political Studies*, 8: 37–47, 37.
25. Leo Strauss, 1971 [1950], "Natural Right and the Distinction between Facts and Values," in Leo Strauss, *Natural Right and History*, 35–80, Chicago and London: University of Chicago Press; see also Leo Strauss, 1959, *What is Political Philosophy?*, New York: University of Chicago Press.
26. See also JaF: 82, 133.
27. But see John G. Gunnell, 1986, *Between Philosophy and Politics: The Alienation of Political Theory*, 164, Amherst: University of Massachusetts Press. Gunnell, for one, calls into question that political theory can find in this quintessential example of contemporary academic philosophy what it seeks because, as he argues, it remains a work about concepts and logic, not about human practice, or practical problems. It is still "meta-theory." I tend to disagree.
28. Robert Nozick, 1974, *Anarchy, State, and Utopia*, 183, New York: Basic Books.

2. A just society

1. PL: 57, 197, 197 note 32, 198 note 33; JaF: 36 note 26, 154, 154 note 29.
2. Rawls notes some distinctions that enable us to understand the meaning of different social contract views and to separate them from one another: the distinction between *actual and non-historical agreements*; the distinction of how the content is determined: by the terms of *an actual contract*, or by *analysis*; the distinction between whether the content of the social contract concerns what people *could do* – or could not possibly do – or what they *would do*; the distinction between whether the content of the social contract specifies when a form of government is *legitimate*, or whether that

content is seen as determining the (*political*) *obligations* that citizens have to their government; LHPP: 14–15. See, for Rawls' lectures on Rousseau, LHPP: 191–248; for those on Locke, LHPP: 103–155; for those on Kant, LHMP: 143–325. See on Kant also John Rawls, 1989, "Themes in Kant's Moral Philosophy," in Eckart Förster, ed., *Kant's Transcendental Deductions; The Three* Critiques *and the* Opus postumum, 81–113, Stanford, CA: Stanford University Press; also in CP: 497–528.

3. During much of the modern period of moral philosophy the predominant systematic view in the English-speaking world had been some form of utilitarianism. One reason for this was, according to Rawls, that it had been represented by a long line of brilliant writers, from David Hume and Adam Smith to F. Y. Edgeworth and Henry Sidgwick. See, for Rawls' lectures on Hume, LHPP: 159–187; LHMP: 21–102; for those on Sidgwick, LHPP: 375–415; for Rawls' lectures on John Stuart Mill LHPP: 251–316.

4. In JaF: 141 the same point is formulated by Rawls as: "the just draws the limit, the good shows the point."

5. As it is, of course, of Kant's ethics. See for Rawls' analysis of Kant's ideas on the priority of right, LHMP: 217–234. This is part of Rawls' broader analysis of Kant: LHMP: 143–324.

6. Rawls often uses, in *A Theory of Justice*, the term "Kantian interpretation." See for instance in TJ and TJR the whole of §40 under the heading "The Kantian Interpretation." For Rawls there is analogy, not identity, between his ideas and those of Kant. To underline this he has, for instance, added in TJR, at the end of this paragraph, that "the Kantian interpretation is not intended as an interpretation of Kant's actual doctrine but rather of justice as fairness" (TJR: 226).

7. See for the enumeration of the primary goods, TJ: 62, 92; TJR: 54, 79; CP: 313–314, 362–363, 366; PL: 181; LoP: 13; JaF: 58–59.

8. As Rawls notes in his introduction to the revised edition of *A Theory of Justice* (the revisions actually made in 1975), there should be no ambiguity as to "whether something's being a primary good depends solely on the natural facts of human psychology or whether it also depends on a moral conception of the person that embodies a certain ideal." It depends on the latter: "[p]rimary goods are now characterized as what citizens need in their status as free and equal citizens, and as normal and fully cooperating members of society over a complete life." The primary goods "are seen as answering to their needs as citizens as opposed to their preferences and desires" (Introduction to TJR: xiii). See also Rawls' article published in 1982, "Social Unity and Primary Goods"; see also CP: 367. Note also, once more, that this introduction is 95 percent identical to the introduction to the earlier published French translation of *A Theory of Justice* (*Théorie de la justice*, Paris, éditions du Seuil), published in 1987. The English

translation of that introduction is part of CP: 415–420. The remark on the primary goods can be found there, at 417–418. For more on "all-purpose means" see chapter 2, the section "The principles of justice and primary goods."

9. See the paragraph on "Principles of Moral Psychology" (TJ & TJR: §75). Rawls has not changed these ideas substantially over the years. See, for instance, JaF, where Rawls repeats the idea that the psychological principles exhibit this reciprocity of disposition (JaF: 196).

10. In TJ: 15, Rawls states, instead of "prevents," "nullifies."

11. See also CP: 316 (originally from "Kantian Constructivism in Moral Theory," 1980: 528).

12. Or "generalizes and carries to a higher level of abstraction the familiar theory of the social contract" (TJ: 11; TJR: 10).

13. James Buchanan, 1975, *The Limits of Liberty: Between Anarchy and Leviathan*, Chicago: University of Chicago Press. For Buchanan, justice is a by-product of efficiency when using Hobbesian anarchy as the starting point of analysis; see Percy B. Lehning, 1978, "Social Contract and Property Rights: A Comparison between John Rawls and James M Buchanan," in P. Birnbaum, J. Lively and G. Parry, eds, *Democracy, Consensus and Social Contract*, 279–294, London and Beverly Hills: Sage Publications; David Gauthier, 1986, *Morals by Agreement*, Oxford: Oxford University Press. Gauthier's view is that social order should mirror the partiality of the natural order. In Rawls' view, the well-ordered society corrects the arbitrariness of natural, social, and accidental contingencies. See, for an argument that Gauthier has missed an important element of what justice is really about, and for a comparison with Gauthier-Rawls: Percy B. Lehning, 1993, "Right Constraints?" in David Gauthier and Robert Sugden, eds, *Rationality, Justice and the Social Contract: Themes from* Morals by Agreement, 95–115, New York and London: Harvester Wheatsheaf.

14. See also TJ: 150–151.

15. Rawls introduces only in later years the terms "narrow" and "wide" reflective equilibrium. But although both terms, "narrow" and "wide," would not have been used in TJ or TJR, the ideas underlying the terms were already present in TJ and TJR. In "narrow" reflective equilibrium we take note only of our own judgment. Rawls started using both terms from 1974 onward; see PL: 8 note 8, 384 note 16.

16. We should note that Rawls himself, in TJ and TJR, in making the two comparisons, does not speak in all instances of a comparison with "utilitarian" principles. In the second comparison it is a comparison between *justice as fairness* and what he calls a "mixed conception." In the "mixed conception" (U2), the difference principle is substituted by

the principle of average utility combined in specific cases with a stipulated minimum; see TJR: xiv; TJ & TJR: §21 "The Presentation of Alternatives"; TJ & TJR: §49 "Comparison with Mixed Conceptions"; see also JaF: 120.

17. See also TJR: xiv.

18. J. C. Harsanyi, 1975, "Can the Maximin Principle Serve as a Basis for Morality?" *American Political Science Review*, 69: 594–606; J. Narveson, 1982, "Rawls and Utilitarianism," in H. B. Miller and W. H. Williams, eds, *The Limits of Utilitarianism*, 128–143, Minneapolis: University of Minnesota Press.

19. Rawls has explicitly replied to Harsanyi's article in his 1978 "The Basic Structure as Subject," 69 note 4; see also PL: 261 note 5; JaF: 97 note 19.

20. The same remark can be found in PL: 53 note 7, and both remarks can also be found at the same place in the editions of PL of 1996 and 2005. It is the same as what Rawls notes in 1982, in "The Basic Liberties and Their Priority," 20–21 note 20, 87 note 80. And in 1985 he had also noted this in "Justice as Fairness: Political not Metaphysical," 237 note 20. It is also to be found in 1999, in his *Collected Papers*, 401 note 20. And, finally, once again in 2001, in JaF: 82 note 2. With regard to the sentence, "The theory of justice is a part, perhaps the most significant part, of the theory of rational choice," Rawls remarks that it should be corrected.

21. See also JaF: 43 note 3.

22. See: JaF: xvii, 43 note 3. And, once again, in part III of JaF: 94 note 17, 97 note 19.

23. In TJ: 62; TJR: 54, Rawls speaks of "social values" instead of "primary goods," and "to everyone's advantage" instead of "the advantage of the least favored."

24. See, for the formulation of the principles of justice, TJ: 60, 250, 302; TJR: 53, 220, 266. See for the priority rules, TJ: 302–303; TJR: 266–267. The correct term is "a lexicographical order," but this is, as Rawls himself notes, too cumbersome. He uses either "lexical" or "serial," TJ: 42–43; TJR: 37–38. We will do the same.

25. TJ: 250, 302; TJR: 220, 266. From 1982 onwards, Rawls no longer uses the formulation "the most extensive" in the first principle of justice, but "a fully adequate scheme." This change in wording is made by Rawls in reaction to criticism formulated by H. L. A. Hart in 1973, in an important article, "Rawls on Liberty and its Priority," *University of Chicago Law Review*, 40(3): 534–555. See for Rawls' reaction, his 1982 "The Basic Liberties and Their Priority," in Sterling M. McMurrin, ed., *Tanner Lectures on Human Values*, volume III, 3–87, Salt Lake City: University of Utah Press, and in a revised version which is part of PL:

289–371. See, for the principle, PL: 5, 291; see also JaF: 42, 111–112. The acknowledgment of the criticism by Hart, and working out revisions to cope with it, are from after 1975. Thus they are not part of the revised edition of *A Theory of Justice* that – although it had been published in 1999 – is based, as we noted earlier, on revisions Rawls had made before that time. The reformulation of the first principle has, it should be stipulated, nothing to do with changes in later days, as in *Political Liberalism*, to be able to cope with a plurality of comprehensive doctrines (a subject of the next chapter of this introduction, "Pluralism and justice").

26. TJ: 302; TJR: 266; CP: 362, 392; JaF: 42–43; PL: 6.
27. See also TJ: 63.
28. See also TJ: 152, 542–543; TJR: 475–476.
29. The last sentences are revisions, compared to the original edition of 1971, but already made in 1975. They can be found in the German translation of TJ, published in 1975: 177; see also TJR: 475.
30. See also TJR: 132.
31. See also TJ: 63.
32. Rawls refers to Jean Drèze and Amartya Sen, 1989, *Hunger and Public Action*, Oxford: Clarendon Press, chapter 13, "The Economy, the State, and the Public"; JaF: 47; LoP: 109.
33. Rawls refers to Amartya Sen, 1981, *Poverty and Famine*, Oxford: Clarendon Press.
34. But also note Rawls' remark: "imagining themselves to be fathers, say, they are to ascertain how much they should set aside for their sons and grandsons by noting what they would believe themselves entitled to claim of their fathers and grandfathers" (TJR: 256).
35. See also PL: 274 note 12; JaF: 160 note 39; Rawls, 1978, "The Basic Structure as Subject": 70 note 11.
36. But precisely the fact that so many factors influence motivation to stimulate the development of natural endowments, such as social position, the situation within the family, and societal circumstances, makes it very difficult to judge if a situation of fair equality of opportunity has been accomplished. Rawls even thinks reaching it in practice may turn out to be impossible; see TJ: 73, 301, 511; TJR: 73, 265, 448; JaF: 43–44.
37. TJ: 250, 203, 205, 244; TJR: 220, 178, 179, 215.
38. TJ: 178–183, §67; TJR: 155–160, §67, 386–391, beginning of §81; see also PL: 318–324; CP: 158, 314, 366; JaF: 60.
39. At the legislative stage. We will return to this issue in the section "Designing a just basic structure: the four-stage sequence" in this chapter.
40. Since a debate in 1974 with the economist Musgrave, Rawls nuances this point; R. A. Musgrave, 1974, "Maximin, Uncertainty, and the Leisure

Trade-off," *Quarterly Journal of Economics*, 88: 625–632. In that debate, Rawls notes with regard to leisure that there may be good reason for including "leisure time" among the primary goods (stipulating once again that the index of primary goods is not a measure of welfare); see CP: 253 (originally from "Reply to Alexander and Musgrave," 1974); see also chapter 5, note 24.

41. Originally "Social Unity and Primary Goods," 1982: 161.
42. Originally "Social Unity and Primary Goods," 1982: 168.
43. Amartya Sen, 1988, "Freedom of Choice," *European Economic Review*, 32: 269–294, 277.
44. Amartya Sen, 1982, "Equality of What?" in Amartya Sen, *Choice, Welfare, and Measurement*, 353–369, 365, Oxford: Basil Blackwell.
45. Over the last twenty years or so this approach of "basic capabilities" has been further developed. Next to Amartya Sen one has immediately to mention here the name of the political philosopher Martha Nussbaum. In many publications written together they have elaborated and deepened this approach. See, for example, Martha Nussbaum and Amartya Sen, eds, 1993, *The Quality of Life*, Oxford: Clarendon Press. See in that volume, for instance, Amartya Sen, "Capability and Well-Being": 30–53. See also Martha Nussbaum, "Human Capabilities, Female Human Beings," in Martha Nussbaum and Jonathan Glover, eds, 1995, *Women, Culture and Development: A Study in Human Capabilities*, 61–104, Oxford: Oxford University Press; Martha Nussbaum, 2000, *Women and Human Development: The Capabilities Approach*, Cambridge: Cambridge University Press. In the latter publication, Nussbaum tries to formulate a potential list of basic capabilities, a list on which among different cultures even an "overlapping consensus" could emerge. In 2006, Nussbaum (in her *Frontiers of Justice: Disability, Nationality, Species Membership*, Cambridge, MA: The Belknap Press of Harvard University Press) collected all her publications with regard to this debate. In this collection it is, once again, explained why she is of the opinion that – in contrast with the "basic capabilities" approach – the classical idea of the social contract, expressed according to Nussbaum in its strongest form by John Rawls, is unable to solve the problem of how to do justice to people with physical and mental impairments. In fact, she calls into question the whole idea of a social contract for mutual advantage as a way of thinking about choosing basic political principles. It simply cannot sufficiently express the dignity of those who give and receive care. Instead of a Kantian image of people, which stresses rationality and reciprocity, she holds a plea to move more to an Aristotelian image, which sees dignity and need as subtly intertwined. In this context we also have to mention the "Human Development Index" (HDI), a (first step in the development of a)

"basic capability index" that the United Nations Human Development Program, in cooperation with Amartya Sen (the principal author of this index), has worked out; see Amartya Sen, 2000, "A Decade of Human Development," *Journal of Human Development* 1: 17–23, 22. We will not elaborate here if indeed the basic capabilities approach provides us an approach that is more useful than a "resource-equality approach." But, for instance, Thomas Pogge has his doubts; see Thomas Pogge, "Can the Capability Approach Be Justified?" in Martha Nussbaum and Chad Flanders, eds, "Global Inequalities," special issue of *Philosophical Topics*, 30(2) (fall 2002, appeared February 2004): 167–228.

46. Sen, "Equality of What?," 368.
47. Ibid, 367.
48. Ibid, 366.
49. Sen, "Freedom of Choice," 278.
50. Amartya Sen, 1984, "Rights and Capabilities," in Amartya Sen, *Resources, Values, and Development*, 307–324, 323, Oxford: Basil Blackwell.
51. See, on "commodity fetishism" in relation to Rawls' primary goods, Sen, "Equality of What?," 366, 367–368.
52. Ibid, 366.
53. Ibid, 368.
54. "Rights and Capabilities," 320.
55. Amartya Sen, 1992, "Justice and Capability", in *Inequality Reexamined*, 73–87, New York: Russell Sage Foundation, Cambridge, MA, Harvard University Press; see also Percy B. Lehning, 1990, "Liberalism and Capabilities: Theories of Justice and the Neutral State," *Social Justice Research*, 4(3): 187–213.
56. Originally from "The Priority of Right and Ideas of the Good," 1988.
57. Originally from "Social Unity and Primary Goods," 1982; Rawls refers here to Sen "Equality of What?"
58. But Rawls also notes that, while acknowledging that he is not considering the more extreme cases, "this is not to deny their importance. I take it as obvious, and accepted by common sense, that we have a duty towards all human beings, however severely handicapped. The question concerns the weight of these duties when they conflict with other basic claims." It raises the question "whether justice as fairness can be extended to provide guidelines for these cases; and if not, whether it must be rejected rather than supplemented by some other conception" (JaF: 176 note 59).
59. JaF: 169–176, where we find Rawls' final reply to Sen.
60. Norman Daniels compares Rawls' use of primary goods with two different targets of egalitarian concern: with Sen's basic capabilities, and with "equal opportunity for welfare" (or "equal access to advantage").

We have followed in this paragraph the analysis of this second comparison: Norman Daniels, 1990, "Equality of What: Welfare, Resources, or Capabilities?," *Philosophy and Phenomenological Research*, 50, Supplement, 273–296; also in Norman Daniels, 1996, *Justice and Justification: Reflective Equilibrium in Theory and Practice*, 208–231, Cambridge and New York: Cambridge University Press.

61. Richard J. Arneson, 1988, "Equality and Equal Opportunity for Welfare," *Philosophical Studies*, 54: 79–95; Richard J. Arneson, 1990, "Liberalism, Distributive Subjectivism, and Equal Opportunity for Welfare," *Philosophy and Public Affairs*, 19(2): 158–194; Richard J. Arneson, 2000, "Luck Egalitarianism and Prioritarianism," *Ethics*, 110: 339–349; Richard J. Arneson, 2008, "Rawls, Responsibility, and Distributive Justice," in Marc Fleurbaey, Maurice Salles, and John A. Weymark, eds, *Justice, Political Liberalism, and Utilitarianism: Themes from Harsanyi and Rawls*, 80–107, Cambridge: Cambridge University Press; G. A. Cohen, 1989, "On the Currency of Egalitarian Justice," *Ethics*, 99: 906–944, 922–923, 930–931 (Cohen is interested in "advantage," a broader notion than mere welfare, but advantage includes welfare); Ronald Dworkin, 1981, "What is Equality? Part 1: Equality of Welfare," *Philosophy and Public Affairs*, 10(3): 185–246; Ronald Dworkin, 1981, "What is Equality? Part 2: Equality of Resources," *Philosophy and Public Affairs*, 10(4): 283–345; both also in R. Dworkin, *Sovereign Virtue: The Theory and Practice of Equality*, 11–119, Cambridge, MA: Harvard University Press; John Roemer, 1994, "A Pragmatic Theory of Responsibility for the Egalitarian Planner," in John Roemer, *Egalitarian Perspectives: Essays in Philosophical Economics*, 179–196, 179–80, Cambridge: Cambridge University Press.

62. G. A. Cohen, 1997, "Where the Action Is: On the Site of Distributive Justice," *Philosophy and Public Affairs*, 26(1): 3–30, 12; G. A. Cohen, 2002, *If You're an Egalitarian, How Come You're So Rich?*, 130, Cambridge, MA and London: Harvard University Press.

63. Dworkin, "Equality of Welfare" and "Equality of Resources."

64. But see, for an extensive analysis of "luck egalitarianism" from the perspective of Rawlsian "democratic equality," Elizabeth Anderson. She argues that "luck egalitarianism" fails the most fundamental test any egalitarian theory must meet: that its principles express equal respect and concern for all citizens; Elizabeth S. Anderson, 1999, "What is the Point of Equality?," *Ethics*, 109(2), 287–337.

65. Of course, these are all basically the same "anti-utilitarian" arguments that Rawls has also used in his fundamental comparison between the difference principle and the principle of average utility constrained by a certain social minimum (everything else remaining the same, thus

recognizing the primary place of the equal liberties), and his eventual choice of the former. The vagueness of the idea of average (or total) well-being, or in general the vagueness of the utilitarian principle, remains troublesome for Rawls. The issue remains of how to establish the interpersonal measure. These are issues Rawls discusses in TJ and TJR: §49 "Comparison with Mixed Conceptions."

66. It is an argument we can find extensively elaborated in "Primary Social Goods as the Basis of Expectations", TJ & TJR: § 15 (TJ: 90-95; TJR: 78–81). "For questions of social justice we should try to find some objective grounds for [the basis of interpersonal comparisons of expectations], ones that men can recognize and agree to. At the present time, there appears to be no satisfactory answer to these difficulties from a utilitarian point of view" (TJ: 90–91).

67. We must, as Rawls later formulates it, "respect the constraints of simplicity and availability of information" (PL: 182).

68. PL: 185 note 15. In viewing preferences and tastes when they become incapacitating as calling for psychiatric treatment, Rawls here acknowledges following Norman Daniels, in Daniels' discussion of two luck egalitarians, Richard Arneson and G. A. Cohen. The reference to Daniels is to "Equality of What?." Daniels refers to Arneson, "Equality," and Cohen, "Currency."

69. And Rawls adds: "And in making this decision, the value of education should not be assessed solely in terms of economic efficiency and social welfare. Equally if not more important is the role of education in enabling a person to enjoy the culture of his society and to take part in its affairs, and in this way to provide for each individual a secure sense of his own worth" (TJ: 101; TJR: 87).

70. See also TJ: 101, 104–105; TJR: 89–90; JaF: 74–77, 124.

71. See also TJ: 78. Throughout Rawls' work, "reciprocity" plays a central role. The term "reciprocity," though, is used by Rawls in different ways. The first use of the term we encountered earlier on, in the context of the principles (or tendencies) of moral psychology, where the basic idea of these tendencies is one of reciprocity without which fruitful social cooperation would hardly be possible. It is "a tendency to answer in kind" (TJ: 494; TJR: 433). It is these (moral) psychological principles that exhibit this reciprocity of disposition (JaF: 196). The specification of the idea of reciprocity given in the quotation this note refers to is the second use of the term "reciprocity." It is the relevant one in this whole section on "The difference principle and reciprocity." It denotes the terms of social cooperation that *justice as fairness* specifies and that benefit everyone in a fair way: it specifies what the fair distributive shares are. Further on we will see that the term "reciprocity" is used in a third way, where it is

formulated as "the criterion of reciprocity" in the context of the idea of public reason and public justification. In those instances we are concerned with (shared) reasons for accepting the principles of justice that specify the fair terms of cooperation, and the requirement of reciprocity is an extension of the contractarian idea. This use of the term we will encounter when we discuss "political liberalism," as well as "The Law of Peoples." The context usually makes it quite clear which use of the term Rawls has in mind.

72. See also TJR: 68.
73. See also TJ: 158.
74. This guarantee for a suitable minimum is, for instance, for the political theorist Philippe van Parijs, the starting point for a "general transfer" that takes the form of an *unconditional* basic income, based on the recognition of the moral right to an equal share in external resources; Philippe van Parijs, 1995, *Real Freedom for All: What (if Anything) Can Justify Capitalism?*, Oxford: Clarendon Press.
75. TJ: 78–80, 104–105, 318–319; TJR: 68–70, 89–90, 280–281; PL: 283; JaF: 62–64.
76. See, on the issue of "optimal taxation," Liam Murphy and Thomas Nagel, 2002, *The Myth of Ownership: Taxes and Justice*, 135–139, Oxford: Oxford University Press; and the economics literature they cite.
77. Kenneth Arrow, 1973, "Some Ordinalist-Utilitarian Notes on Rawls's Theory of Justice," *Journal of Philosophy*, 70: 245–63, 259.
78. In fairness to Rawls it should be added that he, on the other hand, recognizes there is an issue here regarding the relation between (income) tax rates and people's incentives to contribute efficiently: the question of how subsidies and taxes "tilt" in view of their effect on how the surplus of social cooperation is distributed. This is clear, for instance, from a written comment of Rawls on a paper by the economist E. S. Phelps, "Wage Taxation for Economic Justice." Rawls wrote to Phelps: "We should not accept a standard, it seems to me, *whatever* the implications of it. Therefore how [the difference principle] applies to economic questions like taxation is not a matter of *mere* application. One is testing the viability of the conception of distributive justice itself, perhaps not as decisively in this sort of question as some others, but still one is testing it. The kind of exploration you [= Phelps] present is necessary if we are to determine whether the criterion is really reasonable"; Rawls, in reaction to, E. S. Phelps, 1973, "Wage Taxation for Economic Justice," in E. S. Phelps, *Economic Justice*, 417–483, 423 note 11, Harmondsworth: Penguin.

79. S. Gordon, 1973, "J. Rawls's Difference Principle, Utilitarianism, and the Optimum Degree of Inequality," *The Journal of Philosophy*, 70: 275–280, 279.

80. This process of what Rawls has called "the four-stage sequence" has remained unchanged over the years; see TJ: 195–201; TJR: 171–176; PL: 397–398; JaF: 48.

81. It is important to distinguish the four-stage sequence and its conception of a constitutional convention from the kind of view of constitutional choice found in social theory and exemplified by J. M. Buchanan and Gordon Tullock, 1963, *The Calculus of Consent*, Ann Arbor: University of Michigan Press.

82. TJ: 198; TJR: 173. As Rawls notes, the traditional example of "imperfect procedural justice" is a criminal trial. "The desired outcome is that the defendant should be declared guilty if and only if he has committed the offence with which he is charged. The trial procedure is framed to search for and to establish the truth in this regard. But it seems impossible to design the legal rules so that they always lead to the correct result. ... An innocent man may be found guilty, a guilty man may be set free. ... The characteristic mark of imperfect procedural justice is that while there is an independent criterion for the correct outcome, there is no feasible procedure which is sure to lead to it" (TJ: 85–86; TJR: 74–75); see also PL: 73 note 25.

83. This coordination is what Jeremy Bentham thought of as the "artificial identification of beliefs and interests," and what Adam Smith thought of as the work of the invisible hand; TJ: 57, 198, 455; TJR: 49, 173, 399.

84. Rawls assumes "that a variant of majority rule suitably circumscribed is a practical necessity. Yet majorities (or coalitions of minorities) are bound to make mistakes, if not from a lack of knowledge and judgment, then as a result of partial and self-interested views" (TJ: 354; TJR: 311).

85. Restoring persons to good health has, as Rawls remarks, urgency, "whereas cosmetic medicine, say, is not offhand a need at all" (JaF: 174).

86. Rawls refers here to the well-known studies of J. A. Schumpeter, 1972 [1942], *Capitalism, Socialism and Democracy*, London: George Allen and Unwin; and A. Downs, 1975, *An Economic Theory of Democracy*, New York: Harper and Brothers.

87. Originally "The Basic Structure as Subject," 1978: 64.

88. Originally "The Basic Structure as Subject," 1978: 54; see also JaF: 161.

89. Meade starts his fifth chapter, "A Property Owning Democracy," as follows: "Let us suppose that by the wave of some magic wand ... the ownership of property could be equally distributed over all

citizens of the community"; J. E. Meade, 1965, *Efficiency, Equality, and the Ownership of Property*, 40, Cambridge, MA: Harvard University Press.

90. R. A. Musgrave, 1959, *The Theory of Public Finance: A Study in Political Economy*, chapter 1, New York, Toronto, London: McGraw-Hill.

91. See also JaF: 161.

3. Pluralism and justice

1. It should be noted that in *A Theory of Justice*, nowhere is the term "comprehensive doctrine" used.

2. To prevent misunderstanding, the issue in *Political Liberalism* is not that Rawls has eventually come to the insight that society is characterized by a plurality of views. He had, of course, also acknowledged that fact in *A Theory of Justice*. He, for instance, notes in §22, on "The Circumstances of Justice," that "individuals not only have different plans of life but there exists a diversity of philosophical and religious belief, and of political and social doctrines" (TJ: 127; TJR: 110).

3. "Uninteresting Hobbesian": A Hobbesian view would be a perspective from which political institutions are seen to be merely collectively rational, but not as a framework within which the content of the notions essential to ("Rawlsian") social cooperation – that of reasonable self-restraint and that of fairness, where social cooperation is understood as distinct from mere social coordination and organized social activity – can be defined or outlined. The idea of cooperation involves an idea of mutuality and reciprocity (another way to refer to fairness), and a willingness to do one's part, provided others (or enough others) do theirs (another way to refer to reasonable self-restraint) (LHPP: 87–88). Rawls disclaims the Hobbesian ambition of creating stability among egoists (JaF: 82 note 2). In fact, he had already elaborated this point in TJ, for the same reasons: there, as in PL, a well-ordered society is one "whose members have a strong and normally effective desire to act as the principles of justice require" (TJ: 454; TJR: 398); see also TJ & TJR: §76 "The Problem of Relative Stability." But note that the context in TJ and TJR is one in which *justice as fairness* is seen as (part of) a comprehensive doctrine, and thus all members of such a well-ordered society are seen as underwriting the same comprehensive doctrine.

4. See also PL: xx, xxvii, xxxix.

5. See PL: 81–88; or, for that matter, JaF: 185, 196 note 17.

6. Still "Kantian" (although *justice as fairness* is not [any longer] considered as a comprehensive doctrine but as a political conception of justice). Explicitly, Rawls stipulates in the case where *justice as fairness* is (now seen as) political, not metaphysical, "the adjective 'Kantian' indicates

analogy, not identity, that is, resemblance in enough fundamental respects so that the adjective is appropriate" (CP: 388 note 2). There is, however, no resemblance to Kant's views on questions of epistemology and metaphysics. Kant's doctrine is a comprehensive moral view, in which the idea of autonomy has regulative force for all life. Although being indebted to Kant, we should be clear about what Rawls means when saying so. Political liberalism does not *deduce* from a conception of practical reason in the background, but rather *gives content* to an idea of practical reason and three of its component parts: the idea of reasonableness, decency, and rationality. "The criteria for these three normative ideas are not deduced, but enumerated and characterized in each case. Practical reason as such is simply reasoning about what to do, or reasoning about what institutions and policies are reasonable, decent, or rational, and why. There is no list of necessary and sufficient conditions for each of these three ideas, and differences of opinion are to be expected." Thus, "although the idea of practical reason is associated with Kant, political liberalism is altogether distinct from his transcendental idealism. Political liberalism specifies the idea of the reasonable" (LoP: 87). The idea of the reasonable is not, then, an epistemological idea, but refers to the idea of democratic citizenship, to reasonable citizens characterized by their willingness to offer fair terms of social cooperation among equals, and to recognize the burdens of judgment. Political liberalism contrasts political constructivism with Kant's moral constructivism. Political constructivism "constructs" the content of a political conception. It does not presuppose that there is any prior moral order that a theory of justice purports to correspond to or represent. Rather, principles of justice are the product of a procedure that represents reasonable constraints on how rational agents should reason practically about the terms of social cooperation (CP: 388 note 2; PL: 99–101).

7. In his analysis of the doctrine of J. S. Mill, Rawls notes that the content of Mill's principles of political and social justice is very close to the content of the two principles of *justice as fairness* He even remarks: "This content is I assume, close enough so that, for our purpose, we may regard their substantive content as roughly the same" (LHPP: 267). In LHPP, Rawls explains "how, given his apparently Benthamite beginning, [Mill] managed to end up with principles of justice, liberty, and equality not at all that far away from justice as fairness, so that his political and social doctrine – lifted from his overall moral view – could give us the principles of modern and comprehensive liberalism" (LHPP: 313).

8. Michael J. Sandel, 1982, *Liberalism and the Limits to Justice*, Cambridge: Cambridge University Press. A "second edition" from 1998 contains a new

preface, "The Limits to Communitarianism," as well as a new added chapter that discusses the *Political Liberalism* of Rawls.

9. Michael J. Sandel, 1996, *Democracy's Discontent: America in Search of a Public Philosophy*, 13, 290, Cambridge, MA and London: The Belknap Press of Harvard University Press.

10. An idea that Rawls borrows from Wilhelm von Humboldt (1767–1835). It expresses von Humboldt's idea of a situation in which "each individual is enabled to participate in the rich collective resources of all the others"; see Wilhelm von Humboldt, *Ideen zu einen Versuch, die Grenzen der Wirksamkeit des Staates zu bestimmen* (translated in 1969 as *The Limits of State Action*, 16–17, Cambridge: Cambridge University Press); see also TJ: 523, 523 note 4; TJR: 459, 459 note 4; PL: 320–323; JaF: 142; 201 note 22. We will elaborate on the Aristotelian Principle in the section "The social bases of self-respect," in chapter 5.

11. It has quite rightly been argued that "one of the most striking and least-remarked features of the liberal-communitarian debate that occupied a great deal of the attention of political philosophers in the 1980s is that Rawls was a singularly bad choice for demonstrating the flaws that communitarians saw with liberalism." See, for this point and for the references to the relevant literature, Anthony Simon Laden, 2003, "The House that Jack Built: Thirty Years of Reading Rawls," *Ethics*, January, 367–390, 376.

12. See also JaF: 104–105. Note that the same argument is already present in TJ: 207; TJR: 181.

13. Rawls, 1989, "The Domain of the Political and Overlapping Consensus," 251. Also in CP: 473–496, 491; PL: 311.

14. Albeit with an important change in the formulation of the first principle of justice, regarding the basic liberties; see chapter 2, note 25; chapter 3 notes 53, 55; chapter 6, note 4.

15. See also Samuel Freeman, 1994, "Political Liberalism and the Possibility of a Just Democratic Constitution," *Chicago-Kent Law Review*, 69, 619–668, 650.

16. The importance Rawls attaches to the role that "public reason" plays in "political liberalism" is evident from the fact that his article "The Idea of Public Reason Revisited" (originally published in 1997) is not only included in the *Collected Papers* from 1999 (CP: 573–616), but also included in *The Law of Peoples* from 1999, as well as in the newly expanded edition of *Political Liberalism* from 2005. In debating "political liberalism," we have incorporated the ideas developed in "The Idea of Public Reason Revisited," as well as the relevant remarks made in *Justice as Fairness: A Restatement*, with regard to "political liberalism."

In this introduction, "The Idea of Public Reason Revisited" is quoted as published in *The Law of Peoples*, 129–180.

17. These limits of justification are imposed by agreement on the values of public reason. Note here the nearly identical formulation about reasoning in *A Theory of Justice*, where Rawls formulates that we need "evidence and ways of reasoning acceptable to all. It must be supported by ordinary observation and modes of thought (including the methods of rational scientific inquiry where these are not controversial) which are generally recognized as correct" (TJ: 213; TJR: 187). Regardless of whether we interpret *justice as fairness* as a liberal comprehensive doctrine or as a liberal political conception of justice, the appropriate modes of reasoning have not changed. The issue now is rather that, in a situation where there are different comprehensive doctrines, these modes of reasoning have to be a part of the original agreement.

18. It is here we encounter for the first time – in the context of "political liberalism" – the use of the term "reciprocity" linked to the idea of public reason (see chapter 2, note 71).

19. Note that the idea of civic friendship is not a new idea. In *A Theory of Justice*, this idea was linked to the idea of fraternity. The idea of fraternity was in its turn an idea that was expressed in the difference principle; and the difference principle expresses the idea of reciprocity.

20. It should be noted parenthetically that this is a more permissive view of Rawls when compared with the original edition of *Political Liberalism* from 1993 (PL: lii note 25).

21. Ideally, "citizens are to think of themselves *as if* they were legislators and ask themselves what statutes, supported by what reasons satisfying the criterion of reciprocity, they would think most reasonable to enact" (LoP: 135).

22. As mentioned earlier, in *A Theory of Justice* Rawls had not used the terms "narrow" and "wide."

23. See PL: 385–389; JaF: 29–32.

24. See, for an extensive analysis of "reflective equilibrium" before and after "the political turn" made by Rawls, Norman Daniels, 1996, *Justice and Justification: Reflective Equilibrium in Theory and Practice*, Cambridge and New York: Cambridge University Press.

25. Some citizens might not, as Rawls notes, have a comprehensive doctrine, "except possibly a null doctrine, such as agnosticism or skepticism" (PL: 386 note 18).

26. *Political Liberalism* spoke originally of three "features." But, as Rawls explains now, "The term *conditions* is better than *features*, since they define a liberal political conception, as I understand it" (PL: xlviii note 18). But in LoP, Rawls has switched once more, now using the term

"characteristic principles" (LoP: 14, 49). We use that term in the following.

27. Rawls adds that "adequate all-purpose means" refers to primary goods (PL: xliii note 19; see also LoP: 14, 49).

28. PL: xlviii–xlix, 6, 223, 227–230; LoP: 14, 141; JaF: 41, 46.

29. However, it is "inevitable and often desirable that citizens have different views as to the most appropriate political conception; for the public culture is bound to contain different fundamental ideas that can be developed in different ways. An orderly contest between them over time is a reliable way to find out which one, if any, is most reasonable" (PL: 227).

30. Note in these three consecutive sentences the three different ways that Rawls makes use of the term "reciprocity."

31. Again, see what was referred to earlier in chapter 2, note 9; see Rawls: "Principles of Moral Psychology," TJ & TJR: §75 (TJ: 494; TJR: 433).

32. See also JaF: 7 note 6.

33. See T. M. Scanlon, 1982, "Contractualism and Utilitarianism," in Amartya Sen and B. Williams, eds, *Utilitarianism and Beyond*, 103–128, Cambridge and New York: New York University Press; also in T. M. Scanlon, 2003, *The Difficulty of Tolerance: Essays in Political Philosophy*, 124–150, Cambridge: Cambridge University Press (references in the following are made to the 1982 publication).

34. Scanlon, "Contractualism", 116. Or, as Scanlon says: "The contractualist account of moral wrongness refers to principles 'which no one could reasonably reject' rather than to principles 'which everyone could reasonably accept'" (p. 111). To make an impartial judgment "that a principle is acceptable is, one might say, to judge that it is one you would have reason to accept no matter who you were" (p. 120). Note that Rawls' requirement is formulated in a positive way and not, as in Scanlon's case, in a way of non-endorsement. In discussing Rawls' position, Scanlon follows him "in speaking of the acceptability of principles rather than their unrejectability" (p. 120 note 16); see also: T. M. Scanlon, 1998, *What We Owe to Each Other*, chapter 5, Cambridge, MA, and London: The Belknap Press of Harvard University Press.

35. Brian Barry, 1995, *Justice as Impartiality*, 67, Oxford: Clarendon Press (for his remark that a theory of justice that turns on reasonable agreement can be called a theory of *justice as impartiality*, see p. 7). Over the years Barry has extensively elaborated the distinctions between "justice as reciprocity" and "justice as impartiality," as well as those between "justice as mutual advantage" and "justice as impartiality." An enduring element in his work is the argument that a theory of justice can be characterized by its answers to three questions. "First, what is the motive

(are the motives) for behaving justly. Secondly, what is the criterion (are the criteria) for a just set of rules? And thirdly, how are the answers to the first two questions connected?" (pp. 46, 49). In working out these three questions, Barry argues that "justice as impartiality" can offer a satisfactory answer to all three. Barry's work shows a long-term engagement with Rawls' work, especially with *A Theory of Justice*, as it does once again here. His disagreement with Rawls' theory of *justice as fairness* as formulated in *A Theory of Justice* is that the specification of Rawls' original position fails to capture the underlying idea of fairness adequately, based as it is "on a misguided importation of justice as reciprocity that leads Rawls toward the motivational postulate that he puts into the original position" (p. 62). In *Justice as Impartiality*, Barry excises from Rawls' theory any reference to "justice as reciprocity." In doing this, one gets, according to Barry, a coherent theory of "justice as impartiality." In this context it should be noted that Rawls has written with regard to the idea of reciprocity (and thus, to prevent misunderstanding, not with regard to "the criterion of reciprocity" and the related ideas of justification based on the idea of public reason), that this idea "lies between the idea of impartiality, which is altruistic (being moved by the general good), and the idea of mutual advantage understood as everyone's advantage with respect to each person's present or expected future situation as things are" (PL: 16–17, 50). Rawls adds in a footnote that this "thought is expressed by Allan Gibbard in his review of Brian Barry's *Theories of Justice* (1989, Berkeley: University of California Press). Barry thinks justice as fairness hovers uneasily between impartiality and mutual advantage, where Gibbard thinks it perches between, on reciprocity. I [= Rawls] think Gibbard is right about this" (PL: 17 note 18). In his turn, Barry has reacted to Rawls' footnote that in fact – if "justice as impartiality" is correctly understood, following his definition of it – Rawls does subscribe to the theory. The point is that Rawls at the same time subscribes to certain elements of "justice as reciprocity," which, according to Barry, renders Rawls' theory incoherent (*Justice as Impartiality*, 59, 60 note b). The point Barry is arguing for is that the equal baseline that Rawls takes, from which gains are to be calculated, requires the importation of an ethically driven baseline, and the rationale for that cannot come from the idea of reciprocity itself. Eventually, in the text of JaF, Rawls has now (re-)formulated his idea on the location of the idea of reciprocity as follows: "Reciprocity is a moral idea situated between impartiality, which is altruistic, on the one side and mutual advantage on the other" (JaF: 77). Barry would certainly persist in arguing that it is the elements of "justice as reciprocity" which make up for incoherence. All this also helps to explain why, although Rawls' requirement for reciprocity may bear resemblance to Scanlon's contractualism, Barry tries "to make the case that the form of justice as impartiality proposed by T. M. Scanlon provides a superior solution to that put forward by John Rawls in *A Theory of Justice*" (Barry, *Justice*, 111).

36. Ibid, 67.
37. Ibid, 7.
38. Ibid.
39. See also Thomas Nagel. He believes impartiality is egalitarian in itself: "What it means is that impartiality generates a greater interest in benefiting the worse off than in benefiting the better off – a kind of priority to the former over the latter" (Nagel, 1991, *Equality and Partiality*, 66, New York: Oxford University Press). Let us add that we should remember that in *justice as fairness* in Rawls' set-up of the original position, where the veil of ignorance deprives the parties of information, attention also turns first on those who would do worst under the outcome of the unanimously reached agreement: "Because the parties start from an equal division of all social primary goods, those who benefit least have, so to speak, a veto. ... Taking equality as the basis of comparison, those who have gained more than others are to do so on terms that are justifiable to those who have gained the least" (TJR: 131; PL: 282).
40. See also Barry: "[I]t may be argued that the only terms that cannot reasonably be rejected for living together by the adherents of any 'comprehensive view' are those embodied in Rawls's first principle of justice. For only 'equal freedom' is neutral in an appropriate way between different conceptions of the good. Hence, nobody can claim to be unfairly discriminated against by it" (Brian Barry, 1995, "John Rawls and the Search for Stability," *Ethics*, 105: 874–915, 894).
41. Barry for one would be happy if this would be the case, unhappy as he is with the "suspect intermediation" of Rawls' original position, which is regarded by him as "an embarrassment" (Ibid, 895).
42. Scanlon, "What We Owe," 245.
43. Ibid, 245–247, 398 note 49; JaF: 7 note 6.
44. But also recall, not one that is part of the theory of rational choice.
45. See also JaF: 202.
46. Benjamin Constant, 1988 [1819], *Political Writings*, translated and edited by B. Fontana, 307–328, Cambridge: Cambridge University Press; see also TJ: 201; TJR: 177; PL: 299; JaF: 143.
47. See also PL: 420–421. Rawls refers here to Charles Taylor, 1985, *Philosophy and the Human Sciences. Philosophical Papers 2.* 335, Cambridge: Cambridge University Press; see also PL: 206 note 38; JaF: 142 note 8.

48. Rawls refers with regard to this terminology to Cass Sunstein, 1988, "Beyond the Republican Revival," *Yale Law Journal*, 97: 1539–1590; see also JaF: 146 note 16.
49. See also JaF: 148.
50. See, for an elaboration of the distinction between "property-owning democracy" and a capitalist welfare state, R. Krouse and M. McPherson, 1988, "Capitalism, 'Property-owning Democracy,' and the Welfare State," in A. Gutmann, ed., *Democracy and the Welfare State*, 79–105, Princeton: Princeton University Press.
51. This is a permanent issue of attention and concern. The curse of money in political affairs is an issue raised in many publications by Rawls; see, for instance, TJ: 225–228; TJR: 197–200; PL: lviii, 328, 357; LoP: 24 note 19, 50, 139; JaF: 149–150.
52. See also JaF: 150.
53. Although we are here only dealing with the issue of the "fair value of political liberties" that are now included in the first principle of justice, also note that in the way this principle is formulated, the words "the most extensive total system," which were used in *A Theory of Justice*, have been replaced by "a fully adequate scheme." In doing this, Rawls acknowledges the criticism of H. L. A. Hart; PL: 331–332, 341–342; JaF: 111–112. We will discuss this issue in the section "Equal basic liberties: regulation or restriction?"; see also chapter 2, note 25; chapter 3, note 55; chapter 6, note 4.
54. Parenthetically, these ideas on "neutrality" are, for someone like Michael Sandel, another clear demonstration of what is wrong with Rawls' conception of liberalism. Sandel finds an illustration of these ideas in, for instance, the position taken in the "philosophers' brief" on physician-assisted suicide, a brief which we mentioned earlier. Sandel's reaction to the brief, signed by the "Dream Team of liberal political philosophy – Dworkin, Nagel, Nozick, Rawls, Scanlon, and Judith Jarvis Thomson," is that at "the heart of the philosophers' argument is the attractive but mistaken principle that the government should be neutral on controversial moral and religious questions. Since people disagree about what gives meaning and value to life, the philosophers argue, government should not impose through law any particular answer to such questions. Instead, it should respect a person's right to live (and die) according to his own convictions about what makes life worth living. ... Despite their claim to neutrality, the philosophers' argument betrays a certain view of what makes life worth living." Sandel profoundly disagrees with this kind of argument, which turns on autonomy and choice, that enables us to view our lives as our own creations. "Far from being neutral, the ethic of autonomy invoked in the brief departs from many religious traditions

and also from views of the founders of liberal political philosophy, John Locke and Immanuel Kant." See a collection of articles by Michael J. Sandel, 2005, *Public Philosophy: Essays on Morality in Politics*, 113–114, 115, Cambridge, MA and London: Harvard University Press (the article originally was published on July 7, 1997). As for Rawls' rebuttal, it would be that Sandel has missed the point that the argument in the brief was a *political* argument (CP: 618–619). See, for related issues, a review by Sandel of *Political Liberalism* (pp. 211–247, 271–276). Roughly, Sandel's criticism turns, once again, on Rawls' ideas of the priority of the right over the good, now in conjunction with criticism of political liberalism bracketing grave controversial moral questions, and a critique of the use of public reason. See, for a reaction by Rawls, LoP: 174, 174 note 176; CP: 609; 609 note 90. In the index of Rawls' *Collected Papers*, there is one single entry referring to Sandel: "Sandel, Michael: misunderstandings of."

55. Thus it is here that we discuss the result of Rawls' acknowledgment of the criticism of H. L. A. Hart; see chapter 2, note 25.

56. See also PL: 296; JaF: 113–114. In *Political Liberalism*, Rawls extensively debates the limits of "free political speech" in the context of the United States. He illustrates this with jurisprudence from cases of the Supreme Court. It is in this context that he argues that advocacy of revolutionary and even seditious doctrines is fully protected, the basic freedom of freedom of thought being protected (PL: 340–363).

57. Although Rawls is, of course, concerned with political toleration, he wants to illustrate that a defense of toleration can also be based on a different kind of argument, based on a perspective from a religious or nonreligious doctrine. An example of how a religious perspective could do so is, according to Rawls, a study of Abdullahi Ahmed An-Na'im, 1990, *Toward an Islamic Reformation: Civil Liberties, Human Rights, and International Law*, Syracuse: Syracuse University Press. In this study, the traditional interpretation of Shari'a, which for Muslims is divine law, is reconsidered. Focusing on the earlier, Mecca period in interpreting Shari'a, the claim is that this interpretation supports constitutional democracy, equality of men and women, and complete freedom of choice in matters of faith and religion. This idea of toleration, then, is expressed from within a religious doctrine. This is an example of what Rawls calls "reasoning from conjecture." But, once again, this is not, of course, the ground of toleration political liberalism asserts, but a ground to show how it could be asserted and at the same time be consistent with one's own comprehensive doctrine; see LoP: 151 note 46.

58. See in this context the discussion by Rawls of the issue of school prayer in the USA; LoP: 164–165. And see also in this context the disputed question of abortion, where, for instance, Roman Catholics may reject a

decision to grant a right to abortion: PL: lv, lv note 31, 243 note 32; LoP: 169–170, 169 note 80.

59. Note here an example of the consequences of the shift from a comprehensive liberal doctrine of *justice as fairness* in *A Theory of Justice*, to a political conception of justice. In *A Theory of Justice* we are concerned with moral autonomy, interpreted in its Kantian, comprehensive form; in political liberalism we are concerned with political autonomy; PL: xliii note 8, xliv–xlv, 199; LoP: 146.

60. See, for instance, Stephen Macedo, 1995, "Liberal Civic Education and Religious Fundamentalism: The Case of God v. John Rawls?," *Ethics*, 105, 468–496, 486.

61. The place of the family in Rawls' theory (as part of the basic structure; JaF: 162), as well as – more generally speaking – that of the position of women, has always been a controversial issue. Feminist political theory has extensively debated and criticized Rawls' theory with regard to this issue. An example is the work of Susan Moller Okin, who died in 2004. In her final, posthumously published, article she provides an overview of this criticism of Rawls' work (starting with *A Theory of Justice* up till "The Idea of Public Reason Revisited" from 1997); Susan Moller Okin, 2004, "Justice and Gender: An Unfinished Debate," *Fordham Law Review*, 72(5): 1537–1567.

62. See for the same remarks by Rawls: John Rawls and Philippe van Parijs, 2003, "Three Letters on *The Law of Peoples* and the European Union," *Revue de Philosophie économique*, 1(7): 7–20, 14–15, and also 14 note 3.

63. See also: LoP: 169.

64. Joshua Cohen, 1993, "Moral pluralism and political consensus," in D. Copp, J. Hampton, and J. E. Roemer, eds, *The Idea of Democracy*, 270–290, 280, Cambridge: Cambridge University Press.

4. International justice

1. LoP: 10. *The Law of Peoples* is greatly indebted to Kant's idea of the *foedus pacificum*. But because "the law of peoples" is developed out of political liberalism, once again at no point is Rawls deducing the principles of right and justice, or decency, or the principles of rationality, from a conception of practical reason in the background; see: LoP: 86–87; see also chapter 3, note 6.

2. CP: 565–572; LoP: 99–103.

3. This statement is explicitly repeated by Rawls at many other places in *The Law of Peoples*; see, for instance, LoP: 55, 128.

4. This is a crucial point in Rawls' exposition. Rawls does not take the path in which human rights are grounded in a political (moral) conception of

liberal cosmopolitan justice. Here Rawls on the one hand, and political theorists like Brian Barry, Thomas Pogge, and Charles Beitz, part company with their fundamental disagreement on (the grounding of) international justice; see also LoP: 82. Rawls refers here to Brian Barry (1989, *Theories of Justice* Berkeley: University of California Press), who discusses the merits of this procedure. He also refers to the first edition (1979), Part III, of Charles R. Beitz, 1999, *Political Theory and International Relations*, revised edition with a new afterword by the author, Princeton: Princeton University Press. Rawls also refers to Thomas Pogge, who formulates, for instance in 1994, a "global egalitarian principle"; Thomas Pogge, 1994, "An Egalitarian Law of Peoples," *Philosophy and Public Affairs*, 23(3): 195–224. Rawls notes with regard to this egalitarian principle of Pogge's that "it is not a statement of [Pogge's] own preferred view, but one that he sees as internal to *A Theory of Justice*. It states how he thinks the international system should be treated if it were treated as the domestic one is treated in *A Theory of Justice*" (LoP: 115 note 47). But, as argued in the text, Rawls disagrees: this is not the path to be taken, and it is certainly not the path taken by Rawls himself.

5. Rawls refers for this to J. L. Brierly, 1963, *The Law of Nations: An Introduction to the Law of Peace*, 6th edn, Oxford: Clarendon Press. This work contains a list of the familiar and traditional principles of international law. In fact, Rawls had already in TJ, as well as in TJR, referred to the same work, and thus to the same list of principles; TJ: 378; TJR: 332.

6. It is Rawls himself who has dealt with the question what "the Law of Peoples" would say about forming a single federal union between the Netherlands and Belgium; see: LoP: 43 note 53.

7. LoP: 75–78.

8. Rawls refers here to Roy P. Mottahedeh, 1993, "Toward an Islamic Theology of Toleration," in Tore Lindholm and Kari Vogt, eds, *Islamic Law Reform and Human Rights: Challenges and Rejoinders*, 25–36, Copenhagen, Lund, Oslo and Turku/Åbo: Nordic Human Rights Publications; LoP: 76 (the reference by Rawls incorrectly states in the title of the article "Theory" instead of "Theology").

9. LoP: 84, 59, 122.

10. Pointing out the fact that boundaries are historically arbitrary, depending to some degree on historical circumstance, may be true or not, but "to fix on their arbitrariness is to fix on the wrong thing," Rawls argues (LoP: 39).

11. This is, for example, one of the reasons for the disagreement Rawls has with Charles Beitz's "global distribution principle," since Beitz thinks that a global system of cooperation already exists. In a "Rawlsian" sense

it does not, there is no "Rawlsian" "global basic structure" and it is hard
to see there ever will be one, according to Rawls (Rawls refers to Beitz,
Political Theory).

12. LoP: 8, 38–39, 108. But with regard to the "duty of assistance" for
    instance, Pogge notes: "Rawls obscures ... the important causal role
    that the global economic order plays in the reproduction of poverty and
    inequality, suggesting that each society bears sole responsibility for its
    own place in the economic-rank order"; Thomas W. Pogge, 2001,
    "Priorities of Global Justice," in Thomas W. Pogge, ed., *Global Justice*,
    6–23, 16, Oxford: Blackwell.

13. Rawls refers here to a study by David Landes, noting: "This is
    powerfully (if sometimes a little too strongly) argued by David Landes"
    (LoP: 117 note 51); David Landes, 1998, *The Wealth of Nations*, New
    York: W. W. Norton.

14. This "global difference principle" is in fact already being rejected by
    Rawls on three grounds: first, that no agreement will be reached on it in
    a Rawlsian original position on the international level; second because it
    presupposes "a global system of social cooperation" based on a global
    basic structure; and third because it neglects Rawls' "political culture"
    argument. Rawls refers to Beitz (*Political Theory*, 1999 [1979]).
    Thomas Pogge's "global egalitarian principle," which is, according to
    Rawls, similar in many respects to Beitz's "global distribution princi-
    ple," fares not much better. It is rejected by Rawls with the same
    arguments he uses against Beitz's principle. Rawls refers to Pogge,
    "Egalitarian"; LoP: 115.

15. LoP: 109. Rawls refers to Amartya Sen, 1981, *Poverty and Famine*,
    Oxford: Clarendon Press. He also refers to Jean Drèze and Amartya Sen,
    1989, *Hunger and Public Action*, Oxford: Clarendon Press, chapter 13,
    "The Economy, the State, and the Public"; JaF: 47; LoP: 109.

16. Rawls is saying this "because many Muslim writers deny that Islam
    sanctions the inequality of women in many Muslim societies, and attri-
    bute it to various historical causes." Rawls refers here to Leila Ahmed,
    1992, *Women and Gender in Islam*, New Haven: Yale University Press;
    see: LoP: 110 note 39.

5. *Justice as Fairness* in practice

1. Also in CP: 415–420.
2. Anthony Crosland, 1974, *Socialism Now and Other Essays*, London:
   Jonathan Cape.
3. Ibid, 15.
4. Ibid, 17.

5. *The Future of Socialism* was published in 1956, re-published in 2006, London: Constable. References are to this new edition.
6. Crosland, *Future of Socialism*, 191.
7. Ibid, 189.
8. See, for instance, Roy Hattersley, 1987, *Choose Freedom: The Future of Democratic Socialism*, London: Michael Joseph.
9. Crosland, *Future of Socialism*, 159.
10. Stuart Hampshire, 1972, "A New Philosophy of the Just Society," *The New York Review of Books*, 18(3), February 24.
11. Brian Barry, 2002, "The Philosopher Who Transformed his Subject: Obituary of John Rawls," *Financial Times* (London), November 28, 2002, 23.
12. As Harold Wilensky formulates it in his well-known study of 1975: *The Welfare State and Equality: Structural and Ideological Roots of Public Expenditures*, 1, Berkeley: University of California Press.
13. Social democrats are struggling with two ideological alternatives, either to take "the Third Way" – in fact a misnomer for the neo-liberal track – or the classical social democratic one. The text clearly has the classical position in mind.
14. As John Rawls formulates it in one of his letters, in John Rawls and Philippe van Parijs, 2003, "Three Letters on *The Law of Peoples* and the European Union," *Revue de Philosophie économique*, 1(7): 7–20, 15.
15. The context in which Rawls debates the issue of the right to advertise is the one in which advertising is seen as a kind of speech, and that it can be restricted by contract. The "right to advertise" is not an inalienable right, in contrast to the basic liberties.
16. Let us, to prevent misunderstanding, recall that the justice of distributive shares depends on the background institutions and how they allocate *total* income to the least advantaged (wages *plus* other income transfers such that claims of need and an appropriate standard of life are met), as required by the (application of) the difference principle; TJ: 304, 277; TJR: 245, 267; JaF: 59.
17. Richard J. Arneson, 2007, "Does Social Justice Matter? Brian Barry's Applied Political Philosophy," *Ethics*, 117(3), April: 391–412, 401.
18. Brian Barry, 2005, "The Cult of Personal Responsibility," in *Why Social Justice Matters*, Part IV, 131–166, 139, Cambridge: Polity Press.
19. The social-democrat Frank Vandenbroucke has been in the Belgian federal government, "Verhofstadt – I," (1999–2003) Minister of Social Affairs and Pensions.
20. See, on these issues, Frank Vandenbroucke, 1999, "European Social Democracy [and the Third Way]: Convergence, Divisions and Shared Questions," in A. Gamble and T. Wright, eds, *The New Social Democracy*,

37–52, 37–38, Oxford: Blackwell Publishers. Vandenbroucke has substantiated his practical political ideas in an extensive political-theoretical argument in 2001, in his *Social Justice and Individual Ethics in an Open Society. Equality, Responsibility, and Incentives* (Studies in Economic Ethics and Philosophy), Berlin, Heidelberg, New York: Springer-Verlag.

21. Commission on Social Justice, 1994, *Social Justice: Strategies for National Renewal*, 1, 10, London: Vintage.

22. See also *The New Egalitarianism*, a collection of essays co-edited by Anthony Giddens (*auctor intellectualis* of the Third Way) and Patrick Diamond (at the time a special advisor to Prime Minister Tony Blair), published in 2005. The collection encourages reflection on the interface between theory and politics, particularly the connection between social justice and social solidarity. Edward Miliband (MP, appointed in June 2007 as minister for the Cabinet Office and Chancellor of the Duchy of Lancaster; promoted in October 2008 to secretary of State at the newly created department of Energy and Climate Change; at the moment of publication of *The New Egalitarianism* Chair of HM Treasury's Council of Economic Advisers, advising the Chancellor of the Exchequer, in that period Gordon Brown) elaborates in his contribution the deleterious effects of material inequality in terms of individuals' sense of self-respect, affected by their relative position vis-à-vis others in society, the way in which inequality undermines community by producing social atomization, and the dangers of spillover effects from the economic sphere, especially the danger that "greater inequalities will intensify the use of resources to gain political outcomes and probably make more likely different standards of public service provision depending on income" (p. 46). Inequality matters because it has these damaging effects and the focus should be on mitigating them. A welfare system "should be concerned with outcomes as well as opportunities, can prioritize the position of the worst off, and can demand appropriate responsibilities." Otherwise formulated, and the point to note in the present context, is that demanding appropriate personal responsibilities is perfectly compatible with egalitarianism: "Responsibilities are consistent with egalitarianism" (p. 49); Edward Miliband, 2005, "Does Inequality Matter?" in Anthony Giddens and Patrick Diamond, eds, *The New Egalitarianism*, 39–51, Cambridge: Polity.

23. Samuel Scheffler, 1992, "Responsibility, Reactive Attitudes, and Liberalism in Philosophy and Politics," *Philosophy and Public Affairs*, 21(4): 299–323, 301.

24. These remarks have to be situated in the context of the debate on how to handle leisure time. We have already encountered this issue in debating primary goods, more specifically the issue of whether "leisure time"

should be included in the index of primary goods; see also chapter 2, note 40. Rawls' opinion here is that "twenty-four hours less a standard working day [say eight hours] might be included in the index as leisure." Not working, then, means having an extra eight hours of leisure. It is another way of expressing the idea that all citizens are seen in *justice as fairness* as normally and fully cooperating members of society over a complete life and that – in Rawls' view – everybody should do his part in a just society; PL: 181 note 9; CP: 455 note 7; JaF: 179. Philippe van Parijs has elaborated this idea of leisure time. The more importance is attached to leisure time, the more important an unconditional basic income becomes; Philippe van Parijs, 1995, *Real Freedom for All: What (if Anything) Can Justify Capitalism?*, chapter 4, Oxford, Clarendon Press; see also Philippe van Parijs, 1991, "Why Surfers Should be Fed: The Liberal Case for an Unconditional Basic Income," *Philosophy and Public Affairs*, 20(2): 101–131.

25. This exposition also has nothing to do with the issue if we interpret *justice as fairness* as a liberal comprehensive doctrine, as is done in *A Theory of Justice*, or as a variant of political liberalism. The exposition in §48 of *A Theory of Justice*, "Legitimate expectations and moral desert," still fully holds, as is also clear from JaF: 72–79.

26. See the section "Fair background institutions and market arrangements" in chapter 2.

27. TJR: xv–xvi; TJ & TJR: §42 "Some remarks about economic systems"; JaF: 138–139.

28. As noted earlier, the term "property-owning democracy" is borrowed from J. E. Meade, 1965, *Efficiency, Equality and the Ownership of Property*, Cambridge, MA: Harvard University Press. See, for the contrast between "property-owning democracy" and "welfare-state capitalism," TJR: xiv–xv; JaF: 135, 138–140.

29. We can add that a "property-owning democracy" should allow for the possibility of J. S. Mill's idea of a society in a just stationary state where (real) capital accumulation may cease; JaF: 159.

30. One should in this regard not be distracted by the remarks of Rawls in the preface added to the *Revised Edition* of *A Theory of Justice*, in which he discusses among other things the contrast between "property-owning democracy" and a "welfare state." All elements to note the contrast were already in place much earlier in his works.

31. On pure procedural justice see (once again) TJ: 84–89, 272, 274–275, 304, 310; TJR: 73–77, 240, 242–243, 267, 273; JAF: 53, 57, 140. On the four-stage sequence, majority rule, and pure procedural justice: TJ: 202, 362; TJR: 176, 318; PL: 428–431.

32. TJ: 178–183, §67; TJR: 155–160, §67, 386–391, beginning of §81; PL: 318–324; CP: 158; 314, 366; JaF: 60.
33. TJ: §65; TJR: §65; PL: 203, 203 note 35, 207; JaF: 200, 200 note 21.

6. *Justice as Fairness*: a realistic utopia

1. Brian Barry, 1995, "John Rawls and the Search for Stability," *Ethics*, 105: 874–915, 915.
2. Ibid, 878.
3. "John Rawls: For the Record," interview with John Rawls, *The Harvard Review of Philosophy*, 1991 Spring, 1: 38–47, 43.
4. See also chapter 2, note 25; chapter 3, note 14.
5. "John Rawls: For the Record," 43.
6. Ibid, 44.
7. We mention only the main conditions of a "realistic utopia." Rawls in fact reviews seven conditions that are necessary for a realistic utopia to obtain for a reasonable just constitutional democratic society. He next checks whether parallel conditions would hold for a society of reasonably just and decent peoples who honor the Law of Peoples; LoP: 12–23.
8. The term "realistic utopia" only became known to the wider public by its use in *The Law of Peoples* (see, for instance, LoP: 4, 5–6, 11–23), and its use in *Justice as Fairness: A Restatement* (JaF: 1, 13). The term had, however, been used by Rawls since the late 1980s, for instance in a manuscript that contained the main outlines for JaF, eventually published in 2001. But to work out a "realistic idea of justice" has been always Rawls' aim. It may always have been his aim, but more often than not a "realistic utopia" is discussed in the context of Rawls' international theory of justice as formulated in *The Law of Peoples*. See, for instance, Rex Martin and David A. Reidy, eds, 2006, *Rawls's Law of Peoples: A Realistic Utopia?* Malden, MA and Oxford: Blackwell Publishing.

Works by John Rawls: a selection

1950: "*A Study on the Grounds of Ethical Knowledge: Considered with Reference to Judgments on the Moral Worth of Character.*" Unpublished PhD dissertation, Princeton University.

1951: "Outline of a Decision Procedure for Ethics," *Philosophical Review*, 60, 177–197.

1971: *A Theory of Justice*, Cambridge, MA: Harvard University Press (607 pp.).

1974: "Reply to Alexander and Musgrave," *Quarterly Journal of Economics*, 88, 633–655.

1978: "The Basic Structure as Subject," in A. I. Goldman and J. Kim, eds, *Values and Morals: Essays in Honor of William Frankena, Charles Stevenson, and Richard B. Brandt*, 47–71. Dordrecht: Reidel.

1980: "Kantian Constructivism in Moral Theory: The Dewey Lectures 1980," *Journal of Philosophy*, 77, 515–572.

1982: "Social Unity and Primary Goods," in A. Sen and B. Williams, eds, *Utilitarianism and Beyond*, 159–185. Cambridge: Cambridge University Press.

1982: "The Basic Liberties and Their Priority," in Sterling M. McMurrin, ed., *Tanner Lectures on Human Values*, volume III, 3–87, Salt Lake City: University of Utah Press.

1985: "Justice as Fairness: Political not Metaphysical," *Philosophy and Public Affairs*, 14, 223–251.

1987: "On the Idea of an Overlapping Consensus," *Oxford Journal of Legal Studies*, 7, 1–25.

1988: "The Priority of Right and Ideas of the Good," *Philosophy and Public Affairs*, 17, 251–276.

1989: "The Domain of the Political and Overlapping Consensus," *New York University Law Review*, 64(2), 233–255.

1996: *Political Liberalism*, paperback edition with an additional preface, "Introduction to the Paperback Edition," New York: Columbia University Press (464 pp.).

1997: "The Idea of Public Reason Revisited," *The University of Chicago Law Review*, 64(3), 765–807.

1999: *Collected Papers*, edited by Samuel Freeman, Cambridge, MA and London: Harvard University Press (655 pp.).

1999: *The Law of Peoples*, including the paper "The Idea of Public Reason Revisited," Cambridge, MA: Harvard University Press (199 pp.).

1999: *A Theory of Justice. Revised Edition*, Cambridge, MA: Harvard University Press (538 pp.). [Publication of the 1975 revised text, which has been used for all translations.]

2000: *Lectures on the History of Moral Philosophy*, edited by Barbara Herman, Cambridge, MA: Harvard University Press (384 pp.).

2000: "'A Reminiscence: Burton Dreben," in Juliet Floyd and Sanford Shieh, eds, *Future Pasts: Perspectives on the Place of Analytical Tradition in Twentieth-Century Philosophy*, 417–430. New York: Oxford University Press.

2001: *Justice as Fairness: A Restatement*, edited by Erin Kelly, Cambridge, MA: Harvard University Press (214 pp.).

2005: *Political Liberalism*, including "The Idea of Public Reason Revisited," New York: Columbia University Press (525 pp.). [Expanded paperback edition.]

2005: *A Theory of Justice: Original Edition*, Cambridge, MA and London: The Belknap Press of Harvard University Press (607 pp.). [Paperback re-issue of the original version of 1971.]

2007: *Lectures on the History of Political Philosophy*, edited by Samuel Freeman, Cambridge, MA and London: The Belknap Press of Harvard University Press (476 pp.).

Further reading

The first book-length analysis of *A Theory of Justice* was published in 1973 by the political theorist Brian Barry: *The Liberal Theory of Justice: A Critical Examination of the Principal Doctrines in* A Theory of Justice *by John Rawls*, Oxford: Clarendon Press.

For criticism from a *libertarian* point of view, the standard has been set in 1974 by Robert Nozick's *Anarchy, State, and Utopia*, New York: Basic Books.

For a *communitarian* perspective, the study by Michael J. Sandel, 1982, *Liberalism and the Limits to Justice* (Cambridge: Cambridge University Press) is decisive. The study, however, can better be seen as one that formulates the kernel of communitarian thinking than as a critical study of *A Theory of Justice*. It shows too many deficiencies in a correct interpretation of some of the fundamental ideas of Rawls' theory to be considered as such.

An early but still very useful collection of thorough essays on *A Theory of Justice* is: Norman Daniels, ed., 1975, *Reading Rawls: Critical Studies of* A Theory of Justice, Oxford: Basil Blackwell (re-published with a new preface in 1989). This collection contains, among others, the critique of H. L. A. Hart from 1973, a critique that led Rawls to revise the formulation of his first principle of justice.

For a collection of essays on *Political Liberalism* see: Victoria Davion and Clark Wolf, eds, 2000, *The Idea of Political Liberalism: Essays on Rawls*, Lanham, Boulder, New York and Oxford: Rowman & Littlefield.

A collection of essays discussing many of the main features of Rawls' account of justice set out in *A Theory of Justice* and in *Political Liberalism* is a volume edited by Samuel Freeman, 2002, *The Cambridge Companion to Rawls*, Cambridge: Cambridge University Press. This collection also contains an extensive, thematically ordered bibliography of secondary literature.

Charles Beitz and Thomas Pogge have applied the ideas of Rawls to the international arena by extending the thought-experiment of the original position onto a global level. See, for that idea and for a critical analysis of *The Law of Peoples*: Charles R. Beitz, 1999, *Political Theory and International Relations*, revised edition with a new afterword by the author, Princeton: Princeton University Press [first edition 1979]; Charles R. Beitz,

2000, "Rawls's Law of Peoples," *Ethics*, 110(4), 669–696; Thomas W. Pogge, 1994, "An Egalitarian Law of Peoples," *Philosophy and Public Affairs*, 23(3), 195–224; Thomas W. Pogge, 2001, "Rawls on International Justice," *Philosophical Quarterly*, 51(203), 246–253.

For a collection of essays on *The Law of Peoples*, see Rex Martin and David A. Reidy, eds, 2006, *Rawls's Law of Peoples: A Realistic Utopia?*, Malden, MA and Oxford: Blackwell Publishing.

For an analysis of the reception of "John Rawls in Europe," see the special issue published in 2000 of the *European Journal of Political Theory*, 1(2), 129–255. It analyzes the reception of Rawls' work in France, Germany, Great Britain, Italy, Spain, and Portugal, in the Nordic Countries, and in The Netherlands.

Index